Global Dynamics of Shi'a Marriages

T0385760

The Politics of Marriage and Gender:
Global Issues in Local Contexts

Series Editor: Péter Berta

The Politics of Marriage and Gender: Global Issues in Local Context series from Rutgers University Press fills a gap in research by examining the politics of marriage and related practices, ideologies, and interpretations, and addresses the key question of how the politics of marriage has affected social, cultural, and political processes, relations, and boundaries. The series looks at the complex relationships between the politics of marriage and gender, ethnic, national, religious, racial, and class identities, and analyzes how these relationships contribute to the development and management of social and political differences, inequalities, and conflicts.

Global Dynamics
of Shiʿa Marriages

Religion, Gender, and Belonging

EDITED BY
YAFA SHANNEIK
ANNELIES MOORS

RUTGERS UNIVERSITY PRESS

NEW BRUNSWICK, CAMDEN, AND NEWARK, NEW JERSEY, AND LONDON

LIBRARY OF CONGRESS CATALOGING-IN-PUBLICATION DATA

Names: Shanneik, Yafa, editor. | Moors, Annelies, editor.
Title: Global dynamics of Shiʿa marriages: religion, gender, and belonging /
    edited by Yafa Shanneik and Annelies Moors.
Description: New Brunswick: Rutgers University Press, 2021. |
    Series: Politics of marriage and gender: global issues in local contexts |
    Includes bibliographical references and index.
Identifiers: LCCN 2020057853 | ISBN 9781978818460 (paperback) |
    ISBN 9781978818477 (hardcover) | ISBN 9781978818484 (epub) |
    ISBN 9781978818491 (mobi) | ISBN 9781978818507 (pdf)
Subjects: LCSH: Shiites—Marriage customs and rites. | Shīʿah—Customs and
    practices. | Islamic marriage customs and rites. | Shīʿah—Doctrines.
Classification: LCC BP194.4 .G56 2021 | DDC 306.81088/29782—dc23
LC record available at https://lccn.loc.gov/2020057853

A British Cataloging-in-Publication record for this book is
available from the British Library.

♾ The paper used in this publication meets the requirements of the American National
Standard for Information Sciences—Permanence of Paper for
Printed Library Materials, ANSI Z39.48-1992.

www.rutgersuniversitypress.org

Manufactured in the United States of America

CONTENTS

PART THREE
Temporary Marriage:
A Flexible and Controversial Institution

SERIES FOREWORD

The politics of marriage (and divorce) is an often-used strategic tool in various social, cultural, economic, and political identity projects as well as in symbolic conflicts between ethnic, national, or religious communities. Despite having multiple strategic applicabilities, pervasiveness in everyday life, and huge significance in performing and managing identities, the politics of marriage is surprisingly underrepresented both in the international book publishing market and in the social sciences.

The Politics of Marriage and Gender: Global Issues in Local Contexts is a series from Rutgers University Press examining the politics of marriage as a phenomenon embedded into and intensely interacting with much broader social, cultural, economic, and political processes and practices such as globalization; transnationalization; international migration; human trafficking; vertical social mobility; the creation of symbolic boundaries between ethnic populations, nations, religious denominations, or classes; family formation; or struggles for women's and children's rights. The series primarily aims to analyze practices, ideologies, and interpretations related to the politics of marriage, and to outline the dynamics and diversity of relatedness—interplay and interdependence, for instance—between the politics of marriage and the broader processes and practices mentioned above. In other words, most books in the series devote special attention to how the politics of marriage and these processes and practices mutually shape and explain each other.

The series concentrates on, among other things, the complex relationships between the politics of marriage and gender, ethnic, national, religious, racial, and class identities globally, and examines how these relationships contribute to the development and management of social, cultural, and political differences, inequalities, and conflicts.

The series seeks to publish single-authored books and edited volumes that develop a gap-filling and thought-provoking critical perspective, that are well balanced between a high degree of theoretical sophistication and empirical richness, and that cross or rethink disciplinary, methodological, or theoretical boundaries. The thematic scope of the series is intentionally left broad to encourage creative submissions that fit within the perspectives outlined above.

Among the potential topics closely connected with the problem sensitivity of the series are "honor"-based violence; arranged (forced, child, etc.) marriage; transnational marriage markets, migration, and brokerage; intersections of marriage and religion/class/race; the politics of agency and power within marriage; reconfiguration of family: same-sex marriage/union; the politics of love, intimacy, and desire; marriage and multicultural families; the (religious, legal, etc.) politics of divorce; the causes, forms, and consequences of polygamy in contemporary societies; sport marriage; refusing marriage; and so forth.

Global Dynamics of Shi'a Marriages: Religion, Gender, and Belonging offers fascinating insight into why, how, and to what extent Shi'a Muslim marriages have been undergoing transformation in rapidly changing local and transnational contexts as a result of global developments, trends, and processes. Although the main focus is on the complex relationships between marriage practices and preferences as well as religious identities, value regimes, and institutions, the volume convincingly demonstrates that, in the case of Shi'a Muslim marriages, not only religious belonging shapes the meaning and patterns of marriage: nationality, ethnicity, generation, and class can also play a decisive role. Based on a brilliant investigation of the interplay between and context-sensitive hierarchies of religious and other forms of belonging, the volume argues against the widespread essentializing and deceptive practice where the imagination and meaning of being a Muslim is reduced to religious affiliation, commitment, and identity. Through analysis of various forms and aspects of Shi'a Muslim marriages—such as new dating practices, the politics of dowry, temporary marriages, or long-term changes in marriage patterns—the chapters provide the reader with a novel comparative perspective through which major similarities and differences between marriage practices among Shi'a Muslim communities in different parts of the world as well as the consequences of embeddedness of marriage practices within wider contexts of migration, transnationalism, and living in a diaspora can be effectively captured.

Péter Berta
University College London
School of Slavonic and
East European Studies
Budapest Business School
Faculty of International
Management and
Business

Global Dynamics of Shi'a Marriages

Introduction

ANNELIES MOORS
YAFA SHANNEIK

There has been renewed attention in academia and beyond for Muslim marriages in Muslim-majority countries as well as in settings where Muslims are a minority, in the Global North and in the Global South (Afary 2009; Foblets et al. 2014; Grillo 2015; Hasso 2010; Jones and Shanneik 2020; Mir-Hosseini 1993; Moors forthcoming; Shrage 2013). Especially in settings where such marriages have become the focus of public debate, this has engendered a growing body of research. The subjects addressed include unregistered marriages (Akthar et al. 2018; Arabi 2001; Latte Abdallah 2009; Moors et al. 2018), polygamous marriages (Charsley and Liversage 2013; Majeed 2015; Van Wichelen 2009), early/late marriages and singlehood (Johnson 2010; Singerman and Ibrahim 2003; Zbeidy 2018), transnational marriages (Charsley 2013; Schmidt 2011; Sportel 2013), forced marriages (Anitha and Gill 2011; Razack 2004; Welchman 2011), and temporary marriages (Haeri 1989; see further below).

Except for publications on temporary marriages, such research has by and large focused on Sunni Muslim marriages. It is true that after the 1979 Islamic Revolution in Iran more attention has been paid to Shi'a Islam in general, centering on such topics as the historical development of Shi'a Islam (Ayoub 2005; Cole 2002), Shi'a politics and sectarianism (Clarke and Kuenkler 2018; Mattiesen 2013), transnational dimensions of Shi'ism (Gholami 2015, 2018; Scharbrodt 2018), the formation of Shi'a Islamist movements (Louër 2008), and Shi'a ritual practices (Flaskerud 2014; Khosronejad 2014; Shanneik 2017; Spellman 2004). However, very little academic work has engaged with Shi'a marriages, and those studies have, moreover, by and large remained limited to Iran (Afary 2009; Mir-Hosseini 1993). This volume thereby makes important contributions to research on Shi'a Muslims through shifting the focus to marriage practices in those settings that have remained unrepresented in Shi'a studies. This volume fills this gap in academic research by engaging with Shi'a Muslim marriages and relationships in Pakistan, Oman, Indonesia, Norway, and the Netherlands as well as Iran.[1]

This volume sets out to make a substantial contribution to research about Shi'a Muslim marriages, with a focus on how Shi'a Muslims enter into marriage. As marriage is a central institution for the reproduction of families, ethnic and religious groups, and nations, a wide variety of parties are invested in encouraging, transforming, or contesting particular kinds of marriages. The contributors to this volume present the multiple and sometimes divergent points of view of those interested and involved in the process of getting married, such as parents and other kin, religious authorities, state and non-state actors, and the young couples themselves. These marriages not only need to be contextualized within the framework of the nation-state, but also must take into account local communities as well as transnational networks and global connections.

With this contribution we gain insight into the global dynamics of Shi'a marriages in a wide range of contexts. Hegland focuses on long-term changes in marriage practices in an Iranian village, while Walter discusses new dating practices of the Shi'a in northernmost Pakistan. Safar writes about dower and wedding practices among three Shi'a communities in Oman, and Bøe focuses on the function of the dower among well-educated Iranian migrants to Norway. Nisa discusses temporary marriages among the Shi'a minority in Indonesia, while Girard analyzes the discourse of Iranian students in the Netherlands on various forms of relationships. Asgarilaleh and Moors focus on the function of temporary marriage in the case of third-party gametes donation in Iran.

Engaging with such a geographical variety of cases, this volume offers a novel comparative perspective on the diverse marriage practices among Shi'a Muslims in different parts of the world. This includes settings where Shi'a Muslims are the religious majority (Iran), where they are a religious minority within a Muslim-majority context (Pakistan, Oman, and Indonesia), and where they are a minority within a Muslim minority context (Norway and the Netherlands). Shi'a Muslims in these various locations are also related to such communities elsewhere through transnational networks produced through migratory movements of students, traders, and professionals. Thereby, this volume further engages with Shi'a marriage practices embedded within wider contexts of migration, diaspora, and transnationalism and their effect on the changing nature of Muslim marriage practices. It highlights variations and negotiations of individuals' and communities' norms and values in relation to Muslim family lives, spouses' relationships, and gender dynamics. Discussing the multiple forms of belonging implicated in these marriages, the contributions simultaneously provide broader insights into the shifting position of Shi'a Muslims in a rapidly changing world of sectarian violence. Before further positioning the contributions to this volume, we first present a brief note on the historical development of Shi'a Islam.

The Shi'a Context

After the death of the Prophet Muhammad, disputes arouse around who would succeed him and rule over the Muslim community after him. Shi'a Muslims believe that this ruler should have been someone from the Prophet's family (*ahl al-bayt*), who are believed to have a special spiritual and socioreligious standings in society to lead the Muslim community after the Prophet's death. They also believe that the Prophet appointed, during his lifetime, his cousin and son-in-law Ali ibn Abi Talib as his successor and first Imam. Sunnis, however, believe the successor should be appointed from the Companions of the Prophet and accepted Abu Bakr as the first caliph. Ali however became only the fourth appointed caliph. Ali's son Husayn launched a revolt against the Umayyad's ruling caliph Yazid and was killed together with his entourage on the plain of Karbala (south of Iraq) in 680 CE. This battle became a symbol of Shi'a persecution and oppression and plays a central role in Shi'a collective identity and sectarian disputes.

Shi'a Muslims constitute a minority within Islam, with Twelver Shi'a being the largest denomination within Shi'ism. Twelver Shi'is believe in a patrilineal line of succession of the twelve Imams with the last imam believed to have gone into hiding as a child and will appear as the Islamic savior, *Mahdi*, at the end of times (Haider 2014). Shi'a communities are found around the world as a minority within a Sunni majority context, such as in Kuwait, Saudi Arabia, Pakistan, Oman, and Yemen. In Iran, Iraq, Bahrain, and Azerbaijan Shi'a Muslims form the majority but have not always been in power but rather have been ruled and marginalized by the minority Sunni population, such as in Bahrain and, until 2003, in Iraq (Matthiesen 2013).

Religious and spiritual authority is central to Twelver Shi'ism. Every individual is meant to follow and emulate the religious guidance of one senior cleric, also referred to as the source of emulation (*marja' al-taqlid, maraje' al-taqlid* [pl.]) (Walbridge 2001).[2] The most senior and most widely followed *marja' al-taqlid* is the Iranian-born Grand Ayatollah Sayyid Ali Sistani (b. 1930), whose network spreads across the world (Rizvi 2018). These senior clerics set the rules of Shi'a *fiqh* (jurisprudence), and with the influence, and to a certain extent involvement, of individuals and civil society, they initiate the process of *ijtihad* in which legal reasoning is found for new legal questions.[3] Boundaries and parameters regarding marriage and sexuality are negotiated and dictated by these senior Shi'a clerics. They also determine how norms are defined, which may also be translated into state law in Shi'a-majority countries.

Although all contributions to this volume focus on Twelver Shi'a Muslims, the latter adhere to diverse *maraji' al-taqlid* and also follow various customary practices. They use different terms in relation to marriage processes and understandings of marriage practices. Therefore, in this introduction we do not establish a glossary to homogenize Shi'a terms and practices. Rather, this volume illustrates the diversity of individuals' and communities' understandings of terms and practices influenced by global but also local socioreligious, economic, and political contexts.

Shi'a Marriages: Diverse Practices, Multiple Belongings

Whereas this volume engages with Shi'a marriages, we recognize that there is considerable overlap in how Sunni and Shi'a Muslims enter into marriage. For those living in Muslim-majority settings, Muslim family law regulates their personal status and marital relations. Muslim marriages follow a contractual approach that is in many ways similar for Sunni and Shi'a Muslims. Only after a marriage contract is concluded can sexual intercourse be considered religiously and often also legally permitted (Welchman 2007). As for every contract, offer and acceptance are required; that is, both spouses need to consent to enter into the marriage. Many but not all Islamic scholars also consider the approval of the marriage guardian (*wali*) of the bride necessary. For Shi'a Muslims in particular this depends on the *marja' al-taqlid* the couple follows and on whether the bride is entering into her first marriage or has previously been married (Afary 2009; Haeri 1989). A dower, presented by the groom to the bride—known as *mahr* in Arabic or as *mehriyeh* in Persian—is part of the marriage contract. Whereas in Sunni Islam the presence of two witnesses is needed for the contract to be valid, for Shi'a Muslims this is not required by every *marja' al-taqlid*, although it is often recommended. The other main difference between Sunni and Shi'a marriage regulations is that the Shi'a allow for temporary marriages (*mut'a* or, in Persian, *sigheh*), that is, a marriage concluded for a specific period of time. Publications on Shi'a marriages have almost without exception focused on this contested practice. This volume, in contrast, engages with Shi'a marriages in a broader manner and hence also includes Shi'a permanent marriages. Moreover, scholars of temporary marriages place these in the context of the wider array of forms that conjugal relationships may take or point to the multiple and at times novel meanings that temporary marriages have acquired.

Taken together, the contributions to this volume start from an approach that empirically investigates how in specific settings particular forms of identification and difference matter. This means that whereas the focus in this volume is on Shi'a marriages, we do not a priori assume that religious affiliation is the main determinant of Shi'a Muslims' actions or their primary form of identification and belonging. As the various contributions indicate, the extent to which Shi'a Muslims enact a commitment to religious practice varies considerably. For instance, Bøe's work on Iranian migrants in Norway indicates that for her interlocutors it is important to delink national identity from religion, while the Omani Shi'a with whom Safar did research underline how Shi'a Islam is part and parcel of their communal identities.

This volume analyzes to what extent and in which ways Shi'a Muslims participate in, negotiate, or contest religious aspects of marriage and how their marriage practices simultaneously shape and are shaped by other forms of identification and belonging, such as nationality, ethnicity, generation, and class. In Norway the focus is on practices of largely secular well-educated Iranian migrants, while in Oman the Shi'a minority is divided into ethnic groups that also take up different class positions. In Iran the life courses of different generations are markedly divergent, in Pakistan the focus is on emerging practices of Shi'a minority youth, while in Indonesia the views of Shi'a students differ from those of Shi'a elites. Among Iranian students in the Netherlands differences in religiosity matter, and in Iran religious authorities and biomedical experts hold a variety of views on marriage and gametes donation. Moreover, the contributors to this volume not only engage with the impact of national and subnational identifications but also pay attention to how global mobility and transnational relations matter in the field of Shi'a marriages. A number of contributions focus on the marriage ideals and practices of migrants, expatriate traders, and international students. Global connections are, however, produced not only by mobile people but also through mobile ideas, such as Shi'a religious concepts that traveled from Iran to Indonesia and elsewhere in the aftermath of the Iranian Revolution. In other words, this volume engages with Shi'a marriage concepts and practices that are also embedded within contexts of mobility and transnationalism.

All contributions to this volume are based on longer-term empirical field research with Shi'a Muslims. The coherence of this volume is constituted not only through its focus on Shi'a marriages but also by the particular themes highlighted and the ways in which they are in conversation with each other. The volume is divided into three main parts. The first two parts (four chapters) engage with marriage trends and practices that are not specifically Shi'a in a doctrinal sense. The themes they focus on—shifts in generational and gender relations, new forms of dating, and trends in dower registration—are also present among Sunni Muslims. Yet as these contributions indicate, these practices may nonetheless gain a Shi'a connotation because they are accompanied by Shi'a rituals (as with marriage celebrations in Oman), function as a Shi'a identity marker (as with dating practices in Pakistan and with dower practices in Oman), or because our interlocutors need to engage with Shi'a normative structures (as in Iran after the Islamic Revolution or for Iranian migrants in Norway who may want to return to Iran). The third part (three chapters), in contrast, directly engages with a specifically Twelver Shi'a religious institution—temporary marriage. Avoiding an essentialist reading of this institution, this volume shows the very different ways in which these marriages function, how the motivations for women to enter into these marriages and the meanings they attribute to them vary widely, both in Iran and in a minority setting such as Indonesia, and how young Iranians evaluate these marriages in the context of other forms of relationships. In the following sections we bring these contributions into conversation with each other along three thematic lines: gender and generational shifts in dating and marriage; the dower, signifying religion, ethnicity, and class; and temporary marriages as a flexible and controversial institution.

Gender and Generation: New Dating and Marriage Practices

In the Middle East, as elsewhere, major socioeconomic and political transformations, such as nation-state formation, have been accompanied by shifts in household composition, family relations, and the conclusion of marriages (Kandiyoti 1996). By the early twentieth century, among the modernizing middle classes, the ideal of companionate marriages had emerged together with that of nuclear households, centering on the new male citizen, his domesticated wife, and their children (Abu-Lughod 1998; Najmabadi 1993). Gradually, in many locations, processes of urbanization, the spread of education and wage labor, and transnational migration have also lessened the dependence of the younger generation on their elders and have enabled a greater say of the younger generation in the selection of spouses (Latte Abdallah 2009; Moors 1995; Hasso 2010).

This has also engendered a shift in ideals about marriages that is more complex than simply a transition from arranged to love marriage. It is true that marriages arranged by parents in which the parties have at most met each other briefly in the company of others have lost much of their appeal. However, the concept of romantic love has been present in the past as well, while in the case of present-day marriages family involvement and material considerations may also matter both in the Global North and the Global South (Zelizer 2000). An emergent pattern in the Middle East has been a shift toward more companionate forms of marriage that may simultaneously still be presented as arranged (Hart 2007). In strictly religious circles, where gender segregation is considered desirable, the term "Islamic marriage" is sometimes used to refer to marriages where the spouses do not date freely and where religious commitment may matter more than material interests and family concerns (Moors 2013).

The first two chapters focus on changing marriage relations in a village near Shiraz in Iran (Hegland) and on the emergence of forms of dating in a Shiʻa community in Gilgit-Baltistan, in northernmost Pakistan (Walter). Whereas both take the wider context of generational change into consideration, their style of writing is very different. Hegland uses very broad strokes to analyze wider processes of change, also paying attention to its effects on the older generation, while Walter describes emerging dating practices among young people in depth and with much detail.

Hegland's contribution is particularly interesting because she did her initial fieldwork in the village prior to the Iranian Revolution in 1979. Describing in general terms how these rural households were organized at the time, she underlines the strong generational and gender hierarchies. Young men were dependent on their fathers and women married very young and moved in with their in-laws, living in extended family households. Whereas in the early part of their life cycle these young women were highly dependent on their mothers-in-law, once they had children themselves they gradually gained a stronger position and expected, in turn, to become respected mothers-in-law.

It became evident that this cycle had broken down when she returned for fieldwork after the turn of the century. Urbanization, education (for men and for women), and work outside of agriculture (for men) had made sons far less dependent on their fathers and young women more mobile, while ages at marriage had also risen. With the growing importance of consumer culture and status linked to material wealth, marriage had become far more expensive, with most of the costs borne by the side of the groom and sometimes also that of the bride. Not only did these costs entail the dower, gold jewelry, and the increasingly ostentatious wedding parties but brides were also increasingly reluctant to live with their in-laws. Instead, they had come to expect to move into a fully furnished house of their own.

In the case of Iran, the question then arises of how such longer term trends relate to state policies in this Shi'a-majority setting. Under Pahlavi rule, in particular among the middle classes, a strong discourse had emerged about modernization and gender equality along Western lines. After the Islamic Revolution, more conservative ideas about gender relations were promoted. Comparing this with Hegland's findings, it is evident that neither the family law reforms under Pahlavi rule nor the policies of the Islamic regime to promote greater gender segregation had much impact in the village where she did research. Instead, during the past decades the local acceptance of women's mobility and cross-gender relationships has increased, families have become smaller, and the authority of the older generation has weakened.

Longer-term changes were also important in Gilgit-Baltistan in northernmost Pakistan, as Walter points out. These included development schemes, new highways, increased education and mobility, as well as access to satellite TV and video clips (from India) and to mobile phones. This has engendered the emergence of a dating culture, with the mobile phone as an important means of connectivity. A wider range of ideas about love, romance, and marriage, influenced not only by romantic notions of Bollywood but also by Islamic concepts, has transformed the interactions of young couples in the period between concluding the Islamic marriage contract (*nikah*) and the wedding celebration (after which the couple will start to live together). Previously this period was a time of avoidance with especially the girls shy and reluctant to interact with their future husbands. More recently, stricter Islamic (rather than customary) views that after concluding the marriage contract avoidance is unnecessary have gained in strength. Also, the meaning of love has changed. Whereas earlier love referred to passion and the loss of the self, which stood in tense relation to ideals of women's self-discipline and respectability, more recently love has become redefined as conjugal love, as companionship leading to mutual attachment and affection.

Such a longish interval between concluding the marriage contract and celebrating the wedding is also present in other, non-Shi'a contexts, both in Muslim-majority settings (Zbeidy 2018) and in Europe (Moors 2013). Among more conservative Sunni Muslims a marriage contract may be concluded relatively early, with the period up to the wedding functioning as some kind of dating period. In Gilgit-Baltistan, however, Sunni Muslims celebrated the signing of the contract and the wedding very closely together. In that area, then, this practice was specific for Shi'a Muslims and hence functioned also as a marker of Shi'a identity.

Dower Practices: Signifying Religion, Ethnicity, and Class

As mentioned previously, the dower is an intrinsic element of a Muslim marriage contract. It refers to the money, goods, and services that the groom agrees to provide the bride with upon marriage.[4] In some settings it is common to register both an amount that is to be paid up front (the prompt dower, due when the contract is concluded) and an amount that is deferred to widowhood or repudiation (the deferred dower). The amounts registered in marriage contracts may vary from an exceedingly small, largely symbolic amounts to very substantial sums of money. What is registered is always relational and depends on a host of factors, such as class, level of education, age, and other personal characteristics (having been married previously) of the spouses. Amounts often tend to be lower if there is already a strong relation of trust between the parties concerned (such as in the case of endogamous marriages).

Historically, two major shifts in dower registrations and payments have been reported. One marked a strong inflation of the amounts agreed upon, the other the registration of only a symbolic sum of money. There may, however, also be considerable differences between the amounts registered and what the groom's side pays in practice. When, as has been the case in Iran, large amounts that husbands will not be able to pay have been registered, the dower does not function as a source of women's economic security, but rather women may use their husband's indebtedness as a bargaining tool to strengthen their position in the case of divorce (Mir-Hosseini 1993). Registering a very small dower, in contrast, often functions as a claim to modernity and status, but this does not mean that the bride receives fewer gifts than she would have otherwise (Moors 2008). Whereas some women activists have been critical of the dower system, considering it as an old-fashioned institution and comparing it to the sale of women, others have argued that especially for women with limited access to other financial resources, such as a well-paying job, it may function as a source of economic security.

The "marriage crisis" (referring to men unable to marry because of the high costs of marriage) is often seen as the effect of women's desire for a high dower. However, it is not only the dower that engenders such problems (Kholoussy 2010; Singerman and Ibrahim 2003). As Hegland's contribution indicates, wedding parties have become highly commercialized and hence are far more expensive than previously was the case, while especially the costs of housing, which is the responsibility of the groom, have increased tremendously. Some state and non-state actors have expressed concerns that such high costs of marriage have engendered late marriage and singlehood among women and have encouraged men to marry foreign women who demand less. Especially in the Gulf States, with their very small national populations, attempts have been made to support men who marry local women by setting up a marriage fund (Hasso 2010), while elsewhere marriage costs are cut by organizing mass weddings (Jad 2009).

The two contributions of this volume that engage with the dower focus on very different settings. Safar analyzes the dower and marriage rituals among the small Shi'a minority in Oman, pointing to how these rituals produce both a sense of community and internal differentiations among the Shi'a. Bøe discusses how the Iranian Shi'a minority in Norway may reject, transform, or confirm the dower, signifying it as an expression of an Iranian-style belonging. Both cases exemplify the ways in which religion, ethnic/national belonging, and class positions are in various and complex ways intertwined.

In Oman, dower practices and festivities among the small Shi'a minority both set it apart from the Sunni and Ibadi Omanis and enact internal differentiations among the Shi'a depending on their ethnic background (Indian, Arab, or Iranian), which to some extent overlaps with status and class positions. The agreed-upon dower among the Shi'a is comparatively low. This is especially the case among those from Indian backgrounds (the Lawatiya), who often hold prominent political and economic positions. Their marriages tend to be endogamous, with only a small, symbolic amount registered as dower. Next to this, Shi'a belonging is also expressed in the ritual of presenting gifts to the bride at a private women-only party, with specific Shi'a ritualistic elements, such as decorations, prayers, and recitations in honor of the Prophet and the Shi'a imams. Among the well-off the wedding ceremony has become an occasion where class and status are celebrated, as it has become highly commercialized, with a celebration held in a wedding hall and the bride wearing an expensive white bridal gown. This stands in contrast to how among the poorer Shi'a of Iranian backgrounds (the 'Ajam) celebrations of mass weddings have emerged, supported by charitable organizations that help to cut the costs.

Among migrants of Iranian backgrounds in Norway who are generally well educated, often consider themselves nonreligious, and are critical of the Islamic regime, many evaluate the dower negatively. They consider it an old-fashioned institution that contravenes gender equality and the ideal of marriage on the basis of love. Nonetheless, many still include some form of dower when they enter into a marriage, in order to turn it into an Iranian-style marriage. Here Iranian-style does not refer to religious affiliation but expresses a sense of cultural belonging. This is evident in how they signify dower rituals as part of their historical heritage or family tradition. Especially women who do not intend to return to Iran and have an income of their own often opt for a symbolic gift instead of a large sum of money. For those who want to go back, it remains necessary to register their marriage within the Iranian system (with its mandatory dower), as the legal and financial protection this entails is still important.

The ways in which individuals (re)signify dower practices, rituals, and festivities may or may not have a religious connotation. Both in Norway and in Oman the Shiʿa are a minority, and in both cases ethnicity matters, but in very different ways. Whereas many Iranians in Norway ideologically reject the dower, they not only include some form of dower for pragmatic reasons but also resignify the dower as part of their national cultural heritage, rather than as a religious practice. In Oman, where the Shiʿa are a religious minority in a Muslim-majority setting, the Shiʿa resignify dower practices that are in and of themselves not specifically Shiʿa into markers of both Shiʿa religious and ethnic identification through the accompanying Shiʿa rituals.

Temporary Marriage: A Flexible and Controversial Institution

In contrast to a permanent marriage contract, a temporary marriage includes a clause that the marriage is for a particular duration, which is customarily understood to vary from one hour to ninety-nine years. At the end of the contract, no divorce procedures are needed.[5] When a man enters into such a marriage he has to pay a sum of money to his temporary wife, but he does not have maintenance obligations toward her, and the parties do not inherit from each other.[6] Children born out of such a marriage are legitimate, with the same rights to maintenance and inheritance as those born in a permanent marriage. However, as temporary marriages are often not registered and kept secret, if a man denies the marriage it is very difficult to prove its existence and hence the filiation of children (Yasseri et al. 2019).

Temporary marriages are a flexible and, for many, controversial Twelver Shiʿa institution and prohibited within Sunni Islam.[7] Yet Twelver Shiʿa Muslims also hold divergent views on this institution and use it for a variety of aims. Historically, temporary marriages were popular with traveling merchants and pilgrims when they were away from home (Haeri 1989). During the Pahlavi reign this institution became increasingly marginalized, as it did not fit with its project of modernization along Western lines. After the Islamic Revolution, in contrast, the regime attempted to revive the practice, considering temporary marriages both as an opportunity for young war widows to remarry and as a progressive Islamic institution suitable for young couples not yet able to enter into a permanent marriage that may function as an alternative to cohabitation (Haeri 1992).

Women hold a variety of perspectives on the desirability of such marriages. Many secular, urban, middle-class women consider temporary marriage as a relic of the past, as a threat to the stability of the family, as a cover for forms of prostitution, and, more generally, as an institution that is detrimental to the position of women (Haeri 1992). Some young people use it instrumentally to avoid interference by the morality police and to circumvent state regulation (Afary 2009). It may, however, be risky for young women to enter into such marriages. Especially in circles where women are expected to be a virgin when marrying, it may jeopardize their chances of a respectable permanent marriage, while those who enter into a temporary marriage hoping to achieve a meaningful and affectionate relation and companionship may well be disappointed (Haeri 1989). Still, for lower-class divorced women a temporary marriage can be an option to escape the marginality of their status, while for better-off divorced or widowed women a temporary marriage may be socially acceptable (Afary 2009).

Whereas structurally such marriages often concern relationships that are strongly unequal in terms of gender and class, with older wealthy men marrying young, poor women as temporary wives (Moruzzi and Sadeghi 2006), recent explorative research also indicates that some of these temporary marriages become committed longer-term relationships. These include marriages of middle-aged widowed or divorced men and women who seek companionship and intimacy but do not want to go through a permanent marriage and young, never-married adults who enter into a temporary marriage to legitimate an intimate, companionate relationship while postponing a permanent marriage as they prefer to first pursue their education and begin their professional career (Aghajanian et al. 2018). Young people who are not very concerned about religious rules may, in contrast, opt to enter into an intimate relationship without any kind of marriage.

Whereas sexuality is often foregrounded in the case of temporary marriages, that is, their function to legitimate a sexual relationship, there is also a form of temporary marriage that is explicitly nonsexual (Haeri 1989). Often such nonsexual temporary marriages are concluded to avoid the rules of gender segregation, such as when unrelated men and women need to travel together on a pilgrimage or a tourist trip, or in the case of employment that entails close social contact. In strictly religious families, nonsexual temporary marriage may also be used by couples during their engagement to allow for some intimacy (but not for a full sexual relationship), enabling them to spend time together, without concerns that their relationship would, in their own eyes and in those of their social circle, be sinful.

Three contributions to this volume engage with very different forms of temporary marriages, both sexual and nonsexual, with different aims, including procreation, and within different settings. Nisa discusses temporary marriages in Indonesia, the largest Muslim-majority country, where Shi'a Muslims constitute a small religious minority that has increasingly come under attack. Asgarilaleh and Moors focus on how in Iran temporary marriages have been used as a mechanism for procreation in the case of assisted reproductive technologies (ARTs), while Girard analyzes how Iranian students in the Netherlands discuss temporary marriages within the context of a range of other possible relationships.

In Indonesia, as Nisa explains, there are both Shi'a communities with a long-standing presence and those, often university students, who have more recently turned to Shi'a Islam in the aftermath of the Iranian Revolution. With the growing animosity of Sunni groups toward this Shi'a presence, temporary marriages have become a highly controversial issue, rejected by some as a form of "*halal* prostitution." Among Shi'a youth, in contrast, these marriages are often popular as a means to avoid illicit sexual relationships for those not yet able or ready to go through the complicated process of a permanent marriage. Some couples may also enter into a temporary marriage while completing their studies, as a means to get to know each other before entering into a permanent marriage, often with the permission of their families. Shi'a elites, in turn, express criticism of temporary marriages because of their concern that they may harm the reputation of the Shi'a in an already tense situation. Fearing such criticism, couples may well hide the fact that they have entered into such a marriage.

Girard, in turn, investigates how Iranian students in the Netherlands evaluate temporary marriage compared to other relationships, such as permanent marriage, the boyfriend-girlfriend relation, and "white marriages" (*ejdewaj-e sefid* in Persian). These students consider a temporary marriage as more acceptable in the case of single men who want to avoid sinning than with men who are already married. Moreover, they are generally more positive about a nonsexual temporary marriage. Those students who regard themselves as less religious tend to consider temporary marriage as an outdated institution. They regard a girlfriend-boyfriend relationship associated with love rather than with sexuality as permissible and also argue in favor of white marriages, a term used for cohabitation, which they also link to romantic relationships. Using concepts such as love, sex, sin, modernity, and gender equality, their arguments fit well with a wider discourse that highly values companionate marriages, based on love and partnership.

Asgarilaleh and Moors trace how in Iran temporary marriage and third-party gametes and embryo donation have become entangled and disentangled in the course of time. The use of such marriages in the case of third-party donation (what they label as "laboratory *sigheh*") may be considered a new form of nonsexual temporary marriage that aims not at sexual pleasure but at procreation. Whereas some *maraji'* do not require any kind of marriage for gametes donation if there is no gaze or touch, others argue for the need for a temporary marriage for the duration of conception in the laboratory. Yet entering into such a laboratory *sigheh* precludes gametes donation by close kin because of the incest taboo. In the case of stranger donors another problem emerges—the tension between concluding a temporary marriage and the desire for confidentiality, as the donors of the gametes are considered the legal parents. Proposed solutions differ: some biomedical experts argue for developing a stronger bioethical perspective, broadening the scope for social parenthood, while others agree with the tactical use of Islamic formats such as milk kinship and temporary marriage.

In spite of their differences, these cases also point to some common ground. In all cases there is a more positive valuation of temporary marriage if it is nonsexual or concluded as a step toward a permanent marriage. Temporary marriages that are not explicitly linked to sexuality are very much part of the turn toward love-based, more companionate relationships, with those who are less religious also in favor of other types of nonmarital relationships. Interestingly, this fits well with debates among young Sunni Muslims about unregistered marriages, whereas in some settings among the more religious such marriages are similarly employed to allow for a period of getting to know each other (Moors 2013). Those who are less concerned about religious rules may reject such marriages in favor of more equal forms of relationships, including cohabitation (Kolman 2018). In other words, a quintessential Shi'a institution such as temporary marriage is affected by broader societal trends that impact both Sunni and Shi'a marriages.

To conclude, what does this volume as a whole contribute to studies of marriage and Shi'a Islam? In popular debate, especially when tensions between Sunni and Shi'a Muslims are increasing, Shi'a marriages are often reduced to temporary marriages, which are then, in turn, labeled as a form of women's exploitation. Scholars focusing on religious doctrine and legal regulations also tend to highlight differences between Sunni and Shi'a Islam. The ethnographic approach the authors of this volume work with and the wide range of settings where they conducted their research enable a more layered and nuanced view of Shi'a marriages. Their contributions indicate that in many respects Sunni and Shi'a marriages are alike. Those entering into marriage have similar concerns and considerations both with respect to the material aspects of marriage as well as in view of personal and affective relations. The contributions on temporary marriages show the wide range of motivations of those entering into such marriages as well as the different ways in which their social circle and society at large evaluate these marriages.

Whereas it is evident that socioeconomic processes of change have generally allowed the younger generation more say in their marriages, how they enter into marriage is by no means given. An ethnographic approach is helpful as it does not a priori foreground the religious but investigates whether and how religion matters. This becomes visible at various moments in the process of contracting a marriage, such as with respect to the forms of dating they consider licit, whether they would consider alternative relationships acceptable, how dower arrangements are negotiated and valued, and what kinds of celebrations are held. There is a wide range of views both among religious authorities as well as among laypeople on these issues, and social practices fluctuate in concert but also in contrast to legal and theological frameworks.

Finally, the contributions to this volume also convincingly show the need to take into account the multiple positionings and identifications of the parties concerned. Being part of a Shi'a community may be framed in terms of religious belonging but also ethnic or national belonging. Some may, moreover, resignify being Shi'a as a cultural rather than religious heritage. Being Shi'a may bind people together and even connect them through transnational ties, while other axes of differentiation, such as ethnicity or class, may produce internal divisions within Shi'a communities. Whereas outcomes are unpredictable, entering into marriage is always intimately entangled in these multiple forms of belonging.

NOTES

1. As we are covering a diverse range of countries with their own languages and dialects, this volume does not follow a particular system of transliteration.
2. Individual believers may change the particular *marja'* they follow or follow different scholars (see Shanneik 2013).
3. Ayatollah Mohammad Taqi al-Modarresi is one of the senior clerics who supported the involvement of laypeople in the process of *ijtihad.* For more on this, see Razavian (2015).
4. According to Islamic scholars, the dower is either a condition for the validity of a marriage or an effect of a marriage (Welchman 2007).
5. The woman needs, however, to complete a waiting period prior to a next marriage in order to ascertain paternity in the case of pregnancy.
6. The Qur'anic term for the payment to the bride in the case of temporary marriage is *'ajr,* and for permanent marriage *mahr* or, in Farsi, *mehriyeh.* However, many Shi'a scholars and laypeople use the term *mahr* in both cases (Haeri 1989, 220n6). On *mahr* within the Gulf context, see Safar (2015, 2018).
7. Sunni authorities agree that temporary marriage was permitted at the time of the Prophet Muhammad but that the second caliph Omar had prohibited it in the seventh century. The Shi'a hold the opinion that since the Prophet did not ban temporary marriages, it is not permissible to forbid it (Yasseri et al. 2019, 73).

REFERENCES

Abdalla, Mustafa. 2015. "Challenged Masculinities: Sexuality, 'Urfi Marriage, and the State in Dhahab, Egypt." In *Gender and Sexuality in Muslim Cultures,* edited by Gul Ozyegin, 37–54. London: Routledge.
Abu-Lughod, Lila. 1998. "The Marriage of Feminism and Islamism in Egypt: Selective Repudiation as a Dynamic of Postcolonial Cultural Politics." In *Remaking Women: Feminism and Modernity in the Middle East,* edited by Lila Abu-Lughod, 243–269. Princeton, NJ: Princeton University Press.
Afary, Janet. 2009. *Sexual Politics in Modern Iran.* Cambridge: Cambridge University Press.
Aghajanian, Akbar, Sajede Vaezzade, Javad Afshar Kohan, and Vaida Thompson. 2018. "Recent Trend of Marriage in Iran." *Open Family Studies Journal* 10: 1–8.

Akhtar, Probert, and Annelies Moors. 2018. "Informal Muslim Marriages: Regulations and Contestations." *Oxford Journal of Law and Religion* 7 (3): 367–375.

Akhtar, Rajnaara C. 2018. "Unregistered Muslim Marriages in the UK; Examining Normative Influences Shaping Choice of Legal Protection." In *Personal Autonomy in Plural Societies, A Principle and its Paradoxes,* edited by Marie-Claire Foblets, Michele Graziabei, Alison Dundes Renteln, 140–155. New York: Routledge.

Anitha, Sundari, and Aisha K. Gill. 2011. *Forced Marriage. Introducing a Social Justice and Human Rights Perspective.* London: Zed Books.

Arabi, Oussama. 2001. *Studies in Modern Islamic Law and Jurisprudence.* Leiden: Brill.

Ayoub, Mahmoud M. 2005. *The Crisis of Muslim History.* 2nd ed. Oxford: Oneworld Publications.

Charsley, Katharine, ed. 2013. *Transnational Marriage: New Perspective from Europe and Beyond.* New York: Routledge.

Charsley, Katharine, and Anika Liversage. 2013. "Transforming Polygamy: Migration, Transnationalism and Multiple Marriages among Muslim Minorities." *Global Networks* 13 (1): 60–78.

Clarke, Morgan, and M. Künkler. 2018. "De-centring Shi'i Islam." *British Journal of Middle Eastern Studies* 45 (1): 1–17.

Cole, Juan R. 2002. *Sacred Space and Holy War: The Politics, Culture and History of Shi'ite Islam.* London: I. B. Taurus.

Flaskerud, Ingvild. 2014. "Women Transferring Shia Rituals in Western Migrancy." In *Women's Rituals and Ceremonies in Shiite Iran and Muslim Communities*, edited by Pedram Khosronejad, 115–134. Berlin: Lit Verlag.

Foblets, Marie-Claire, Mathias Rohe, and Prakash Shah, eds. 2014. *Family, Religion and Law: Cultural Encounters in Europe.* Farnham: Ashgate.

Gholami, Reza. 2015. *Secularism and Identity: Non-Islamiosity in the Iranian Diaspora.* London: Routledge.

Gholami, Reza, and A. Sreberny. 2018. "Integration, Class and Secularism: The Marginalization of Shia Identities in the UK Iranian diaspora." *Contemporary Islam*, https://doi .org/10.1007/s11562-018-0429-7.

Grillo, Ralph. 2015. *Muslim Families, Politics and the Law: A Legal Industry in Multi-cultural Britain.* London: Routledge.

Haddad, Yazbeck Yvonne, and Jane Idleman Smith. 1994. *Muslim Communities in North America.* New York: State University of New York Press.

Haeri, Shahla. 1989. *Law of Desire: Temporary Marriage in Iran.* London: I.B. Taurus.

———. 1992. "Temporary Marriage and the State in Iran: An Islamic Discourse on Female Sexuality." *Social Research* 59 (1): 201–223.

Haider, Najam. 2014. *Shi'i Islam: An Introduction.* Cambridge: Cambridge University Press.

Hart, Kimberly. 2007. "The Ambiguity of 'Spouses Choices' in a Turkish Village." *Journal of the Royal Anthropological Institute* 13 (2): 345–362.

Hasso, Frances. 2009. "Shifting Practices and Identities. Nontraditional Relationships Sunni Muslim Egyptians and Emiratis." In *Family, Gender, & Law in a Globalizing Middle East and South Asia*, edited by Kenneth M. Cuno and Manisha Desai, 211–222. New York: Syracuse University Press.

———. 2010. *Consuming Desires: Family Crisis and the State in the Middle East.* Stanford, CA: Stanford University Press.

Jad, Islah. 2009. "The politics of group weddings in Palestine: Political and gender tensions." *Journal of Middle East Women's Studies* 5 (3): 36–53.

Jones, Justin, and Yafa Shanneik. 2020. "Reformulating Matrimony: Islamic Marriage and Divorce in the Contemporary UK and Europe." *Journal of Muslim Minority Affairs* 40 (1).

Johnson, Penny. 2010. "Unmarried in Palestine: Embodiment and (Dis)Empowerment in the Lives of Single Palestinian Women." *IDS Bulletin* 41 (2): 106–115.

Kandiyoti, Deniz, ed. 1996. *Gendering the Middle East: Emerging Perspectives.* London: I.B. Taurus.

Kholoussy, Hanan. 2010. *For Better, for Worse: The Marriage Crisis That Made Modern Egypt.* Stanford, CA: Stanford University Press.

Khosronejad, Pedram, ed. 2014. *Women's Rituals and Ceremonies in Shiite Iran and Muslim Communities.* Berlin: Lit Verlag.

Kolman, Iris. 2018. "Beyond Non-Registration: Women Opting for Cohabitation in Tunis." *Sociology of Islam* 6 (3): 381–400.

Latte Abdallah, Stephanie. 2009. "Fragile Intimacies: Marriage and Love in the Palestinian Camps of Jordan (1948–2001)." *Journal of Palestinian Studies* 38 (4): 47–62.

Louër, Laurence. 2008. *Transnational Shia Politics: Religious and Political Networks in the Gulf.* London: Hurst.

Majeed, Debra. 2015. *Polygyny: What It Means When African American Muslim Women Share Their Husbands.* Gainesville: University Press of Florida.

Matthiesen, Toby. 2013. *Sectarian Gulf: Bahrain, Saudi Arabia, and the Arab Spring That Wasn't.* Stanford, California: Stanford Briefs, An Imprint of Stanford University Press.

Mir-Hosseini, Ziba. 1993. *Marriage on Trial: A Study of Islamic Family Law: Iran and Morocco Compared.* London: I.B. Tauris.

———. 1996. "Women and Politics in Post-Khomeini Iran: Divorce, Veiling the Emerging Feminist Voices." In *Women and Politics in the Third World*, edited by Haleh Afshar, 142–170. London: Routledge.

Moors, Annelies. 1995. *Women, Property, and Islam: Palestinian Experiences, 1920–1990.* Cambridge: Cambridge University Press.

———. 1999. "Debating Islamic Family Law: Legal Texts and Social Practices." In *The Social History of Women and Gender in the Modern Middle East*, edited by Marlee Meriwether and Judith Tucker, 141–175. Boulder, CO: Westview Press.

———. 2008. "Registering a Token Dower: The Multiple Meanings of a Legal Practice." In *Narratives of Truth in Islamic Law*, edited by Baudouin Dupret, Barbara Drieskens, and Annelies Moors, 85–104. London: I.B. Taurus.

———. 2013. "Unregistered Islamic Marriages: Anxieties about Sexuality and Islam in the Netherlands." In *Applying Shari'a in the West*, edited by Maurits Berger, 141–164. Leiden: Leiden University Press.

———. Forthcoming. "Women and Marriage in the Middle East." In *Handbook on Women in the Middle East*, edited by Suad Joseph and Zeina Zaatari. London: Routledge.

Moors, Annelies, Rajnaara Akhtar, and Rebecca Probert. 2018. "Contextualizing Muslim Religious-Only Marriages." *Sociology of Islam* 6 (3): 263–273.

Moruzzi, Claire Norma, and Fatemeh Sadeghi. 2006. "'Out of the Frying Pan, Into the Fire.' Young Iranian Women Today." *Middle East Report* 36 (4): 22–28.

Najmabadi, Afsaneh. 1993. "Veiled Discourse—Unveiled Bodies." *Feminist Studies* 19 (3): 487–518.

Ozyegin, Gul, ed. 2015. *Gender and Sexuality in Muslim Cultures.* London: Routledge.

Razack, Sherene. 2004. "Imperilled Muslim Women, Dangerous Muslim Men and Civilised Europeans: Legal and Social Responses to Forced Marriages." *Feminist Legal Studies* 12 (2): 129–174.

Razavian, Pooya Christopher. 2015. "The Discursive Self: Rethinking the Relationship between Autonomy and Tradition in Shi'i Thought." Doctoral thesis, University of Exeter. https://ore.exeter.ac.uk/repository/handle/10871/23295.

Rizvi, Sajjad. 2018. "The Making of a *Marjaʻ*: Sistani and Shiʻi Religious Authority in the Contemporary Age." *Sociology of Islam* 6 (2): 165–89.

Sachedina, Abdulaziz. 1994. "A Minority within a Minority: The Case of the Shiʻa in North America." In *Muslim Communities in North America*, edited by Yvonne Yazbeck Haddad and Jane Idleman, 3–14. New York: State University of New York Press.

Safar, Jihan. 2015. "Mariage et Procréation à Oman et au Koweit. Une étude générationnelle dans le contexte des Etats rentiers." PhD dissertation, Sciences Po. https://spire.sciencespo.fr/notice/2441/alvbjak559kv9vdqrjhvo1uf8.

———. 2018. "Explaining Marriage Payment. *Mahr* among Omanis." *HAWWA* 16: 90–143.

Scharbrodt, Oliver. 2018. "A Minority within a Minority?: The Complexity and Multilocality of Transnational Twelver Shia Networks in Britain." *Contemporary Islam*, https://doi.org/10.1007/s11562-018-0431-0.

Scharbrodt, Oliver, and Yafa Shanneik, eds. 2020. *Shiʻa Muslim Minorities in Contemporary World: Migration, Transnationalism and Multilocality*. Edinburgh: Edinburgh University Press.

Schmidt, Garbi. 2011. "Law and Identity: Transnational Arranged Marriages and the Boundaries of Danishness." *Journal of Ethnic and Migration Studies* 37 (2): 257–275.

Shanneik, Yafa. 2013. "Gendering Religious Authority in the Diaspora: Shii Women in Ireland." In *Religion, Gender and the Public Sphere*, edited by Niamh Reilly and Stacey Scriver-Furlong, 58–72. New York: Routledge.

———. 2017. "Shia Marriage Practice: Karbala as Lieux de Mémoire in London." *Social Sciences* 6 (3). http://www.mdpi.com/2076-0760/6/3/100.

Shrage, Laurie. 2013. "Reforming Marriage: A Comparative Approach." *Journal of Applied Philosophy* 30 (2):107–121.

Singerman, Diane, and Barbara Ibrahim. 2003. "The Costs of Marriage in Egypt: A Hidden Dimension in the New Arab Demography." *Cairo Papers in Social Science* 24 (1/2): 80–116.

Spellman, Kathryn. 2004. *Religion and Nation: Iranian Local and Transnational Networks in Britain*. New York: Berghahn Books.

Sportel, Iris. 2013. "Because It's an Islamic Marriage Conditions upon Marriage and after Divorce in Transnational Dutch-Moroccan and Dutch-Egyptian Marriages." *Oñati Socio-Legal Series* 3 (6): 1091–1110.

Van Wichelen, Sonja. 2009. "Polygamy Talk and the Politics of Feminism: Contestations over Masculinity in a New Muslim Indonesia." *Journal of International Women's Studies* 11 (1): 173–188.

Walbridge, Linda S, ed. 2001. *The Most Learned of the Shiʻa: The Institution of the Marjaʻi Taqlid*. Oxford: Oxford University Press.

Welchman, Lynn. 2007. *Women and Muslim Family Laws in Arab States: A Comparative Overview of Textual Development and Advocacy*. Amsterdam: Amsterdam University Press.

———. 2011. "Muslim Family Laws and Women's Consent to Marriage: Does the Law Mean What It Says." *Social Difference Online* 1: 63–79.

Yaghoobi, Claudia. 2018. "Mapping Out Socio-cultural Decadence on the Female Body: Sadeq Chubak's Gowhar in Sange-e Sabur." *Frontiers* 39 (2): 206–223.

Yasseri, Nadjma, Lena-Maria Möller, and Marie-Claude Najm, eds. 2019. *Filiation and the Protection of Parentless Children: Towards a Social Definition of the Family in Muslim Jurisdictions*. The Hague: Asser Press.

Zbeidy, Dina. 2018. "Marriage Registration among Palestinians and Syrians in Jordan: Debating Identity, Society, and Displacement." *Sociology of Islam* 6 (3): 359–380.

Zelizer, Viviana A. 2000. "The Purchase of Intimacy." *Law and Social Inquiry* 2 (3): 817–48.

PART ONE

Gender and Generation

New Dating and Marriage Practices

1

Marriage Modifications in Aliabad

Social Change Overrides Clerical Directives

MARY ELAINE HEGLAND

From the 1970s through the second decade of the twenty-first century, procedures and contents of marriages in the community I call Aliabad have been
transformed, influenced by social change, economic permutations, changes in
gender dynamics, and closer contact with nearby Shiraz, the rest of the country,
and other societies through media and travel. These marriage modifications
have allowed greater autonomy and self-determination for young couples and
many advantages for brides and young wives. These changes have also resulted
in a decline in the authority and power of the older generation and especially
mothers-in-law, many of whom have been left on their own when widowed and
sometimes socially isolated and neglected.

The hierarchies in family and marriage have been resisted as offspring,
daughters-in-law, and wives have found voice and are much less willing to accept
the authority of those who in previous decades would have been in much firmer
control over them. In yet another refusal to submit to hierarchy, the younger generation and females, especially, are acting to change marriage parameters and
male-female relationships against the expectations and directives of the clerics
ruling the Islamic Republic of Iran.

This investigation is based on anthropological participant observation and
in-depth, open-ended interviewing and discussion while I lived in Aliabad near
Shiraz for sixteen months in 1978 and 1979, with more than an additional year
of fieldwork among Aliabadis in seven more research visits between 2003 and
2018. As a sociocultural anthropologist, I aim to look at the realities of marriage
in a Shi'i Muslim community as understood through ethnography, rather than
at ideals or expectations from the Shi'i Muslim religion as interpreted by various religious sources, clerics, theologians, and laypersons.

Aliabad Marriage during the 1970s

The following, based on my fieldwork in Aliabad between August 1978 and December 1979, is provided in order to outline a generalized picture of earlier marriage with which to contrast the dramatic changes in the twenty-first century. Becoming an adult—a full member of society—required marriage. Females were—and still are—called "girls" until they are married, and males are "boys" until marriage, no matter what age. Marriage brought access to sexual relations, the crucial production of children, and a partner of the opposite sex to perform gender-defined work. With the strict gender division of labor, females needed males for economic support, and males needed females for domestic work.

Parents arranged the marriage of a son, bringing in a relatively uneducated young girl, generally aged between nine and fifteen, to the courtyard to help her mother-in-law. A friend told me how he found out whom he would marry about forty-six years ago. While he was away in his military service, his father wrote him a letter saying they had found him a bride and included a photo of the girl. Neither the thirteen-year-old girl nor my friend would have thought to resist their parents' arrangement. Even in the 1960s and 1970s, parents generally maintained easy control over marital arrangements for their offspring. Usually economically dependent upon their fathers for their marriages, marital rooms, and still sometimes their income-producing activities, sons listened to their parents' opinions. Daughters, cloistered at home and able to go out only to attend school or in the company of older relatives, had little opportunity to come in contact with males outside of the family.[1] Girls attended school in Aliabad for a few years and then, at about puberty, were taken out to wait for offers of marriage. Girls pretty much had to say yes to what their parents decided, even if they did put up a fuss initially. Very few managed to refuse a suitor when parents decided in his favor. In one example, a girl was able to refuse a suitor based on the persuasive argument that he lacked economic resources and prospects.[2]

Wedding and marriage expenses at that time fell far below those of the later period. Weddings were celebrated in courtyards, with local-style line dancing in a nearby open area. Women of the families cooked the wedding feast, perhaps excepting a large caldron of rice or two prepared by a hired male cook.[3] For the bridal home, at most an additional mud-brick room, if not already available, was built in the groom's father's family courtyard hidden from the alleyway by a high mud-and-straw wall. The bride's family provided necessities for the bridal room, such as fold-up, locally made mattresses, pillows, and quilts, a few dishes, and minimal household equipment. The bride and groom ate with his family after the bride helped her mother-in-law with food preparation and other household chores.

The bride and groom did not spend time together before the wedding. During the wedding celebration at her parents' home, the bride was expected to be passive and subdued. She sat quietly, looking down, did not interact with others, and did not eat—at least not in front of others. Celebrations were held separately at the homes of the bride and groom. After the celebration in the bride's father's home, the bride was brought to the groom's home late at night. There, a room had been decorated, walls covered with pretty cloth—the *hejleh* or bridal room.

The consummation of the marriage took place here late at night. Sexual relations were not to take place outside of marriage, most crucially for females. The bride was relatively ignorant about sexuality, and the groom was generally inexperienced as well, but the male had to perform and the bride had to be penetrated. The marriage night ended with required and often forced intercourse,[4] often traumatic for the bride and perhaps the groom as well,[5] and could be injurious to the bride, as the following story illustrates.

In the summer of 2008, I commented to a friend that the woman we had just visited must have been young when she married. My friend then told me this story. It happened that the groom's family lived in the courtyard next door to my friend's family. My friend's mother looked out her window into the groom's parents' courtyard the morning after the wedding. The bride's mother was there, washing out her daughter's bloody skirts. As she worked, the mother paused at times to beat her chest, surely in grief, knowing how difficult the night before had been for her daughter. My friend added, "There were a lot like that," acknowledging how common bridal injuries from the abrupt, required intercourse of the marriage night had been. Others controlled the sexual activity and expression of young females and even, to a degree, that of young men.

Brides were expected to work hard under the supervision of their mothers-in-law after the first few days of remaining in the bridal room receiving guests, congratulations, and gifts. Brides held low status in the father-in-law's courtyard. They were to obey their in-laws and husband without question. A child as soon as possible, especially a male baby, brought a bride some improved consideration in the household.[6]

Generally, husbands and wives did not have much to do with each other during the day. In-laws, work obligations, and social expectations restricted interactions between a young husband and his wife. Males and females went about their daily work in different areas—the men in the fields, in shops, or on itinerant trade routes and females with domestic tasks. People did not consider marriage primarily to attain companionship or an intimate relationship. The young couple generally maintained separate, same-sex social circles.[7] Other women became women's important social outlets, confidants, and companions. Women and men stayed in separate rooms or courtyards for social events; couples generally did not look or speak to each other while in the company of others, and especially not in public settings. They were not to give attention to each other or show affection in front of the older generation, even at home, as that would demonstrate a lack of respect for elders. A groom's parents assumed that his main loyalty, attention, and resources should fall to them and not to his bride. She also should devote herself to the interests of her father-in-law's family.

Girls were married at a young age and had much less education and sophistication than today's brides. When I interviewed some elderly women, they talked about how their mothers-in-law decided when they would go to the public bath house and when the bride's hair would be taken out and combed. They even sometimes controlled when the young couple had sexual relations. Living in their courtyard, the young couple remained accessible to the groom's parents. Women sometimes complained that mothers-in-law, and perhaps sisters-in-law too, treated them badly. They sometimes said the mother-in-law encouraged her son to beat his wife.

Before the Iranian Revolution, at the time of my fieldwork in Aliabad in 1978 and 1979, in spite of no laws or state policies against women's mobility, local culture dictated that brides must remain inside the husband's and father-in-law's courtyard. They could not leave without permission. Girls and women had to be accompanied by a chaperone to go any distance out of the home. They could not take the bus into Shiraz on their own.

Eventually, a couple might be able to move to a separate home. Especially in earlier years of marriage, such a step might be the focus of serious conflict between brides and grooms' parents, each wanting the groom's attention, affection, and resources. Fierce discord, a bride fleeing to her father's home several times, and even violence might be part of the power struggle before a couple could move to a separate home.[8]

Changes Affecting the Hierarchal Relationships between Parents and Offspring

More Freedom of Choice for Young People

The nuclear family has become more important. Husband, wife, and children usually spend a great deal of time together, go out on picnics, to other cities, and on pilgrimages and *hajj*. Husbands and wives now place more importance on companionship with each other. As young people usually decide on their own spouses, sexual attraction often plays a greater part in marital relations. A relationship of caring sexual intimacy may develop, instead of the rushed and unemotional sexual congress, especially initially, that some women of earlier generations complained about, bringing the young couple closer to each other.

Kinship relations and interactions with people outside of the nuclear family have declined in importance. These days young people resist control by the groom's parents and take over control of much of their own lives. A family goes into their home and shuts the door behind them, older people commented, and waxed nostalgic for the old days of closer bonds among relatives.

Now the resources of the married couple are used mainly for themselves, their homes, and their children. The wife shops for herself and the children; money is more easily available (before the economic downturn of the past few years; now complaints about the economy and financial issues are pervasive). She can run her own home as she wishes, rather than taking orders from her mother-in-law.

Life has become much more expensive. Expectations for homes, cars, and furniture are high. Children have become expensive to raise; they must have nice clothes, toys, computers, and English classes in the city. Clothes, cars, a home, and education for the children are all part of gaining status, and social status is extremely significant for a family. Especially because of great expectations to demonstrate status through materialism, the young couple wants to use their resources for their own family.

The greater autonomy and higher standard of living for the bridal couple translate into lost influence, status, and resources for the parental generation. The decline in attention and social position for mothers-in-law is particularly noticeable. Usually more educated, comfortable in wider settings, and working in situations away from fathers, sons also have gained power in relationship to their parents. Young men will not perform farm work or even respond to a father's request for help in their small orchards.

More Responsibilities for Parents

Young people of today seem more able to do as they like, comparatively unrestrained by parental pleading and pressure. Many parents are supportive of their children, feeling the regime has been too repressive of young people and their opportunities for enjoyment of their youth have been too restricted. Instead of parents pressuring children, often children are pressuring their parents—to provide cars, spending money, motorcycles, chic clothing for males and outings, fashionable clothing and makeup, jobs, travel, education, and opportunities to go out with friends for females. Sometimes children complain and compare what their friends and relatives get from parents to the lesser benefits provided to them by their own parents.

Parents face extremely high expenses to set their offspring up in life. Expectations on parents have risen dramatically while young couples pretty much have free rein to attain their married lives; wedding expenses start with engagement gifts including expensive gold jewelry for the bride as well as sets of clothing. These days the bride's family typically stages an engagement party. Social pressure and the need to hold one's head up and maintain family reputation mean that people cannot get away with a modest, quiet wedding celebration. Close observation by others in the community, evaluative commentary, and the now-prevalent cultural practice of needing to outdo others (*cheshm ham cheshmi*— looking at others to compare what they have) require great expenditures to marry children off. Families must spend for visits to a beauty parlor for the bride and female relatives of the bride and groom to get their hair, makeup, and fingernail polish done. Now even a groom is expected to get makeup applied professionally, have his eyebrows shaped, and sport a modern hairstyle.

Wedding clothes are extravagant: the bride's family rents an elegant, white, strapless gown for her. Family and relatives buy new clothing. The groom's father pays for the elaborate wedding celebration in a rented garden—only one now instead of both sets of parents hosting one at their homes. The groom's father also provides the home for the newlywed couple and usually a car as well; the bride's parents are responsible for upscale, comprehensive home furnishings and supplies. Then the bride's mother must handle all the needs for the couple's first child. In the case of divorce the bride's parents take her in, and her father copes with her expenses. In order to marry their children off, to be able to raise their heads, and to get good matches for their other children, parents must spend.

Young Women Finding Voice and Resisting Hierarchy in the Twenty-First Century

In recent decades, Aliabad females have been gaining more education, have been marrying later, and are becoming more assertive about their own opinions and interests. By means of satellite dishes, both males and females watch TV programs that feature romantic relations in other countries, although the regime frowns on satellite dishes that bring TV stations from all over the world and on any public romantic, physical interaction. Media and communication raise expectations for romantic, loving relationships, especially among females.

As early as 2003, when I first returned to Aliabad after an absence of twenty-three years, I noticed girls' different behavior. Girls no longer sat quietly, not moving or speaking if guests were present. Now they spoke up, actively continued their own preoccupations, or even playfully disrupted guests' discussions or activities. By 2008, I noted how some young women spoke up and even complained about their lack of freedoms. Most young people do not appreciate the extended family influence or decision making for the benefit of the entire family. They are more individualistic and centered on self-interest rather than on dedication to family welfare.

With desires for a wider life and the greater voice they have in family dynamics, many younger females have sometimes been able to exert pressure for greater freedoms and mobility. If parents do not support their wishes enough, they may complain and nag endlessly until they obtain what they want. For example, one young woman carried on a campaign to get a nose job for several years, despite her parents' opposition, and finally was successful. Now young Aliabad women have won this battle, and nose jobs (generally paid for by the father, as most young women do not work) have become a necessity.

By 2008, this same young woman complained endlessly about always having to be with her parents and family and not being able to go off with her friends on her own. By 2014, she was able to manage going out without her parents when she became engaged to a neighbor in their Shiraz suburb; she eventually married him.[9]

Through schooling at high schools in Shiraz and acceptance at institutions of higher education in cities, many Aliabad females gain autonomy, interactions with people from outside of the village, and knowledge about the wider world. Some younger females have become outspoken, insistent, and determined to persuade their fathers and relatives to accept their own decisions. As practices change, social control has weakened, and in any case these females are often outside of the surveillance of locals for at least a period as they are away at school. Some parents are supportive of their daughters and accept their education and even their wishes to put off marriage, even if they feel it unwise.

Some Aliabad young women have been joining the Iranian youth culture, based on social media, information from outside of Iran, and more opportunities to interact with young people other than close relatives and neighbors. Often, they have ideas about falling in love before they would consider marrying someone. Females especially have gained views about relations with the opposite sex and marriage more in tune with a culture of "developmental idealism" (see Thornton et al. 2015) including more open, egalitarian interactions, marital intimacy, and partnership rather than emphasis on extended family loyalty, procreation, practical division of labor, and generational, gender, and marital hierarchy.

Young Women Flouting Gender and Marital Hierarchies

Young Aliabad women are bringing about transformations in marriage procedures. They have resisted earlier marriages, refusing their parents' choices, turning suitors down, pressuring for more education, and, among a minority, finding means to meet potential marriage partners at educational institutions, work, and encounters elsewhere.[10] Opportunities for young people to meet and get to know others, less pressure to marry early, far less emphasis on marriage for political alliance and economic cooperation, additional experiences of interacting with nonfamily members and members of the opposite sex, more relaxed and informal social interaction, less hierarchical gender and generational dynamics, somewhat less separation of female worlds from male worlds, greatly enhanced opportunities for engaged couples to spend time together, and a more gradual transition to sexual intimacy bring potential advantages of warmer, more partner-like, egalitarian marital relationships.

These days a couple can talk together a great deal before the wedding and even have differences of opinion. Contact and affect build up over a period.

Couples can spend time together before their marriage, hopefully developing affectionate, more intimate relationships before marriage. Engaged couples visit relatives' homes together, go into Shiraz to shop, and may stay overnight at each other's homes and even take trips together. One bride stayed at her fiancé's home for two weeks, looking comfortable, leaning affectionately against her mother-in-law-to-be. Another young woman stayed with her in-laws-to-be frequently. The groom stayed at the home of his bride—his mother's sister's daughter. In 2008, the couple seemed comfortable and affectionate and talked intimately. At the home of the groom, they seemed to have a room assigned to them. Sexual relations had apparently been initiated.

Initiation into sexuality proceeds more gradually. Sexual relations are generally expected to be more mutually enjoyable, especially by the bride, rather than abrupt and painful for the female and heavily male- and family-dominated. The sexual and social aspects of the relationship are under the control of and belong to the bridal couple to a greater degree. The groom's parents have lost closeness with and authority over the bridal couple. Instead of a room in the groom's family's courtyard allocated for their use, these days the bride requires a separate house, apart from the groom's parents, completely prepared for them with everything they could possibly need in place. Brides are adamant that they will not live with the mother-in-law. Many will not even stay there one day; they will not even have the traditional *hejleh* or bridal bower in their in-laws' home.

A groom's parents may still attempt to keep their sons with them, but generally it does not work out. Sometimes the two sides develop acrimonious feelings toward each other. The bride and her family have gained more power over the residence of the newlyweds. The groom's father is duty bound to help his son get a wife, and so he is in a dilemma; usually he will end up footing the bill for their separate housing. Most young people do not appreciate the extended family influence or decision making for the benefit of the entire family. They are more individualistic and centered on their self-interest rather than on the family welfare.

Now at wedding celebrations brides do not act any differently from any other guests. They saunter around, dressed in a white strapless dress, talking with people, dancing, eating, and flirting with the groom. They do not seem to feel their behavior must become passive and quiet. They look self-confident and lively. They are not expected by others to display innocent modesty and fear of sexual initiation. They know the groom, are more knowledgeable about sexuality, exchange affectionate physical gestures with him, and perhaps have already experienced sexual relations. Many marriage celebrations, even in Aliabad, feature illegal gender-mixed parties. In other, more conservative weddings, men go over to the female areas at least to dance—and dancing in mixed company is an even worse taboo.

Females go to high school and even higher education in Shiraz or in other cities—perhaps living elsewhere in a dorm—and may even have a university degree. They have become much more assertive and talkative in mixed company, expressing themselves, disagreeing, and making demands. Their modes of social interaction have dramatically evolved from those of forty years ago, and these have become habits that they carry over into marriage. Their behavior, postures, movements, talk, and mobility are less restricted than those of young women forty years previous. They are better able to negotiate with their husbands. Legally and customarily, women are supposed to obtain the husband's permission before leaving the house. In some families, women abided religiously by this rule. Some women, however, go out without asking. A few younger Aliabad women use the resources of feminist ideology and critique about gender conditions to guide and explain their resistance to their situations.

Married couples may now have much more contact with each other; they talk and laugh together even in front of others. Men can openly show affection to their wives. A husband may put his arm around his wife's shoulder during a family gathering. A wife may lean against her husband and give him affectionate looks. In contrast to forty years ago and expectations of the older generation, younger people now may openly show consideration to their spouses. While I was visiting a butcher and his wife and child in 2007, his mother came upstairs for a little while. The butcher considerately placed some freshly barbequed kebab on his wife's plate; his mother muttered, "She can't even help herself to the meat?"

Marriages are becoming more companionate and cooperative. In most marriages, especially those of younger people, gender dynamics have changed to some degree. Females marry much later; less of an age gap separates husbands and wives; wives do not live with their in-laws; couples have few children—usually only one or two; many women enjoy modern conveniences in their home; and women have much greater access to the wider world outside of their home, kin group, and community than Aliabad women did in the 1970s. All of this has the result of empowering women compared to the situation of women in the 1960s and 1970s. However, while young women have been able to bring about more or less radical changes in marriage procedures, the great majority of young Aliabad women live in marital situations that are a mixture of more and less transformed aspects.[11]

For some young people who are able to attain marriage, marriages have become cauldrons within which women—enabled by education and degrees, more say in choosing a mate, wider worlds, a greater sense of power and entitlement, changed gender dynamics, more experience, the internet, social media, and phone access and know-how, access to mobility and travel, higher age and greater maturity, more interaction with nonfamily males, more voice, less age difference with husbands, and independent, nuclear family residence—continue the work of transforming marital and gender relationships, which in turn contributes to developing more egalitarian gender relations in society in general.[12]

Compared with 1978–1979, quite a few Aliabad marriages these days are sites of more intimate, caring, cooperative, and relatively egalitarian friendships. Many marriages are characterized by relatively traditional gender divisions of labor but also respect and affection. Of course some marriages do not work well, often due to conflicting visions and lifestyle expectations or financial or addiction problems and may be fraught with conflict or end in divorce.[13]

Women Disregarding Gender, Generational, and Marital Hierarchies—and Shiʻi Islamic Clerics and Culture at the Same Time

Growing up in this larger world, despite the Islamic Republic of Iran (IRI) officials' laws and policies, women come into marriages these days prepared to wield more power and influence in the marriage relationship. This reality contrasts profoundly with the rules, regulations, and desired culture of the IRI government; Shiʻi Muslim women, the ruling clerics proclaim, should obey and submit to their husbands. They should devote themselves to their husbands' comfort, raising children and taking care of the home. In order to accomplish these tasks and in order to fulfill the requirements of modesty and separation from nonfamily males, they should stay at home.

Although initially after the Iranian Revolution of February 11, 1979, women's mobility, dress, and interaction with nonfamily males became more restricted, little by little women's subtle pushing against these rules has gradually eroded the restrictions. Although at times the morality police cracked down, over time women began to use makeup and nail polish and to wear shorter and tighter pants, shorter, tighter, and more colorful tunics, and more colorful and fashionable scarves covering less and less of their often extreme hairstyles. Aliabad women—as well as other Iranian women—have also become all the more mobile and out in public, although more or less covered with tunic and scarf.[14] Aliabad females, even young, unmarried ones, now freely take the bus and other vehicles into the city on their own. Whereas in the years after the revolution females always sat in the back of a car, now even while with unrelated males, they sit in the front. Some Aliabad women drive, and a few even own their own cars.

According to informants and sometimes according to specific information I have received as well, sexuality is no longer necessarily contained within marriage, even for females but especially for males. Even Aliabad young people in high school, according to the local critics, have boyfriends and girlfriends (insinuating that sexual activity is part of the relationship). Marriage and parenthood have been somewhat separated from full adulthood and have become a matter more of choice, not as necessary to becoming full social beings, full members of society.

In Aliabad, most people did not pay much attention to various pronouncements about marriage and family. As an exception, people pointed to the regime's recent pressure for a higher birth rate, sarcastically asking such questions as "And where is the money for more children coming from? Will they give us the money? We can't even handle the expenses of the children we have now."[15]

IRI laws and policies provide females with fewer rights, protections, and opportunities than males. All these negative messages about their self-worth surely affect women's sense of well-being and personal freedom at some level. However, since the 1979 revolution, other economic, social, and cultural changes have more dramatically influenced Aliabad marriages than have the changed laws and regulations of the IRI government.

For example, IRI laws have lowered the legal age of marriage for females to thirteen and for boys to fifteen, although with permission from the father or a judge they can legally be married before this. The average age for female first marriage in 2015 was twenty-four (according to government statistics) (Zimmt 2016). Although child marriages apparently have been taking place elsewhere in Iran and might well occur among the Afghans and others living in Aliabad, I have not heard of early marriages among Aliabad people these days.[16]

Despite IRI laws about marriage and family, I found discussion about marriage issues in Aliabad generally focused more on economic and financial issues, the inflation of expectations, and varying social and cultural influences than on Shi'i regulations and IRI laws and policies. Several women, especially those whose husbands or they themselves are overtly at least supporters of the government, demonstrate more adherence to the rules and regulations proclaimed by Shi'i clerical government officials to be Islamic. The great majority, however, go about their day-to-day lives much as would have Aliabad women before the Iranian Revolution, with, however, a great deal more mobility, freedom of action and choice of public and private dress, and say in marriage and family than did village women before 1979.[17]

Economic, Social, and Cultural Influences Override Governmental Directives: Discounting Shi'i Culture and Clerics

For this preliminary research project, I started out at the community level, focusing on everyday discussions, commentaries of individuals, lived experiences, and everyday decision making, interactions, and strategies rather than beginning at the level of religious specialists and—in the case of the IRI—the clerical figures in power and their laws and policies regarding Shi'i Muslim marriage. By focusing on lay commentaries and lived experiences and taking a holistic perspective, the extremely heavy impact of economic permutations, transformation in gender dynamics, social change, world cultures, and people's own changing views and wishes became apparent.

The government highly disapproves of the many changes in gender behaviors, male-female relationships, and marriage. Marriage has become the focus of discussion, debate, concern, blaming, and anxiety—not only among parents and young people of Aliabad but also in the country in general and among IRI government personnel who have tried to develop policies to encourage marriage as they believe it should be.

The Iranian government is striving mightily to push marriage in the direction of earlier, more fecund, universal, hierarchical, lifelong, sexual-labor-divided, traditional husband working and wife/mother at home, and straight marriage. For the past few years, clerical governmental leaders have been mandating for a higher birth rate, no longer subsidizing birth control—and in fact trying to make it difficult to gain access to birth control and condemning abortion. Sexual relations must be confined to marriage.

In spite of this heavy drive to regularize Iranian marriages according to the ruling clerics' versions of Shi'i Muslim culture, Iranians are moving in the direction of marriages similar to trends in many other countries—later marriages, less dramatic age differences between partners, more empowered brides, delayed parenthood, birth control (see Loeffler and Friedl 2009, 2014) and even illegal abortions to limit family size, birth rates lower than two, occasional decisions to forego children, climbing divorce rates, more people remaining single, communication and interaction among unmarried males and females, sexual activity before and even outside of marriage, homosexual self-identification and activity, cohabitation without marriage, more female-headed households, more women living alone, and less hierarchical marital relationships.[18] Although such changes have occurred to a much greater degree in Tehran, especially in the upper-middle and middle classes, most of these trends are visible among Aliabad people as well. I have not heard of the cohabitation of unmarried Aliabad people. Forgoing marriage is extremely rare among Aliabad people. I have not heard of Aliabad couples deciding to remain childless and staying with the decision. Otherwise, Aliabad society is moving in the same direction as the rest of the country regarding marriage, if at a slower pace than in Tehran especially among the upper, upper-middle, and middle classes.

Women in Iran and the families who want the best for them are working within narrow parameters to improve their situations. Even when not directly stymied by a law or policy, women face severe gender discrimination and pressure to fit into restrictive frameworks. Yet females are making amazing progress toward greater voice within marriages and more intimate, egalitarian relationships, empowered by transformation in gender dynamics and their own modified ideas about gender and marriage.

Brides generally come into marriage with more resources, empowerment, and status than they did forty years ago. Although legally they have fewer rights regarding marriage than their husbands, within the framework of the marriage wives are now more equipped to negotiate and/or pressure their husbands, nag them, and utilize other tactics to influence them—as in earlier decades.[19] These days, though, many wives feel enabled to be more verbal and direct in communicating and negotiating with their husbands. In some households I visited, I have been treated to extensive family discussions. Husband and wife and teenaged or older offspring, especially daughters—who now have attained higher levels of education than their fathers, brothers, and, even more so, their mothers—exchange differing ideas. Even in Aliabad many females, especially but not only among the young, do not accept the regime's pronouncements about women, their seclusion and covering, and the limits on their mobility and behavior.[20] Under everyday conditions, economic conditions and considerations, social change, youth culture, more power and sense of entitlement in the hands of young people, and global culture more effectively than the clerical rulers' ideas about Shi'i Muslim marriage influence how many people think about and take action regarding marriage.

IRI clerical rulers are putting a great deal of effort into molding Iranian marriages, from the top down, into their image of Shi'i Muslim marriage. Despite IRI officials' push for earlier marriage and more children, economic factors and desires for better lives push people to put off marriage, delay having children, and have small families. Economic considerations, social changes, and cultural influences enabled by communication and mobility have brought about marriage expectations and behavior more in line with "developmental idealism" (see Thornton et al. 2015; Abbasi-Shavazi and Askari-Nodoushan 2012) than with the IRI rulers' vision of Shi'i Muslim marriage. For many Aliabadis as well as other Iranians, marriage perceptions and practices are moving in the direction of choice, companionship, and greater equality and focus on the interests of the individuals, couples, and nuclear families. In many cases people themselves, from the grassroots up, are transforming mainstream Iranian Shi'i marriages into more what they want for themselves. With marriage as well as with other areas of life, many Aliabadis and other Iranians are moving away from the Shi'i Islamic culture promoted by conservative clerical leaders toward a more secular, individualistic culture (also see Faramarzi 2017 and Mir and Khaki 2015).

In recent years IRI officials have become greatly disturbed by the direction of marital changes in Iran. They are concerned about the much later age for marriage, greatly lowered birth rates, premarital relationships and sexual activity, women's insubordination in marriage, lowered rates of marital fidelity, greatly increasing rates of divorce, "white marriage" (living together without marriage formalities), and the lack of female modesty in dress, mobility, and interaction with nonfamily males.[21] They have sponsored several in-depth and broad studies about gender relations and marriage. According to several researchers and policy makers at the 2018 First International Conference on Social Policy in the

Islamic World, IRI officials are so concerned about marriage that they are pressuring researchers and students to focus their work on marriage.

According to studies, economic problems and sexual dysfunction are among the most common reasons for marital difficulties and divorce. The government has tried to address these issues, mandating courses on sexuality for engaged couples. Before the regime's push for higher birth rates in the past few years, premarital procedures included information about birth control. Government classes (and Shi'i teachings as well) contain the expectation that intercourse should be mutually pleasurable. Radio programs deal with marital relationships and ways to improve communication and cooperation. The government offers loans for marriage and other loans as well and provides a small stipend to families for each member. Officials sometimes sponsor group weddings and have made efforts to place a limit on the amount of money to be available to a bride as agreed upon in marriage contracts. They post advertisements about the benefits of large families and encourage more children in every way possible. However, as several people said to me in the spring of 2018, "We don't listen."

Conclusion: Rebuffing Hierarchies in Gender, Marriage, and Clerical Authority

In the areas of gender dynamics and relations, marriage, and religion, despite the rule of the Shi'i clerics of the IRI, hierarchies are eroding. Due to ongoing social change, many women feel more empowered to assert themselves in aspects of marriage in spite of clerical rules that wives must obey, serve, and submit to their husbands. Women are marrying later, having few children, and in some cases becoming more mobile and self-actualizing instead of staying at home and keeping busy with domestic tasks only. Probably most Iranians, at least in some areas, are not listening to the Shi'i clerics who declare themselves to be representatives of God on earth, whose laws and directives must be followed by all Shi'i Muslims.

Of course Iranians have widely differing views and practices regarding marriage and other areas as well. In Aliabad, most people of the population from 1978–1979 have been more integrated into general Iranian society and aspects of culture shared by many countries. Most of the less well-off people living in Aliabad are in-migrants, such as Afghans and Lurs from more rural areas and other places. I do not know much about their cultures but assume that they hold more conservative, traditional views. Of course many other Iranians take a relatively conservative stance about gender issues, religion, and the IRI government. Nikki Keddie's commentary about the two cultures in Iran continues to be relevant, although the more modern, secularist, world-culture-influenced category has grown much larger in the past few decades (Keddie 2006).[22] An anthropologist based in Tehran and cited by Faramarzi estimates the two groups to be about evenly split (Faramarzi 2017). Election results of May 19, 2017, also suggested the more modernist, reformist sector of the population to be somewhat larger. Conservative Hojjat al-Islam Ebrahim Raisi, who promised that "his government would enhance women's dignity within the family, because women should be 'good mothers and wives'" (Davachi 2017), lost to the more moderate then incumbent president Hassan Rouhani.

World dynamics—in economics, education, media, and social and cultural influences—are impacting Iranian Shi'i marriages—arguably to a greater extent than Shi'i rules and regulations and more than the laws and visions of the IRI government and the rulers' own ideal marriage culture. These global dynamics are resulting in Iranian and Aliabad marriages moving in the same direction as trends in marriages elsewhere (see Yount and Rashad 2008)—including in the Western countries condemned by the Iranian government.

Recent national-level developments, however, have brought uncertainty to movements away from marriage as defined by the IRI regime. In the June 18, 2021 presidential election, the hardliner Chief Justice Ebrahim Raisi, known for his involvement with mass executions in 1988, who lost to the more moderate President Hassan Rouhani in 2017, won—with a record-breaking low turnout. Many saw his victory this time as engineered by the Council of Guardians, backed by Supreme Leader, Ayatollah Khamenei. With this push for more rigidity and apparent approval for more punitiveness against critics of the regime, what can we expect to happen to marriage expectations and practices in the near future? The course of action Raisi will take remains to be seen. Will he take the politically rigid approach espoused by Khamenei and clamp down further on women and their lives? Or will he adopt a pragmatic approach hoping to expand his now poor base of support, for the next presidential election in 2025?

NOTES

1. Aliabad women and girls did not do animal herding or agricultural work.
2. She later married someone from another city, considered to be a less positive marital situation. Another girl wept and resisted a suitor as she felt herself too young and greatly wished to continue her education, at least to earn a diploma. She was eventually persuaded into the match with the promise she could continue her schooling. The wedding photos show a sad little bride. The promise did not materialize. Much later, when her children were studying at the same level, she decided to take correspondence classes and finally received her diploma.
3. For description of weddings in Lar, see Gianfortoni (2009).
4. See "The Little Changes That Happened When Simin Became Avdal's Wife," in Friedl (1991).
5. Although one hears stories of wedding nights from females, I do not know of wedding night experiences from the male point of view. Sexuality is a relatively new field in Middle East anthropology, and issues of sexuality from the perspectives of male informants are even less researched.

6. For other studies on Iranian marriages, see Friedl (1991, 2014), Tremayne (2006), and Vieille (1978).

7. See "Watching the World from Sarah's Loom," in Friedl (1991), Friedl (2014), Hegland (2003), Tapper (Lindisfarne) (1978), and Wright (1978).

8. For a case study of such a conflict, see Hegland (1999).

9. Others expressed the opinion that it was more a desire to get out without parental interference rather than a sincere desire to form a lifelong union that prompted the girl to marry.

10. Miri Ghaffarzadeh (2016) found some similar changes in mate selection and weddings in the Iranian city of Urmia.

11. Regarding Aliabad gender dynamics, education, and marriage from 2003 to 2015, see Hegland (2009 and 2014). See also Friedl (2014).

12. Also see Kian (2007, 2014).

13. For discussion about the current problems and challenges of some present-day marriages, see Hegland (2021).

14. Several movements in Iran are openly resisting forced hijab; some women have been removing and defiantly waving their scarves in public.

15. Given the severity of economic problems for middle- and lower-class Iranians these days in addition to the attitudes of discouragement, even despair, among so many, in spite of clerical propaganda, real conditions do not encourage people to have more children. See Kamali Dehghan (2018) and Khosravi (2017).

16. Many Lurs, Afghans, and people from elsewhere now live in Aliabad. I do not have much interaction with the in-migrants and would not know about early marriages among them.

17. Before the 1979 Revolution, all Aliabad women always wore a *chador* (a large semicircle of cloth, centered above the face and falling to the ground all around, held together in front with a hand) when going outside of their courtyards. Now the great majority of women wear a scarf and a tunic, a less cumbersome and covering outdoor outfit, with only a few more elderly women continuing to use a *chador*. Many young women do not want to use any of these, and the great majority do not feel hijab should be forced. Also see Anonymous (2018).

18. A recent report from the Iranian Parliament found that 80 percent of Iranian women are sexually active before marriage. See Ahmadian (2014).

19. For creative and intriguing tactics applied by wives several decades ago in a Lurish village, see Friedl (1991).

20. For studies of questioning, negotiating, and resisting IRI laws and pronouncements about females and gender among women elsewhere in Iran, see Afary (2009), Gerami (2012), Gerami and Lehnerer (2001), Haghighat (2014), Kian (2010), Kian-Thiébaut (2005), Mahdavi (2009), Mahdi (2003), Moaveni (2006, 2010), Sadeghi (2008, 2010), and Torab (2007).

21. I know of no white marriages either in Aliabad or among Aliabad people who live elsewhere. However, knowledge about the concept of white marriage has reached Aliabad; in spring 2019 several people in Aliabad referred to it. More dramatically, two young women whose families are from Aliabad but who are living outside of Aliabad said that they would like to be in a white marriage, that such an arrangement would allow them better acquaintance with a young man to really know whether or not he would be the right marriage partner for them.

22. Abbas Milani has referred to this current culture clash with active, determined pro-
    tagonists on each side as "trench war in the digital age" (Milani 2017). A recent survey
    found 82 percent of Iranians supporting "separation of religion and state," whereas in
    the MENA survey the statistic was only 24 percent. See Afary and Friedland (2018).

REFERENCES

Abbasi-Shavazi, Mohammad Jalal, and Abbas Askari-Nodoushan. 2012. "Family Life and
    Developmental Idealism in Yazd, Iran." *Demographic Research* 26: 207.
Afary, Janet. 2009. *Sexual Politics in Iran*. New York: Cambridge University Press.
Afary, Janet, and Roger Friedland. 2018. "Critical Theory, Authoritarianism, and the Poli-
    tics of Lipstick: From Weimar Republic to the Contemporary Middle East." *Critical
    Research on Religion* 6: 243–268. https://doi.org/10.1177/2050303218800374.
Ahmadian, Alireza. 2014. "Iran's Gender Double Standards." *IranWire*. https://iranwire.com
    /en/features/665.
Anonymous. 2018. "Official Report: Support for Compulsory Hijab Plummets." *IranWire*.
    https://iranwire.com/en/features/5433.
Davachi, Azadeh. 2017. "What Iranian Women Want: President Hassan Rouhani's Second
    Term Is His Chance to Live Up to Iranian Women's Hopes." *U.S. News & World Report*,
    May 24. https://www.usnews.com/news/best-countries/articles/2017-05-24/in-iran
    -women-want-rights-jobs-and-a-seat-at-the-table.
Faramarzi, Scheherezade. 2017. "In Iran's Presidential Elections, Reformists' Hopes Are
    Limited: They Have United Many Formerly Opposed Voters—But for Now the Fight for
    Personal and Political Freedoms Is Taking a Back Seat." *The Nation*. https://www
    .thenation.com/article/in-irans-presidential-elections-reformists-hopes-are-limited/.
Gerami, Shahin. 2012. "De-territorialized Islamisms: Women's Agency of Resistance and
    Acquiescence." In *Routledge Handbook of Political Islam*, edited by Shahram Akbarza-
    deh, 191–204. New York: Routledge.
Gerami, Shahin, and Melodye Lehnerer. 2001. "Women's Agency and Household Diplomacy:
    Negotiating Fundamentalism." *Gender & Society* 15 (4): 556–573.
Gianfortoni, Emily Wells. 2009. "Marriage Customs in Lar: The Role of Women's Networks
    in Tradition and Change." *Iran and the Caucasus* 13: 285–298.
Friedl, Erika. 1991. *Women of Deh Koh: Lives in an Iranian Village*. London: Penguin.
———. 2014. "A Thorny Side of Marriage in Iran." In *Everyday Life in the Muslim Middle East*,
    edited by Donna Lee Bowen, Evelyn A. Early, and Becky Schulthies, 22–132. Blooming-
    ton: Indiana University Press.
Haghighat, Elhum. 2014. "Iran's Changing Gender Dynamics in Light of Demographic, Politi-
    cal and Technological Transformations." *Middle East Critique* 23 (3): 313–332.
Hegland, Mary Elaine. 1999. "Wife Abuse and the Political System: A Middle Eastern Case
    Study." In *To Have and to Hit: Cultural Perspective on Wife Beating*, edited by Dorothy
    Counts, Judith Brown, and Jacqueline Campbell, 234–251. Urbana: University of Illi-
    nois Press.
———. 2003. "Talking Politics: A Village Widow in Iran." In *Personal Encounters: A Reader in
    Cultural Anthropology*, edited by Linda S. Walbridge and April K. Sievert, 53–59. Bos-
    ton: McGraw-Hill.
———. 2009. "Educating Young Women: Culture, Conflict, and New Identities in an Iranian
    Village." *Iranian Studies* 42 (1): 45–79.
———. 2011. "Aliabad of Shiraz: Transformation from Village to Suburban Town." *Anthro-
    pology of the Middle East* 6 (22): 21–37.

———. 2014. *Days of Revolution: Political Unrest in an Iranian Village.* Stanford, CA: Stanford University Press.

———. 2021. "Changing Perceptions and Practices of Marriage among People of Aliabad from 1978 to 2018: New Problems and Challenges." In *Iranian Romance in the Digital Age: From Arranged Marriage to White Marriage*, edited by Janet Afary and Jesilyn Faust, 174–196. London: I.B. Tauris.

Kamali Dehghan, Saeed. 2018. "'Desperate to Find a Way Out': Iran Edges towards Precipice." *Guardian*, July 20. https://www.theguardian.com/world/2018/jul/20/desperate-to -find-a-way-out-iran-edges-towards-precipice?CMP=Share_iOSApp.

Keddie, Nikki. 2006. *Modern Iran: Roots and Results of Revolution.* New Haven, CT: Yale University Press.

Khosravi, Shahram. 2017. *Precarious Lives: Waiting and Hope in Iran.* Philadelphia: University of Pennsylvania Press.

Kian, Azadeh. 2007. "Women and Politics in Post-Islamist Iran: The Gender Conscious Drive to Change." *British Journal of Middle Eastern Studies* 24 (1): 75–96.

———. 2010. "Islamic Feminism in Iran: A New Form of Subjugation or the Emergence of Agency?" *Critique Internationale* 46 (1): 45–66. http://www.cairn-int.info/abstract-E _CRII_046_0045--islamic-feminism-in-iran-a-new-form-of-s.htm.

———. 2014. "Gender Social Relations and the Challenge of Women's Employment." *Middle East Critique* 23 (3): 333–347.

Kian-Thiébaut, Azadeh. 2005. "From Motherhood to Equal Rights Advocates: The Weakening of Patriarchal Order." *Iranian Studies* 38 (1): 45–66.

Loeffler, Agnes, and Erika Friedl. 2009. "Cultural Parameters of a 'Miraculous' Birth Rate Drop." *Anthropology News* 50 (3): 13–15. https://doi.org/10.1111/j.1556-3502.2009 .50314.x.

———. 2014. "The Birthrate Drop in Iran." *HOMO—Journal of Comparative Human Biology* 65: 240–255. https://www.academia.edu/32428246/The_birthrate_drop_in_Iran.

Mahdavi, Pardis. 2009. *Passionate Uprising: The Sexual Revolution in Iran.* Stanford, CA: Stanford University Press.

Mahdi, Ali Akbar. 2003. "Iranian Women between Islamization and Globalization." In *Iran Encountering Globalization: Problems and Prospects*, edited by Ali Mohammadi. New York: RoutledgeCurzon.

Milani, Abbas. 2017. "A Trench War in the Digital Age: The Case of Iran." *Caravan* 1714. http:// www.hoover.org/research/trench-war-digital-age-case-iran.

Mir, Gousia, and G. N. Khaki. 2015. "Globalization and Post-Islamic Revolution: A Changing Iranian Woman." *Journal of Globalization Studies* 6 (1). http://www.socionauki.ru /journal/articles/281744.

Miri Ghaffarzadeh, Shamsi. 2016. "Traditional vs. Modern Wedding Ceremony in Urmia City of Iran." *Social Sciences* 11 (14): 3543–3548.

Moaveni, Azadeh. 2006. *Lipstick Jihad: A Memoir of Growing Up Iranian in America and American in Iran.* New York City: PublicAffairs.

———. 2010. *Honeymoon in Tehran: Two Years of Love and Danger in Iran.* New York: Random House.

Osanloo, Arzoo. 2009. *The Politics of Women's Rights in Iran.* Princeton, NJ: Princeton University Press.

Sadeghi, Fatemeh. 2008. "Negotiating with Modernity: Young Women and Sexuality in Iran." *Comparative Studies of South Asia, Africa and the Middle East* 28 (2): 250–259.

———. 2010. "Bypassing Islamism and Feminism: Women's Resistance and Rebellion in Post-revolutionary Iran." *Féminismes Islamiques* 128 (December): 209–228. https://remmm .revues.org/6936?lang=en.

Shahshahani, Soheila. 2007. "Wedding Ceremony in Turmoil." *Anthropology of the Middle East* 2 (I): 103–108.

Tapper (Lindisfarne), Nancy. 1978. "The Women's Sub-society among the Shahsevan Nomads." In *Women in the Muslim World*, edited by Lois Beck and Nikki Keddie, 374–398. Cambridge, MA: Harvard University Press.

Thornton, Arland, Shawn F. Dorius, and Jeffrey Swindle. 2015. "Developmental Idealism: The Cultural Foundations of World Development Programs." *Sociology of Development* I (2): 277–320.

Torab, Azam. 2007. *Performing Islam: Gender and Ritual in Iran.* Leiden: Brill.

Tremayne, Soraya. 2006. "Modernity and Marriage in Iran: A View from Within." *Journal of Middle East Women's Studies* 2 (I): 65–94.

Vieille, Paul. 1978. "Iranian Women in Family Alliance and Sexual Politics." In *Women in the Muslim World*, edited by Lois Beck and Nikki Keddie, 451–472. Cambridge, MA: Harvard University Press.

Wright, Sue. 1978. "Prattle and Politics: The Position of Women in Dushman-Ziari." *Anthropological Society of Oxford* 9: 98–112.

Yount, Kathryn M., and Hoda Rashad, eds. 2008. *Family in the Middle East: Ideational Change in Egypt, Iran and Tunisia.* New York: Routledge.

Zimmt, Raz. 2016. "Marrying Late: Young Adults and the Marriage Crisis in Iran." Forum for Regional Thinking. http://www.regthink.org/en/articles/marrying-late-young-adults -and-the-marriage-crisis.

2

The New Marital Romance

How Bollywood, Islamic Doctrines, and Mobile Phones Dissect the Imperative of Spouse Evasion

ANNA-MARIA WALTER

"Morek thay nay, ma sath morek thay." In 2014's most popular Shina song, both a girl and a boy sing "talk to me."[1] It was one of the first times that a female voice was commercially recorded in the local language of Gilgit in Pakistan's high mountain area. The young generation enthusiastically listened and danced to the song while elders frowned upon the decay of morals. In a society where distance between the genders is expected, "morek thay" perfectly captures the current disposition of change in intimate relationships. Public debates that oscillate between gender, love, and respectability often revolve around the mobile phone as the epitome of change.

In contemporary Gilgit-Baltistan, various customary, Islamic, and imported Indian or globalized ideas and discourses intersect and contest each other. However, gender relations are generally shaped by *parda* (literally meaning curtain), the segregation of men and women. In varying forms *parda* is prevalent all over South Asia and in many Muslim societies (Abu-Lughod 1986; Jeffery 1979; Mandelbaum 1988; Mernissi 1987; Papanek and Minault 1982; Ring 2006; Vatuk 1982). In private houses and extended families, I discovered the intimate side of this public phenomenon and was startled by how loving many arranged marriages are. "Love or arranged marriage?" was an important subject for my interlocutors: Most women take an eager interest in marital relationships, as mothers who are responsible for their offspring's future, as girls[2] assessing their own standpoint, as mature women narrating their love stories, or all of them together gossiping about others. The tone often switched back and forth between accounts of romance and regrets about the perceived degeneration of morals, which people often correlate with the relatively newly introduced technology of mobile phones. In one of the valleys, I collected a poem in Shina even personifying the mobile phone as the devil's little brother: "Shertane chuno ṟa mobile alun" (Satan's little brother, the mobile, has come).[3]

As so many conversations in the field centered on negotiations of norms and expectations concerning arranged marriages, this chapter explores the background of the ongoing changes in love concepts in the area of Gilgit. For further insights, I draw on works on love and marriage in South Asia and, with the help of ethnographic examples, illustrate women's motivations and emotions by contextualizing them in the wider framework of embodied norms and values. To integrate new influences into their lives, women navigate along their incorporated perception of modesty as well as maneuver their personal agency and contribute to changes of morality in their communities.

The Field Setting

My findings are based on fourteen months of research in Gilgit-Baltistan, the remote arid high mountain area of the former princely state Kashmir, which is still disputed between Pakistan and India and does not have constitutional representation in domestic politics. In the city and suburbs of the capital Gilgit, the region's three sects of Islam—Shi'a, Sunni, and Ismaili—as well as various language and ethnic groups settle next to each other. Pakistan's national language Urdu serves as the lingua franca. In both urban and rural areas, I was accepted as a family member into several houses but mainly worked within the local Shina-speaking Shi'a community, which accounts for much of the area. Although there are minor religious variations among the sects, lifeworlds of women concerning moral concepts of marriage and love are much alike. Most of the population is very much attached to their valleys of origin and sustains a quite rural lifestyle in the city. However, Gilgit-Baltistan has witnessed tremendous changes within the past thirty years (Walter 2014): The Karakoram Highway has connected the region to Chinese markets and Pakistani centers and has increased people's mobility. Besides strong religious links to Shi'ite Iran (or the Ismaili leader Aga Khan and the Sunni missionaries from Tablighi Jamaat) and occasional violent outbursts of sectarian tensions, the region has been shaped by multiple developmental projects, especially by the Aga Khan Development Network, the rapid improvement of education for both genders, and the introduction of media and new communication technologies, such as the mobile phone in 2006.

Working with women in Gilgit-Baltistan was most productive in less formal settings provided by participant observation. To adapt to females' behavior, for me as a young woman in Gilgit *sharm*, (modesty, respectability) emerged as the most relevant parameter. I identify *sharm* as an expressive aspect of the *parda* habitus of many Muslim societies to which numerous authors (in)directly relate to in their ethnographic writings on women in Gilgit-Baltistan (Azhar-Hewitt 1999; Besio 2007; Cook 2007; Gratz 2006; Halvorson 2005; Mahrhoffer-Wolff 2002; Walter 2016; Varley 2010, 2012).[4] Since there is less social stratification in

Gilgit-Baltistan's society than in most other parts of South Asia, *parda* is not primarily a means to express economic or caste hierarchies. In urban settings, however, the seclusion of women can lately also be regarded as an indicator of education and "modernity" that follows stricter interpretations of Islam (Besio 2007).[5] After introducing the female concept of *sharm* as respectability, I describe a new and hybrid form of romance that exemplifies local people's struggle to navigate in the multiplicity of social, cultural, economic, and religious factors and lead morally good lives.

Modest Women and Lovesick Men

Sharm does not easily translate with shame but rather caters to a broader concept of modesty that can be understood only through local epistemology. As a preobjective expression of social categories and their constant bodily enactment, chaste thoughts and modest behavior discipline mind and emotions. Consequently, shame, or rather its avoidance, is truly experienced through an omnipresent set of feelings (Walter 2016).

In Gilgit, *sharm* as women's fear of exposure is always connected to the (potential) presence of men, and shy behavior serves as a role model of femininity. *Sharm* is an expression of proper behavior, of modesty, and does not signal wrongdoing but on the contrary displays and perpetuates a person's self-esteem, social standing, honor, and pride (Abu-Lughod 1986; Randall 2013, 79). I often had the impression that the emotion of shame works as a reminder to restrain oneself, to (re)position oneself in line with social norms of the collective when individually raising too much attention. Just as Saba Mahmood described for trends of piety among Egyptian women, "action does not issue forth from natural feelings but creates them" while at the same time "it is through repeated bodily acts that one trains one's memory, desire, and intellect" (2012, 383–384).

Appropriating mobile telephony into their daily lives, women from in and around Gilgit navigate along their embodied sense of *sharm*. For example, when the call of a stranger with an "unknown number" reaches a girl's mobile phone, she intuitively feels that it is not appropriate to answer and perceives the man imposing himself on her (*tang karna*—to irritate). However, the ambiguous new space of mobile connections also serves as a platform to renegotiate existing norms and values. So when the girl is with cousins or friends in a cheerful, exuberant atmosphere, she might be confident and daring, pick up the phone, and for fun fool the boy who just passes time trying to hook up with any random woman. He now is the culprit while the girl has witnesses to her transparency.

But why do women have to struggle to discipline themselves to this extent? Many wives are in love with their husbands and hope the same for others, but to publicly show one's feelings would be a scandal; it would mean that a woman is not in control of her emotions. In contrary to men, who can be ill tempered and let their anger or jealousy erupt in public, women learn to guard their hearts from early childhood on (Ring 2006, 109). The attitude of modesty seems to be an overcorrection of implicit believes in female emotionality and "savagery." Men are associated with reason and moral behavior (*'aql*), while women succumb to desire and passion (*nafs*); the balance between these all human inherent traits is hard to obtain (Ask 1993, 211). In her ethnography on Pakhtun women in Pakistan, Benedicte Grima (2007) reports how gender roles are cemented by assigning to women attributes of weakness that are associated with emotionality, the feminine in need of male control. From the westernmost side of South Asia to its eastern edge, the same discourse is prevalent in Bangladesh (Rozario 1992): because women are not in control of their own bodies during menstruation or pregnancy, they are considered to be closer to nature, hence not as evolved as males. Islamic scholars, such as the Indian-Pakistani Sayyid Maududi, have proliferated this view: "In short, a woman's mental and nervous system becomes lethargic and disorderly during menstruation. Her limbs do not quite obey her will; rather her will and the decision power are overwhelmed by some involuntary force within her" ([1936] 2011, 80).

Qur'anic teachings stress the importance for people to follow the right path given by Allah to overcome natural distractions and temptations. So to uplift their own status, women demonstrate their "civilized" manner in regulating supposedly "natural" emotions (Abu-Lughod 1986, 152). This perception was never explicitly voiced in any of my encounters in Gilgit, but it was omnipresent implicitly, for example when women do not comfort each other in moments of despair, gossip about a sentimental neighbor, and take pride in accurately running their household. Women's emotional self-discipline partly signals their ability to navigate the established framework. It is also an expression of embodied morality, which is constantly reinforced by Islam's detailed rules of purification, meant to overcome the natural states of menstruation, sexual intercourse, childbirth, and so on. It not only guides women's public behavior but also serves as an embodied discipline of the thoughts and feelings that protect them against being emotionally overpowered.

Young men, on the other side, are more impulsive and emotional. They get angry easily and let go of their guard to fall in love. In the north of the Indian subcontinent, many famous love tales, like those of Laila-Majnun or Heer-Ranjha, narrate the story of passionate lovers who are struck by love from a distance, only at the sight of the other's gentleness. Because of social or hierarchical obstacles, they do not have a joint future and must undergo a lot of suffering (Ask 1993, 219). Chastity and pain are two crucial aspects of such passionate love, *'ishq*, the subject of many famous lyrical and filmic adaptations.

Some men romanticize a girl from their youth all their life. Although they have never established a relationship with her, they project desires unto her and worship her in an imaginary shrine. As I once read in an SMS by a married lover, "She [his wife] is my obligation, you are my love." His beloved girl asserted that he does not expect any physical or long-term commitment from her; she seems to be the canvas for his projection. Charles Lindholm remarks in this regard for Pakhtun lovers that "pure" love and mundane acts of sexuality exclude each other: "In general, sexuality is downplayed, and the emphasis is on the spiritual qualities of the beloved and the deep yearning of the lover. . . . The ideal romance in Pukhtun verse and myth cannot be consummated, for consummation means the end of the quest and the loss of the ideal. . . . Sexual penetration is an act of power; submission is acceptance of inferiority" (2008, 190).

In her very insightful ethnography on life in an apartment complex in Karachi, Laura Ring (2006) notes that women strive to establish close, loving relationships with their husbands but do not want to fall into irresponsible, unpredictable love. The term 'ishq is understood to be a loss of self, of willpower, of one's agency; the afflicted is overpowered by emotions and will surrender everything to the cause of love. As women formally always depend on men, they fear their only sphere of self-determination, the control of their inner life, fading (Ring 2006, 148–152). Ring explains, "Purdah, then—restriction on visibility and vision, but also the prevention of self-exposure through reticence, silence, downcast eyes, and closed mouth—is aimed in part at protecting and preserving those most human (read: culturally valued) of faculties: reason, will, agency" (148).

Female passivity entails men's active pursuit of women: to win a woman's attention he must take the initiative. While girls mostly do not respond to romantic offerings, an absence of objection suggests a form of consent (Ahearn 2001, 249–250). Although this form of courtship is not very widespread in Gilgit-Baltistan, TV and film disseminate it into every valley, deeply influencing young people's imaginations: "He [the young lover] will pass long, intense letters to the girl, begging for a photograph, a meeting, a return letter confirming her love for him. He will pine, profess loss of appetite and enrage his friends in long discussions about the best way to win the girl over. . . . The youth now takes the part of the humble and ardent suitor, whose happiness (indeed, whose life) totally depends upon the favors of his beloved" (Osella and Osella 1998, 199).

Women's mastery at guarding their heart from 'ishq might even be a way to subvert the patriarchal gender ideology: women are goddesses, who resist seduction and "enslave" men. But hierarchies still exist, and one could also interpret women's passivity as self-closure to prevent greater damage. To give in to irresponsible, passionate love really proves to be dangerous for youngsters, who dishonor family loyalties, as cases of honor killings in Gilgit-Baltistan show (Israr 2015). To escape the threat of an illicit relationship, some couples elope to a big city, which means breaking off all natal ties. Most people surrender their longing to outer circumstances and only in rare cases embrace the idea of passionate love. Having embodied reserve and *sharm*, this seems to be no difficult task for women. But many stories of lovesick men who turn insane (*vo mukamal pagal ho gia*) circulate in the area. Interestingly, these men are dealt with lenience; in one case, the brokenhearted man many times tried to commit suicide, stole the family's money, gambled it away, even cast a curse on his beloved— in short, he acted in complete contradiction to conventional ways without being outcast (Lindholm 2006, 8).

In other parts of Pakistan, *'ishq* is often also associated with Sufism, the purity of an asexual love for God. This spiritual branch of Islam hardly exists in Gilgit-Baltistan. There, mysticism is traditionally associated with fairies, the purest of all beings who live on the mountain tops as a counterscheme to the mean, polluted world of (wo)men. People in Gilgit tell—literally—fairy tales of pure spiritual beings who get involved in love relationships with humans occasionally (Marhoffer-Wolf 2002). These stories of prolonged, troublesome adventures serve as warning that one will encounter pain and grief when embracing desire. Although passionate, self-negating *'ishq* clearly belongs to Bollywood movies, Indian dramas, or local folk tales, ideas of this type of ideal and pure love influence people's imaginations.

Between the Weddings

Contrary to that stands grown conjugal affection, which my interlocutors often referred to as *mohabbat*-love among family members more generally. The maxim declares, don't marry who you love but love who you marry! All over South Asia, love should not precede a marriage. However, in Gilgit-Baltistan future spouses usually are not total strangers to one another as most marriages are endogamous, meaning people marry within the widely extended family network of either of their parents. Nevertheless, boy and girl usually have not had much interaction before. To give one's daughter to an unknown family is considered very risky: multiple layers of family bonds keep children close to home, protect them from abuses, and secure a similar environment in their in-law's house. Compatibility through a shared background is taken as a guarantee for happiness (Robinson 2014, 230). Few families marry their daughters to strangers because they aspire to upward mobility through a good match in terms of education and wealth.

Western-style love marriage is often depicted as selfish, individualistic, and antisocial. Romantic love is portrayed as being in opposition to arranged marriages, which cater to the values of family duties and parents' authority (Mody 2008). "As many young people live in joint families, marriage cannot possibly be seen as a private matter, as it affects the lives of parents and the equilibrium of the whole household" (Donner 2008, 70). If young people chose a partner themselves, they alone would be responsible for the decision in times of trouble. Many

Gilgitis feel that parents are better fit for a rationally informed choice and not misguided by romantic feelings. Additionally, the "marriage market" is strictly in the hands of mothers and, although they discuss matters in agreement with their husbands, is one of the most important spheres of influence for women. They insist on exercising their right to search for a daughter-in-law who will perform the daily household chores along with themselves.

Nevertheless, most of my close acquaintances mutually fell in love with their spouses after their arranged wedding. Affection grows over time and through increasing intimacy. Despite common beliefs in the spontaneity of love, my observations show that "choosing to fall in love does not negate the emotion" (Twamley 2014, 104) and can still serve as a precondition for a marital bond. In the life of most Gilgitis physical intimacy and personal disclosure between women and men take place only within the conjugal relationship, thus the bonds created through this companionship often lead to mutual attachment. Although spouses demonstrate distance in front of others, they might risk brief expressions of their mutual affection within the household. The Shina term for grown affection, *khush*, covers the whole spectrum of socially acceptable love(s), from brotherly affection to friendship and parents' love for their children as well as spouses, and used in different contexts simply means happiness.

Shazia grew up in a village in the early 1990s. Her family received a first *rishta* (marriage proposal) for her when she was around ten years old and at thirteen married her to a relative stranger. In those days girls were not involved in the decision-making process and were mostly too young to understand its dimensions. Through *nikah* (Islamic marriage contract) families used to reserve the "good matches" early. Some years later big wedding celebrations signaled the social implementation of the marriage, when the bride moved to the groom's house, at the occasion of the couple's *shadi*. Until then girls were given time to grow up and young men to finish their studies, return to their parents' farm, or find an occupation. The young husband could visit his wife's family, but she would bashfully hide from him, even escaping the house when he was present. Women describe how *shermati* (shy, reserved) they felt in such situations and perceived the young man as a great threat of taking them away from their family.

Shazia's new husband, a distant relative, was studying in Karachi to become a high school teacher and a *sheikh* (religious leader). Being exposed to religious teachings, he argued that through *nikah* they were legally married by Islamic law and wanted to interact with his wife when he returned home to the valley for his holidays. Shazia was trapped in the difficult position of owing obedience to both her parents and her new husband and found a solution in secretly exchanging letters with him. Her inner tensions during this time caused her to fall seriously ill, a state often recounted for girls after their *nikah* in the older times, and she soon pressed for a quick *shadi*. She was only fifteen then. Looking back at that time, she stated her dilemma, while on the other side she described how she fell in love with her husband, how they developed a personal, intimate relationship step by step.

Lately, religious authorities have played an important role in propagating contact of spouses after *nikah* and nowadays even permit sexual relationships of their own grown-up children before celebrating *shadi*. This relaxation has enabled a wide array of dating practices. Ways of relating that would have been wholly inappropriate some fifteen years ago are now acceptable within certain limits. Morality always depends on the framework of judgment and is subject to ongoing negotiations—from letters as means of communication to mobiles.

Here is a current story: Rokiya is from an old neighborhood in Gilgit. She is in her mid-twenties, studied at the local university, and had a personal mobile phone for a safe commute but as a decent and obedient girl never used it to get in touch with boys. When her parents showed great interest in a *rishta* (marriage proposal) by a very promising young man from a well-known family, Rokiya immediately agreed to her mother's request of consent. I was stunned by how unspectacular, without any fuss or curiosity, this conversation was; Rokiya stayed very calm and demonstrated ostensible indifference. The young couple never saw one another until after their *nikah*. Rokiya did not even get a photo; she completely trusted her parents and brothers to make the right choice for her. Whenever I tried to investigate more, she fended me off and refused to take responsibility for the decision of whom to marry.

After they were married by *nikah*, I began to realize that Rokiya benefitted from her strategy of noninvolvement. Because she emphasized her pious devotion, modesty toward men, and commitment to family, she could actively pursue a love relationship with her husband shortly after their *nikah*. The commendably arranged marriage would help her counter any potential criticism of their growing intimacy. The two quickly started to develop a romance over the mobile phone and stayed in almost constant touch through messages and hours of nightly conversations, and after a few months of shy visits at his wife's house, the young man also stayed overnight. They really seemed to fit together well and took an eager interest in each other. Although the age at marriage has increased, many parents in remote valleys still do not give their consent for a sexual relationship before *shadi* but cannot prevent their exchange of intimacies on mobile phones. Nowadays, spouses actually strive to establish a romantic relationship before they move in together, while twenty years ago especially girls, younger in age and less educated, were much too shy and afraid to communicate with their husbands and young husbands would not have approved of a scandalously "free" wife either.

Establishing Intimacy

Some authors (Robinson 2014; Twamley 2014) frame the latest developments in South Asia's marriage patterns with the term "companionate marriage" (Simmons 1979), which refers to a monogamous relationship of one's choice that focuses on the nuclear family and needs continuous confirmation of emotional attachment (Wardlow and Hirsch 2006, 5). Others demolish monolithic Orientalist perceptions of love and arranged marriages by joining both terms (Donner 2016; Mody 2008). By blurring the lines of seemingly contradictory systems of relationship they successfully demonstrate that most marriages encompass aspects of both sides. Even better is the strategy of many Gilgiti women: by using the Urdu phrase *pasand ki shadi* when referring to love marriages distorting the association with Western-style love bringing marriages into Gilgiti context. As *pasand* plainly translates with liking, the stress lies on emotional attachment rather than irresponsible, impulsive passion, an attachment that can very well be established also after an arrangement. Difference to grown family affection, however, is young people's active involvement in the process of cultivating romantic feelings and marital intimacy. When Gilgit's youth express their love for a partner in SMS, they often resort to the English phrase "I love you," which suggests novelty and modernity. The most decisive factor of arranged-love marriages in the area of Gilgit is the increased emphasis on the couple as a unity. Kathrin Gratz illustrates in her detailed ethnography about women's lives in the city of Gilgit that as early as the 1990s an extra room within the household of the extended family was constructed for newlyweds (2006, 545). Individualization and self-determination are literally poured in concrete.

This point can be demonstrated with another case. Aliya's *nikah* took place in 2015, when she was about twenty years old, and marked the happy end of a long love story. The affair had developed between second cousins of about the same age who spent a lot of time in their childhood and teenage years together. When they were young teenagers they started to exchange flirting looks, later also letters on the way to school. While they could interact quite freely within their families, their romantic feelings would have been a subject of great distaste to their parents. Siblings were accomplices though. Over the years their communication channels extended to phone calls on landline and later to SMS, for which Aliya used her illiterate mother's mobile.[6] While this gave her a sense of security, her mother's phone in her hand for many hours also attracted gossip among related women who attentively monitor potential daughters-in-law. Because Aliya is a very beautiful girl from an honorable family, her parents had received many marriage proposals for her. To the misery of her parents, who had to deal with upset relatives, she rejected all of them. At last, Ibrahim successfully contrived their arranged marriage.

Aliya still points out that she would die of shame if her mother ever knew of the whole dimension of their premarital attachment. Although it never included any physical intimacies, the fact that she did not exercise her agency to control her feelings was shameful enough. Nevertheless, Aliya always emphasizes that her parents did not have to set strict rules for their children because they could "trust" them. With "trust" she stresses her confidence in the decency and innocence of her actions, although she herself had developed a love relationship. It shows how confident she is of the decency of her behavior, at least since she managed to convert her romance into an honorable relationship. Based on embodied *sharm* and the omniscient indirect social control through the absence of privacy, Gilgiti girls usually feel unwell when they do things in secret. By emphasizing the English concept of trust, they strive to appease the potential threats of invisible mobile phone communication; on the one hand they use and exploit it for their interests, and on the other they have to make it socially acceptable in front of others and for themselves. By choosing a desired spouse from the circle of potential candidates and maintaining "innocent" communication, which she could have with any cousin, Aliya has perfectly aligned new ideas of romantic love and intimacy with kinship solidarity, Islamic teachings, and her own interests.

Another woman, who got married a few years ago, in retrospect wraps her engagement period in an account of a love narrative. She romantically portrays how she had favored her husband even before the official marriage request and how she had engaged her older sisters to recommend this man to her parents. Although their married life now does not reflect deep affection, it appears that young women increasingly want to see their choice of partner influenced by themselves and do not consider the relationship between spouses valuable without preexisting attraction. Henrike Donner (2012, 3) summarizes similar developments throughout South Asia over the past two decades: "Earlier practices of love and romance, which were not expected to lead to marriage, have been substituted with the notion that love promotes emotional intimacy and this in turn represents the preferable basis for match-making as much as it is a necessary ingredient for successful modern marriages." The strive for agency, to take part in a complex decision-making process instead of heedlessly taking choices alone, seems to be a perfectly appropriated form of individualism, valuing the local framework of collective orientation. Ammara Maqsood (2021) reports a similar manner from her middle-class interlocutors in the Pakistani metropolis of Lahore. Framing secret courtships preceding marriage as having come to an "*understanding*" with a potential spouse, they want to signal "sincerity and seriousness of intention" (5). When developing a relationship within familiar networks, these young and educated women combine reasoned decision with romantic intimacy thus successfully integrate—but also reaffirm—individual as well as collective interests.

Over the past thirty years Gilgitis have had to appropriate various developments into existing social and cultural systems: integration into global markets,
introduction of governmental institutions, initiatives of development projects,
increased mobility, exposure to "downcountry" Pakistan, Urdu and English
schools, the propagation of various Islamic doctrines, new technologies, and
much more. Many people mention Indian dramas or Bollywood films, which are
enthusiastically watched by young women, as negative moral influences in recent
years. Due to lengthy power cuts and diverse interests of household members,
TV is only partly the prior medium for that; video clips are passed on from
mobile to mobile. On the other hand, exposure to conflicting normative models
from Islamic or school education are rarely identified as playing a role in current processes. Growing rates of higher education, often with English curricula
and in Pakistan's bigger cities, as well as programs by developmental institutions inspire ideas of individuality and gender equality. More and more women
take up jobs, work as teachers outside of the house, and gain confidence through
the little everyday struggles they encounter as well as the masculine role they
embody by contributing to the household with their salary. High numbers of
suicides by women in Gilgit's neighboring district Ghizer depict how a high
level of education within an environment of social and economic restrictions
causes young women to despair (Jaffery 2015)—or also how supposedly drown-
ing oneself in a river might cover up honor killings after girls struggled for
self-determination.

Within the opacity of this fast-changing environment, locals must juggle
various normative models while striving for orientation. To be "modern" in contrast to "primitive" and "backward" (*jangli*) or "ignorant" (*jahil*), to uplift their
communities' economic condition and take part in world's politics is clearly the
aspired agenda in Gilgit-Baltistan (Walter 2014, 33–34). This rhetoric fits with
women's strive to be "civilized." Instead of confusing these processes with West-
ernization, local struggles for individualization, gender equality, and romantic
love represent indigenized quests to carve their own place in a contemporary
"modernity" (Donner 2008, 67; Wardlow and Hirsch 2006, 14). Although older
generations in Pakistan often depict love marriages as Western infiltration that
threatens to destroy families' cohesion, reinterpretations of existing practices
do not occur detached from cultural values. As we have seen, they are appropriated within family networks, hierarchical structures, Islamic teachings, and
embodied emotions. Discourses and slight changes in practices penetrate locals'
body and mind, thus affecting the modulation of established ideas, which will
then gradually be embodied as "normal."

With growing age at marriage, increasing rates of girls' school and university
education, and the ability to connect through mobile phones, love is becoming
more commonplace now. Romances, which have always existed in affairs parallel to marriage, have become associated with wedlock and are even perceived

as essential for marriage. Passionate extramarital desire is tamed and domesticated as romance that can lead to marriage. What is changing in South Asia is not love concepts in general but love's place and meaning within marriage. A possibly short-lived passion gets transformed into a lifelong bond that justifies sexual involvement. My Shi'a interlocutors enact the pursuit of spontaneous, romantic love by turning the norm of spousal avoidance into an acceptable courtship phase in between *nikah* (Islamic wedding) and *shadi* (social wedding). As Katherine Twamley notes in her study on Gujarati marriage practices, "The engagement period is the main 'site' of romance; they are given the time to fall in love before marriage, but the decision to marry is taken first" (2014, 104). Youngsters' enthusiasm and strive for self-determination seem to have found a valve; they readily evoke and embrace love after a match is arranged. Sunni and Ismaili communities in Gilgit-Baltistan lack this "free" period; they usually celebrate *nikah* and *shadi* in one wedding. To a certain extent these couples develop intimacy after a formal engagement, but their relationships are more confined. For them the wider ideological trend toward individuality and romantic love poses an even greater threat to chastity and local tradition.

Interestingly, romance as a precondition for wedlock does not obstruct young people's views of marriage per se. Many see lifelong companionship in a rather "realistic" light of upcoming struggles and family compatibility (Donner 2016; Robinson 2014; Twamley 2014). Many of my friends and interlocutors in the area of Gilgit found that love matches risk the perspective for a more promising, functional partnership. Men often mistrust a girlfriend who fell in love with them and suspect she could become weak again, this time with another man. Many Gilgiti boys study in the big cities of Pakistan, where they can interact with girls more freely before their engagement at home, and sometimes stay attached to their beloved for decades. Nevertheless, most of them do not want to marry these "time pass" girlfriends but prefer a respectable girl. Santi Rozario (2012, 163) has made a similar observation among Bangladeshis: "They wanted a woman whose purity was beyond doubt, and who after marriage would remain pure and chaste."

Conclusion

Throughout the chapter I traced the fuzzy edges of established and embodied social norms and values. Abstract concepts are enacted through negotiations. Oversimplified models of Islam, morality, or intimacy fall short of capturing a more diffuse and flexible reality; they do not live up to the wide range of possible settings, cultural repertoires, contexts, and individual personalities and grasp love and marriage only on a normative level. Everyday situations constantly demand our (re)assessment and (re)enactment while each of them offers opportunities for (re)formulation of the same moral or cultural ideas. I depict these

negotiations as forms of continuous embodiment of all the diverse factors that
we tend to—or that tend to us.

In Gilgit-Baltistan public debates about modernity, love, and the decline of
values often manifest themselves in discussions about mobile telephony, while
most actual relationships among young couples mirror socially acceptable connections. They are appropriated into the existing cultural framework. As *parda*
serves as one of the most important aspects of local people's habitus, *sharm* as
quality of women's emotional life serves as an intrinsic scale of judgment. Women
navigate along *sharm* and therefore transgress social restrictions only in rare
cases. Through ongoing debates about new influences, they test and adjust
boundaries. While exercising social roles, people's performance leaves a mark
on their emotions and minds. The embodiment model offers room for creative
variation, or rather for a constant modulation of who one is after every few
minutes. Annemarie Mol puts it this way: "The opposition between surface
appearance and deep reality has disappeared. And people's identities do not precede their performances but are constituted in and through them" (2002, 37).
Just as our environment has a great influence on our perceptions, our experiences contribute to changes in practices and values and penetrate established
structures. We all know this phenomenon: once someone points something out
to us that we have never thought about before, we start noticing it everywhere
and our opinion gradually starts adapting.

With ethnographic examples from northern Pakistan, I showed how mobile
phones facilitate negotiation processes but cannot solely be blamed for the aspiration to do so. However, discourses revolve around the advantages and disad-
vantages of mobile phones and their connection to premarital relationships.
Most of the circulating stories of eloping daughters seem greatly exaggerated but
mirror local people's fears. The highly delicate matter of romantic love as pre-
requisite for marriage is creatively integrated into a system of arranged marital
bonds. While people interchangeably employ different yet never exhaustive
terms for love, many young women describe their marriage with the vernacular
pasand ki shadi. A marriage literally based on "liking" distorts associations of
passionate love and brings them into the Gilgiti context of attachment and fond-
ness that can very well be established after the arrangement. It is generally
understood that mutual affection grows between spouses over time and passionate love used to be projected onto unreachable persons. With the help of mobile
phones and drawing from different discourses for justification, such as Indian
soap operas or Islamic teachings, young women and men in Gilgit-Baltistan
prove highly skillful in maneuvering their individual identities and interests
through a web of social expectations and obligations. More than combining the
stereotypes of love and arranged marriage, something novel emerges here: an
amalgam of older values and contemporary currents. *Pasand* is not as all-
consuming as fervent *'ishq*, the persons involved are still in control of their

lives: couples rather cultivate the experience of a mutual feeling of connected-ness that they consciously embrace and let happen. The important factor is that the relationship is perceived as being self-directed since it happens before the implementation of the marriage through *shadi* and displays a strong focus on the couple, giving them time to build up an emotional bond before family responsibilities take over. This way, young generations succeed to shape and express contemporary, moral lives.

NOTES

1. Music by Jabir Khan, D. W. Baig, and Haroon Sharoon, lyrics by Zafar Waqar Taj; sing-ers are Salman Paras and an anonymous woman; released in February 2014. Available on YouTube, https://www.youtube.com/watch?v=ggzZTDJcsnA.

2. Referring to "girls" is not meant to belittle young women in contrast to a "full woman" with legal rights but reflects the local usage of the term to describe a young, unmar-ried woman who depends on her family for economic means and protection.

3. Poem written by Sher Alam from Sinaker, Bagrote valley.

4. There is not one uniform or consistent Muslim womanhood. Since Islam has spread all over the world, its women greatly vary by geographic origin, ethnicity, history, class, age, education, etc. To not create an artificial entity, I struggle with this gener-alization (Kirmani 2013) and only stress aspects that are applicable for women in Gilgit-Baltistan. A certain degree of simplification is needed to keep findings present-able to a wider audience and guarantee anonymity of my research partners.

5. Emerging from the philosophic tradition of the enlightenment, the term "modernity" is closely related to rationalism and stands in opposition to the perception of an inseparable, codependent body and mind as presented in this chapter. "Modernity" further implies the opposition between supposedly "traditional" and "modern" socie-ties and the cultural project of modernization that has led to a neo-imperial agenda of disseminating "western" ideas and hegemony. Although I am very critical of blind associations connected to "modernity," it structures people's perception of the world and was reflected in many conversations in Gilgit (Walter 2014).

6. Literacy used to be rather low in Gilgit-Baltistan but is increasing steadily. The last offi-cial numbers date back to the late 1990s when only 22 percent of women and 53 percent of men were able to read and write. Among the urban population the gender divide was less obvious and rates higher than in rural sites (Population Census 2001, 51). However, many people without any formal education learned to read the Qur'an. Newer surveys show that almost 90 percent of Gilgit-Baltistan's children attended schools in 2015 (Karim 2016).

REFERENCES

Abu-Lughod, Lila. 1986. *Veiled Sentiments: Honor and Poetry in a Bedouin Society.* Berkeley: Uni-versity of California Press.

Ahearn, Laura M. 2001. *Invitations to Love: Literacy, Love Letters, and Social Change in Nepal.* Ann Arbor: University of Michigan Press.

Ask, Karin. 1993. "Ishq aur Mohabbat: Ideas about Love and Friendship in a Northern Pakistani Community." In *Carved Flesh/Cast Selves: Gendered Symbols and Social*

Practices, edited by Vigdis Broch-Due, Ingrid Rudie, and Tone Bleie, 207–223. Oxford: Berg.

Azhar-Hewitt, Farida. 1999. "Women of the High Pastures and the Global Economy: Reflections on the Impacts of Modernization in the Hushe Valley of the Karakorum, Northern Pakistan." *Mountain Research and Development* 19 (2): 141–151.

Besio, Kathryn. 2007. "Depth of Fields: Travel Photography and Spatializing Modernities in Northern Pakistan." *Environment and Planning D: Society and Space* 25 (1): 53–74.

Cook, Nancy. 2007. *Gender, Identity, and Imperialism. Women Development Workers in Pakistan.* New York: Palgrave Macmillan.

Donner, Henrike. 2008. *Domestic Goddesses: Maternity, Globalization and Middle-Class Identity in Contemporary India.* Hampshire: Ashgate.

———. 2012. "Love and Marriage, Globally." *Anthropology of this Century* 4. http://eprints.lse.ac.uk/43388.

———. 2016. "Doing It Our Way: Love and Marriage in Kolkata Middle-Class Families." *Modern Asian Studies* 50 (4): 1147–1189.

Gratz, Katrin. 2006. *Verwandtschaft, Geschlecht und Raum. Aspekte weiblicher Lebenswelt in Gilgit/Nordpakistan.* Cologne: Köppe.

Grima, Benedicte. 2007. *The Performance of Emotion among Paxtun Women: The Misfortunes Which Have Befallen Me.* Karachi: Oxford University Press.

Halvorson, Sarah J. 2005. "Growing Up in Gilgit: Exploring the Nature of Girlhood in Northern Pakistan." In *Geographies of Muslim Women: Gender, Religion, and Space*, edited by Ghazi-Walid Falah and Caroline Rose Nagel, 19–43. New York: Guilford.

Israr, Israruddin. 2015. "Honour Killing Cases on the Rise in GB, 44 Killed in 2015." *Pamir Times* (blog), December 10. http://pamirtimes.net/2015/12/10/honour-killing-cases-on-the-rise-in-gb-44-killed-in-2015.

Jaffery, Shumaila. 2015. "Ghizer ki khatun khudkushi kyon kar rahi han?" *BBC Urdu*, http://www.bbc.com/urdu/pakistan/2015/06/150610_ghizer_women_suicide_rwa?SThisFB&b_ref=Default.

Jeffery, Patricia. 1979. *Frogs in a Well: Indian Women in Purdah.* London: Zed Press.

Karim, Fida. 2016. "Status of Education in Gilgit-Baltistan, Pakistan." *Pamir Times*, April 27, 2016. http://pamirtimes.net/2016/04/27/status-of-education-in-gilgit-baltistan-pakistan/.

Kirmani, Nida. 2013. *Questioning the Muslim Woman: Identity and Insecurity in an Urban Indian Locality.* New Delhi: Routledge.

Lindholm, Charles. 2006. "Romantic Love and Anthropology." *Etnofoor* 19 (1): 5–21.

———. 2008. "Polygyny in Islamic Law and Pukhtun Practice." *Ethnology* 47 (3): 181–193.

Mahmood, Saba. 2012. "Feminist Theory, Agency, and the Liberatory Subject: Some Reflections on the Islamic Revival in Egypt." In *Handbook of Gender*, edited by Raka Ray, 368–400. New Delhi: Oxford University Press.

Mandelbaum, David G. 1988. *Women's Seclusion and Men's Honor: Sex Roles in North India, Bangladesh, and Pakistan.* Tucson: University of Arizona Press.

Maqsood, Ammara. 2021. "Love as Understanding: Marriage, Aspiration, and the Joint Family in Middle-class Pakistan." *American Ethnologist* 48 (1): 1–12.

Marhoffer-Wolff, Maria. 2002. *Frauen und Feen. Entwicklung und Wandel einer Beziehung. Besessenheit in Yasin/Nordpakistan.* Cologne: Köppe.

Marsden, Magnus. 2007. "Love and Elopement in Northern Pakistan." *Journal of the Royal Anthropological Institute* 13 (1): 91–108.

Maududi, Sayyid Abu A'la. [1936] 2011. *Purdah: The Status of Woman in Islam.* Translated by Al Ash'ari. http://jamaatwomen.org/images/library/e-library_purdah.pdf.

Mernissi, Fatima. 1987. *Beyond the Veil: Male-Female Dynamics in Modern Muslim Society.* Bloomington: Indiana University Press.

Mody, Perveez. 2008. *The Intimate State: Love-marriage and the Law in Delhi.* New Delhi, Oxon: Routledge.

Mol, Annemarie. 2002. *The Body Multiple: Ontology in Medical Practice.* Durham, NC: Duke University Press.

Osella, Caroline, and Filippo Osella. 1998. "Friendship and Flirting: Micro-Politics in Kerala, South India." *Journal of the Royal Anthropological Institute* 4 (2): 189–206.

Papanek, Hanna, and Gail Minault. 1982. *Separate Worlds: Studies of Purdah in South Asia.* New Delhi: Chanakya.

Population Census Organization, Statistics Division, Government of Pakistan. 2001. "1998 Census Report of Northern Areas." Islamabad: Census Publication No. 157.

Randall, Peter. 2013. *The Psychology of Feeling Sorry: The Weight of the Soul.* New York: Routledge.

Ring, Laura A. 2006. *Zenana: Everyday Peace in a Karachi Apartment Building.* Bloomington: Indiana University Press.

Robinson, Teresa Platz. 2014. *Café Culture in Pune: Being Young and Middle Class in Urban India.* New Delhi: Oxford University Press.

Rozario, Santi. 1992. *Purity and Communal Boundaries: Women and Social Change in a Bangladeshi Village.* London: Zed.

———. 2012. "Islamic Marriage: A haven in an Uncertain World." *Culture and Religion* 13 (2): 159–175.

Simmons, Christina. 1979. "Companionate Marriage and the Lesbian Threat." *Frontiers: A Journal of Women Studies* 4 (3): 54–59.

Twamley, Katherine. 2014. *Love, Marriage and Intimacy among Gujarati Indians: A Suitable Match.* Hampshire: Palgrave Macmillan.

Varley, Emma. 2010. "Targeted Doctors, Missing Patients: Obstetric Health Services and Sectarian Conflict in Northern Pakistan." *Social Science & Medicine* 70 (1): 61–70.

———. 2012. "Islamic Logics, Reproductive Rationalities: Family Planning in Northern Pakistan." *Anthropology & Medicine* 19 (2): 189–206.

Vatuk, Sylvia. 1982. "Purdah Revisited: A Comparison of Hindu and Muslim Interpretations of the Cultural Meaning of Purdah in South Asia." In *Separate Worlds: Studies of Purdah in South Asia,* edited by Hanna Papanek and Gail Minault, 54–78. New Delhi: Chanakya.

Walter, Anna-Maria. 2014. "Changing Gilgit-Baltistan: Perceptions of the Recent History and the Role of Community Activism." *Ethnoscripts* 16 (1): 31–49.

———. 2016. "Between 'Parda' and Sexuality: Double Embodiment of 'Sharm' in Gilgit-Baltistan." *Rural Society* 25 (2): 170–183.

Wardlow, Holly, and Jennifer S. Hirsch. 2006. "Introduction." In *Modern Loves: The Anthropology of Romantic Courtship and Companionate Marriage,* edited by Jennifer S. Hirsch and Holly Wardlow, 1–31. Ann Arbor: University of Michigan Press.

PART TWO

Dower Practices

Signifying Religion, Ethnicity, and Class

3

The Dower (*Mahr*) and Wedding Ceremony among the Shiʿa of Oman

Religion, Class, and Ethnicity

JIHAN SAFAR

In the wake of the Arab uprisings in February 2011, young Omanis took to the streets asking for more jobs and less corruption. They also called for the creation of a marriage fund (*sunduq zawaj*) to lessen the suffering of men forced to accumulate large sums of money to finance their marriage. In particular *mahr*, which is the sum of money given by the groom to the bride according to the Muslim marriage,[1] and the wedding ceremony (*ʿirs*) constitute the two most important components of marriage expenses. In Oman, the amount of *mahr* reaches on average OMR 6,200 (USD 16,125),[2] and the *ʿirs* expenses record even higher amounts (Safar 2018). The cost of marriage represents a real burden on young Omanis from different religious and ethnic backgrounds and remains one of the main reasons for rising ages of marriage and increasing celibacy rates in the country (Hasso 2011; Singerman and Ibrahim 2003). The high cost of marriage hence poses a significant challenge in a society where marriage is the fundamental institution for legitimizing sexuality, building a family, and reproducing the community.

Focusing on the Shiʿa minority in Oman, this chapter describes the marriage rituals and their social meanings, particularly with respect to *mahr* practices and wedding ceremonies. This still underexplored research topic highlights some main distinguishing features of the Shiʿa marriages compared to other sectarian or ethnic groups in the country (Barth 1983; Eickelman 1984; Limbert 2010). Empirical evidence highlights three main significant features of Omani Shiʿa marriages. First, relatively low amounts of *mahr* are found among the Shiʿa communities in comparison to Sunnis or Ibadis within the Omani society. Particularly for the Shiʿa, who represent a religious minority in the country, low dowers are likely the result of endogamous unions—that is, marriage within the same community where people have trust in one another and hence can afford to have a relatively moderate *mahr*.[3] Low dowers appear as a marker of religious identification for the Shi'a communities, bonding families and maintaining their collective identities. Second, women's celebration of "giving the (*taslim al-mahr*), in which *mahr* and gifts are displayed and laid out in front of the guests, is another feature of Shi'a marriages. This material and symbolic display of generos-ity is seen as a distinctive social and religious marker among non-Ibadi minori-ties in Oman.[4] The "giving of the *mahr*" thus represents a marker of minority group identification. A third element of Shi'a marriages relates to expensive wed-ding celebrations for the upper strata, which stand in stark contrast to their low amounts of *mahr*. The net result is that nowadays the wedding party has become more expensive than the *mahr*. While the *mahr* and the ceremonial display of gifts act as a symbolic way for connecting families and the community, lavish weddings are more of a sign of status distinction. The functioning of these two parallel but partly contradictory processes is described; each payment hence encompasses a different meaning to Shi'a communities in Oman. At the same time, differences in wedding ceremonies show and produce divisions between the different Shi'a groups. Two patterns are clearly identifiable: the upper strata who organize modern and Westernized weddings and the lower strata who have started to organize collective marriages to counter high marriage expenses. In this regard, the wedding ceremony represents a marker of economic class and social status.

In brief, marriage practices both unite and divide the Shi'a in Oman, bring-ing the communities together around the *mahr* rituals and Shi'a elements dur-ing the ceremony, but also dividing the community, particularly around the wedding performance. This chapter describes the reproduction of the Shi'a com-munities through marriage practices and at the same time reveals the internal differences among the Shi'a themselves, in particular along the lines of ethnic-ity and class. Shi'a marriages therefore show how religion, class, and ethnicity are intertwined within Omani society.

There have hardly been studies on marriage practices and expenses in Oman, let alone on marriage across sectarian or ethnic lines (Safar 2018). Some research on the *mahr* in Arabian Peninsula countries (Al Naser 2009; Dahlgren 2005) and in other Arab countries (Moors 2003; Singerman and Ibrahim 2003) or on the *mehrieh* in Iran (Farzanegan and Gholipour 2017; Rezai-Rashti and Moghadam 2011) are available however. Other studies have investigated Shi'a marriage rituals (Khosronejad 2014), notably in regard to Shi'a transnational communities (Bøe 2018; Shanneik 2017).

This chapter is based on ethnographic fieldwork conducted in Oman. In addition to participant observation and informal conversations with Shi'a and non-Shi'a interlocutors, thirty-nine semistructured interviews were conducted in the country. Among these interviews, eight were carried out between June 2015 and January 2016 with Shi'a men and women, in the capital Muscat and in Sohar situated in the northern governorate of Al-Batinah.[5] Five WhatsApp and Skype conversations were also conducted in 2017 with Shi'a interlocutors. Also, an online questionnaire with 1,195 women of various social, educational, professional, and religious backgrounds was implemented.[6]

The Shi'a of Oman: Heterogeneous Communities

Oman is a diverse country in terms of ethnicity, sects, and linguistic communities. Ibadism, the third sect of Islam, is central to Omani identity.[7] Unofficial sources estimate that 45 to 50 percent of Omanis are Ibadis, while around 40 to 45 percent are Sunnis.[8] The Shi'a are estimated to constitute around 3 percent of the Omani population, counting 80,000 in 2018.[9] However, in spite of their relatively small demographic size, the Shi'a exert disproportionate influence in the political and economic realms (Peterson 2004, 31).

The Shi'a community, all Twelver Shi'a (*ithna 'ashari*), does not form a homogenous group and may be divided into three distinct groups, the Lawatiya (of Sindhi origin), the Baharna (of Arab origin), and the 'Ajam (of Persian origin).[10] Each of the three groups has its own elected leadership committee that manages community affairs according to the Shi'a Ja'fari jurisprudence; and this includes the community's endowments and charity associations (Majidyar 2013, 22). They also have their own mosques, *ma'tam* (Shi'a religious center), and *husseiniyya* (Shi'a communitarian space).[11] The large majority of Omani Shi'a follow the Iraq-based Ayatollah Ali al-Sistani as their religious source of emulation (*marja'iyya*) (Valeri 2010).

In the following section, the three distinct Shi'a groups are described, giving a better understanding of some main features of Shi'a marriage practices.

The Lawatiya (Sindhi Origin)

With around thirty thousand members, the Lawatiya (sing. Lawati) are the largest Shi'a group and the wealthiest in Oman.[12] They are concentrated on the Batinah coast (Liwa, Barka, Sohar, Saham, Al Khabura, Masna'a) but reside predominantly in the capital districts (Muscat, Ruwi, Mutrah). The presence of this Indian-Muslim community, believed to have originated from the regions of Hyderabad (Sindh), attests to more than three-century-old ties between Muscat and the Indian subcontinent.[13] However, some members of the community claim Arab descent: "Some Lawatis, apparently responding to a sense that a distinctively 'Arab' genealogy confers greater social status, have claimed ancestry originating from the Omani interior" (Jones and Ridout 2012, 31–32). According to another narrative they lost their Arab and tribal identity by residing in India for centuries after the Islamic conquest of the subcontinent.[14] Originally Ismailis, a Shi'a subgroup following Aga Khan (Louer 2008), most of the Lawatiya of Oman converted to Twelver Shi'a in the nineteenth century after their excommunication following a dispute over the legitimacy of the Aga Khan's succession in the

1860s (Peterson 2004, 43). The community, known for its prominent merchants, was traditionally linked to commercial activities of the souk in Mutrah and to trade in incense, jewelry, and textiles. They held a monopoly over pearls, dry fish, and dates as well as the import and export of seeds and textiles between Oman and India. The Lawatiya occupied a separated quarter in Mutrah called *sur al Lawatiya* (*sur* meaning "fortified enclosure"), which had for a long time denied access to non-Lawatiya, marking "their distinct identity" by maintaining this "largely exclusive urban community in Mutrah" (Jones and Ridout 2012, 32). The five hundred houses built on the Mutrah corniche close to each other testify to their material wealth and to their seclusion and endogamy (Graz 1981). As a result of new infrastructure and development, the Lawatiya moved in the past decades to more modern suburbs (Peterson 2004, 42). However, men and women continued to attend the *majalis* of the many *ma'atim* in the enclosure as well as those in the main mosque, particularly during Ramadan, Muharram, and Safar, the important months of Shi'a devotional life that are closely linked to the mourning rituals and ceremonies of Ashura, the tenth day of Muharram that is dedicated to the commemoration of the martyrdom of Imam Hussein and his followers in the Battle of Karbala (Sachedina 2013, 158). Their language, the *lawati* dialect (or *khojki*, based on Sindhi and Kutshi), isolates them further from Omani society, though the young generations are losing *lawati* to Arabic. The Lawatiya are considered one of the most educated communities in Oman. Their knowledge of south Asian languages, Arabic, and English has largely contributed to their economic success.[15] They also hold senior positions in government, including cabinet ministers, members of the royal court, and ambassadors to the United States and European countries.[16] Lawatiya women such as Rajiha bint 'Abd al-Amir, the first female minister of tourism, and Khadijah Hassan Al Lawati, the first female ambassador (with a post in the Netherlands), have held influential positions, a sign of the empowerment of Lawatiya women.[17]

As mentioned above, most of Omani Twelver Shi'a follow the Iraqi spiritual leader Ali al-Sistani and are not tied to the Islamic Republic of Iran. However, "[s]ome Lawatiya in Muscat used to follow the Lebanese cleric Muhammad Hussein Fadlallah (who passed away in 2010), and follow the Iranian Ayatollah Ali Khamenei. But, unlike some of their counterparts in Muscat, most of the Lawatiya of Sohar follow Ali al-Sistani," explains an interlocutor from Sohar.[18] The geographical differences between the Lawatiya of Muscat and those living in Al Batinah illustrate the heterogeneity of the Lawatiya community; such differences are also visible in matrimonial practices (notably in regard to *mahr* amounts, as will be discussed below).

The Baharna (Arab Origin)

In addition to the Lawatiya, another powerful Twelver Shi'a community is the Baharna (sing. Bahrani). In Oman, the term *baharna* simply refers to the Arab

Shi'a (Peterson 2004, 44) who migrated from Iraq or from other Gulf countries (Bahrain, eastern Saudi Arabia) and seldom from Iran. The Baharna are exclusively concentrated in the capital Muscat. Before 1970, only a dozen Bahrani families were living in Muscat, and their presence goes back to only six to eight generations (Peterson 2004; Valeri 2010). Though demographically small—not exceeding a few thousand—the Baharna are politically and economically very powerful.[19] Throughout history, their loyalty to the sultans of Muscat remained unwavering. In 1970, 'Asim al Jamali became the first minister of health; in 1995, Ahmad Bin Abdul Nabi Makki was the designated minister of finance and economy until his dismissal in March 2011, following social protests calling for his resignation.[20]

Baharna women were among the first girls enrolled in schools before 1970, notably at the American missionary school in Mutrah, situated in al-Baharina quarter.[21] They were also pioneers in entering the job market and the voluntary field after 1970,[22] the year when the late Sultan Qabous bin Sa'id came to power and started building the nation-state.[23] The Baharna maintain close contacts with Baharna communities in other Gulf countries; following the 1991 Gulf War and the 2003 U.S.-led invasion of Iraq, for example, the Omani Baharna accommodated relatives fleeing Iraq and Kuwait (Valeri 2010, 255). Most of the Baharna also follow the Iraqi spiritual leader Ali al-Sistani.

The 'Ajam (Persian Origin)

The capital Muscat, Al Khoudh suburb, and Al-Batinah region (Sohar, Saham, Suwayq, al Khabura) host a third Shi'a group, the 'Ajam, who originate from Persia. This community is limited to approximately twenty thousand members (Valeri 2010). As they come from different regions of southern Iran (Lar, Bandar Abbas), the geographical proximity with Oman had certainly facilitated their arrival, notably amid the Persian occupation in the eighteenth century and during the reign of the Persian king Nadir Shah. In Sohar where the 'Ajam represent an important ethnic group, the longevity of their presence varies from one to eight generations. Unlike the 'Ajam in Kuwait who constitute an important group and still speak Persian (Safar 2015), the 'Ajam in Oman are smaller in number and maintain limited familial contacts with Iran (Valeri 2010). They have assimilated well into Omani society; many have intermarried with other communities and have taken Arab family names. Compared to the Lawatiya and the Baharna, the 'Ajam are less socially visible and are underrepresented in Oman's political and economic spheres. Compared to other Shi'a, they very often belong to the lower strata. Many members serve in the lower ranks of Oman's security forces. They have their own mosques and charities with the majority of 'Ajams following the *marja'iyya* of Ali al-Sistani.

The diversity of the Shi'a communities by origin, ethnicity, and class is also reflected in the diversity of marriage practices and their attitudes toward *mahr*.

Although sharing a similar "Shi'a ethos" (Pandya 2010, 35) and similar marriage rituals, the Lawatiya, the Baharna, and the 'Ajam have their own matrimonial practices. The next section highlights this dual process of reproduction and distinction among the Twelver Shi'a communities. Next to this, it is also necessary to consider the national setting in Oman to better understand the transformations that have occurred in the marriage institution over the past decades. The institutional restrictions imposed in the mid-1990s on mixed marriages—applicable to all Omanis regardless of their origin, sect, or class—had an impact on the transnational marriage unions.[24] Our interviews conducted for instance with Baharna women revealed a high transnational (Shi'a) endogamy among those married in the seventies and eighties. At that time, matrimonial networks and flows extended beyond the national borders, to Bahrain, the south of Iraq, Saudi Arabia, and Kuwait.[25] In contrast, due to the restrictions imposed on marrying a foreigner, today it remains extremely complicated for a (Shi'a) Omani to marry someone from Iran, Iraq, Pakistan, or some other countries.

The *Mahr* of the Shi'a: Reproduction and Differentiation

The Omani Personal Status Law stipulates that *mahr* (or *sadaq*) is an essential tenet to seal the marriage contract, along with the offer and acceptance, the marriage guardian (*wali*), and two witnesses.[26] However, a Shi'a marriage does not necessarily require the presence of two witnesses (Clarke 2001, 226): "It has become a custom (*'urf*) in Oman to have two witnesses and to register officially their names, but this is not essential. What is essential is to have the offer and acceptance (*ijab wa qabul*). Witnesses are mandatory when it comes to divorce", explains a Shi'a respondent from Sohar. Also, for the Shi'a the absence of a specific *mahr* does not void the contract of marriage (Badareen 2016; Tamadonfar 2015, 69). However, the *mahr* remains a key marker of identification for the Shi'a minority in Oman.

Analyzing the *mahr* institution among the Twelver Shi'a communities provides useful information on religious, class, and communal elements. It shows how the *mahr* helps to reproduce and bond the Shi'a communities but also to differentiate between the Shi'a groups along the lines of class and ethnicity. *Mahr* differentials appear also in complex ways within each subgroup depending on the type of marriage (e.g., cross-sectarian, interethnic, mixed, arranged, or kin marriages).

Reproducing the Shi'a Communities through Low *Mahr* and Endogamy

To start with, finding data on the *mahr* in Oman remains an arduous task. Unlike many Arab countries, the *mahr* amount is not registered in the marriage contracts.[27] To fill this gap, our ethnographic fieldwork gains some insights on the *mahr* amount and its negotiation by religion, ethnic group, and class. Fieldwork revealed that relatively small amounts of *mahr* are observed among the Shiʻa, in comparison to Sunnis or Ibadis who reveal higher amounts throughout the country. Of course it should be noted that establishing reliable comparisons is difficult since the sect variable crosses with other geographical, ethnic, or religiosity variables. As stated by a number of respondents, the *mahr* of the Shiʻa—and regardless of their socioeconomic background—hardly ever exceeds OMR 4,000, an amount below the national average *mahr* that stands at around OMR 6,200: "The *mahr* of the Shiʻa is the lowest in Oman; it is around 4,000 rials. Some (non-Shiʻa) tribes ask for 7,000 or 8,000 rials, but Shiʻa fight against (*yuharibu*) the increase. Even if tribes increase it, our main objective is to combat it," explains a Shiʻa man. Indeed, in Al-Batinah, notably in the cities of Sohar and Shinas—where a majority of ʻAjam and some Lawatiya and Baharna live—the *mahr* appears lower for the Shiʻa in comparison to Sunnis or Ibadis: "The Shiʻa, notably the ʻAjam, have the cheapest *mahr* in Al Batinah," confirms an interviewee from Sohar. "The city of Shinas [in Al Batinah] is known for having one of the highest *mahr* in the country. But for the ʻAjam, it's the lowest amount in the city," adds another respondent. In some areas, Sunnis pay a *mahr* at least 25 percent higher; and the Ibadis in northern regions such as Al Dhahirah pay a *mahr* 50 percent higher. Northern cities close to the United Arab Emirates (UAE) register among the highest *mahr* in Oman; this is in part due to the influence of the UAE and a desire for imitation (Safar 2018). The Lawatiya, for their part, have the lowest amounts in Oman, situated at a fixed amount of OMR 401 (see details later).

Imposing a low *mahr* upon the groom can be justified by the trust factor within in-group marriages. As a matter of fact, when people trust each other—which is often the case with in-group marriages—members will allow for a lower *mahr*.[28] Since Shiʻa frequently marry within the same community and have trust in one another, the *mahr* is likely to be low.

Agreeing to a low *mahr* by the bride's family can also be explained by the desire of the Shiʻa families to facilitate endogamous marriages and to strengthen group cohesion. In fact, low dowers are likely to incite Shiʻa men to marry within the community rather than choosing a non-Shiʻa woman who usually "costs" more than a Shiʻa woman. Hence, low dowers help in maintaining endogamous unions and in reproducing the community and the family.[29]

In addition to the reproduction of the Shiʻa community, a low *mahr* can be explained by the modern attitude of the bride's father. Shiʻa fathers are reputed for having economic and cultural capital, especially Lawati and Bahrani, the majority of whom are wealthy businessmen. One ʻAjami man explains that the changes in paternal attitudes among some Sunnis follow suit in the same direction: "The *mahr* of the Shiʻa is the least expensive in Sohar; but today, our Sunni brothers are getting 'infected' [in'adu] by us and their *mahr* is starting to decrease. The father's cultural level has changed; there is now a social awareness that the daughter's husband is like a son [al zawj ibnahom]."

A low *mahr* can be also credited to women's attitudes and self-perceptions. Some Shiʻa women declared that a high *mahr* does not valorize a woman and leads to the perception of her as merchandize (*silʻa*). In particular, Lawati and Bahrani women, who are pioneers in gaining access to education and in participating in the building of the nation-state since the seventies, believe that a high *mahr* is part of a marriage contract where the bride is "sold" to her husband. Moreover, women in the upper strata consider *mahr* as a symbolic issue rather than a financial asset, as they have other means of securing their property and wealth (Bøe 2015, 34). Lawati and Bahrani women in particular do not identify *mahr* as ensuring a security function. This is exactly what Moors (2003) explains for educated and urban women in Palestine who consider registering a token dower as a sign of modernity.

More Gifts and More Gold

Having a low *mahr* does not prevent the groom from contributing to other forms of payments and gifts to the bride. One must take into consideration the increase of other items offered by the groom, such as gifts and gold. The distinction between *mahr* and gifts allows for a better understanding of the changes that are taking place in marriage practices. "It is commonly known that for the Shiʻa of Sohar, our limit is 4,000 rials; but the sum can reach 6,000 rials when gifts are included," explains one ʻAjami woman.[30] "In Sohar, the commonly known *mahr* is 4,000 rials for Shiʻa, but without the gifts." Usually, both families agree on whether gifts are incorporated or not. "They gave me the entire amount of 4,000 rials as *mahr*, and I received 3,000 rials as gifts," explains one woman from Sohar. "In our neighborhood, we ask for 4,000 rials, but in reality, the man pays much more with the *shabka* and the gifts.[31] Some pay 5,000 rials, all included." As explained by a Lawati man, "For us, the legitimate *mahr* (mahr sharʻi) is 401 rials, but the groom pays for the dress and the gold; so the amount can easily reach 4,000 rials. For us, the *mahr* and the gifts are two different things." In her writing on Jabal Nablus (Palestine), Moors (2003) elaborates on the registering of a token dower, where a "complete disjuncture" is observed between the very small sum registered in the contract (often one JD) and the value of gifts provided by the groom. Registering a token dower is an indication of trust; and the link between wealth and trust is particularly salient for urban and wealthy men and women. More than dower, gifts have become increasingly central in marriage prestation (Moors 2003, 91) with professional women preferring to register a deferred part (*muʼakkhar*).[32] However, registering a deferred part is not common in Oman, where the *muʼakkhar* remains surprisingly a hardly discussed issue.[33] Both Shiʻa and non-Shiʻa Omani women are not really aware of its impor-tance, and the amount of only 300 or 500 rials is sometimes written by conven-tion. "There is no *muʾakkhar* for the Shiʻa, at least for the Lawatiya who impose some conditions, but not a *muʾakkhar*. We do not have this idea of *muʾakkhar*," explains one Lawati man. "In Sohar, there is no *muʾakkhar* for the Shiʻa," con-firms one ʻAjami man. The neglected aspect of the deferred part can be related to low expectations of divorce within the Shiʻa communities in Oman.[34]

Mahr Differentials by Types of Marriage

If the *mahr* limit settles generally around OMR 4,000 among the Shiʻa groups, particularly in Sohar, this amount can be either lower or higher depending on the type of marriage (arranged or love marriage, kin or distant marriage, etc.). Empirical results reveal that love marriages and non-kin marriages register a higher *mahr* compared to arranged and kin marriages (Safar 2018). The case of one ʻAjami man from Sohar gives insights into the *mahr* amount when marriage is arranged by the family. In fact, the respondent paid a *mahr* of only OMR 3,500: "I was expecting 4,000 or 4,500 rials; this is usually our price." His parents selected the prospective bride for him, which explains the easy family negotia-tions on the *mahr* and its relatively low amount. "While going to perform the Hajj, my parents met the girl and her parents in the bus. She's our neighbor. I've heard about the girl, but I never saw her. At the time, I was travelling to Salalah com-pletely depressed because my uncle refused my proposal to marry his daughter, that I loved. . . . During their trip, my parents agreed with the girl's parents on our marriage. I then accepted the proposition. . . . I trust my family's choice." However, as a counterpart to such moderate *mahr*, the bride's father imposed one condition for the marriage: his daughter must live in her own home, sepa-rately from her in-laws. Residing in an independent house is a condition very often discussed during the marriage negotiations, particularly among the Shiʻa. Requesting a moderate *mahr* can hence be counterbalanced by high costs of housing imposed on the groom. More important than the *mahr*, the conditions imposed to the groom often reflect the woman and her family's aspirations to live in a modern, nuclear, and independent unit. In this regard housing remains an important part of the marriage costs for the groom.

Mahr differentials within the community appear also between kin and non-kin marriages. Kin marriages have generally a lower *mahr* than exogamous marriages. One ʻAjami mother indicates, "My third daughter received 5,000 rials in 2013 in addition to gifts, but she married a man from outside the family and is now living in Muscat. He is from Liwa. He first wanted to pay 4,000 rials but the family told him: 'It is commonly known that our *mahr* is 5,000 rials because the girl has no father; besides you are not from the same neighborhood or region, you are from outside [*min barra*] and distant [*baʻid*] from the family.' He finally gave 5,000 rials." This example shows that in addition to non-kin and distant marriages, the absence (death) of the bride's father is likely to increase the *mahr* amount, considering that a girl without a father would need extra protection, a phenomenon also observed among other (non-Shi'a) communities in Oman. In addition to (communal) endogamy, kin marriages help decreasing the *mahr* amount, testifying to the importance of considering in- and out-group forma-tions when analyzing marriage dynamics.[35]

Mahr and Ethnic Differences among the Shi'a Communities

If low dowers in Oman correlate with a sectarian argument—namely that Shi'a register the lowest amount in the country on average—differentials between the three ethnic Shi'a groups are also noticeable. *Mahr* is seen as a marker of iden-tification for the Shi'a communities but also of differentiation, particularly along lines of class and ethnicity. For the overwhelming majority of the inter-viewees, ethnic and class-based factors indeed seem significant in explaining *mahr* variations. Variations are observed in regard to the three ethnic Shi'a groups classified by their geographical origin. In such an ethnic scale, the Lawatiya of Muscat, who are economically very powerful, are known for asking an extremely low and fixed *mahr* situated between OMR 399 and 401. The Baharna in Muscat are known for asking higher dowers than the 'Ajam and the Lawatiya. "But in all cases, Shi'a ask for lower *mahr* compared to others," confirms a Lawati man in Muscat. "The Lawatiya pay exactly 401 rials, and not 400, to assess the agreement," explains one Bahrani man. For the Lawatiya, "*mahr* has always been 401 rials. This amount was written in old marriage contracts but ceased to be written today in the official marriage certificate signed by the notary," adds this Lawati man. This fixed amount is believed to be the *mahr* of Fatima al-Zahra' (the Prophet's daughter and wife of Ali ibn Abi Talib). Designated by *mahr al-fatimi,* it is also believed to be the sum paid by the Prophet to his wives. "For the Lawatiya, it is 399 or 401 rials for all; rich and poor; like in the time of the Prophet, but their marriage celebration is very costly compared to other ethnic groups," declares an 'Ajami man. In the same vein, a respondent adds, "The Lawatiya have a fixed *mahr* [*mahr thabit*] of 401 rials. But, this is only a number; the true value is linked to gold that men have to pay!" The Lawatiya living in Al Batinah seem however closer to the 'Ajam customs in terms of the *mahr* amount, as they do not pay 401 rials like for those in Muscat. "In Sohar, some Lawatiya intermar-ried with Baharna and 'Ajam because they are only a few Lawatiya families com-pared to a much bigger number in Muscat. Here, the Lawatiya generally follow the trends in Sohar, even when it comes to marriage customs," explains a Bulushi man from Sohar, testifying to *mahr* differences within a same ethnic group as to the geographical area.

More than the *mahr*, the wedding costs are perceived as a distinctive sign of Lawatiya's financial economic power and class distinction. This is, as already mentioned, very similar to what happened in the West Bank (Moors 2003), where among the highly educated, gold was no longer registered as obligatory *mahr* but was a freely provided gift. Although the West Bank Palestinians are Sunnis, it seems that being part of a modernizing and professional upper echelon of society is the most important criterion to explain this phenomenon, as will be explained further below.

Also, the Lawatiya, Baharna, and 'Ajam do not frequently intermarry, although intermarriages are more frequent in the Al Batinah region. Few marriages are observed between the 'Ajam and the Lawatiya, who form two distinct groups in terms of ethnicity and class, notably in Muscat.[36] With the introduction of private English and American schools in Muscat, however, young Baharna and Lawatiya seem to interact with each other more.

Kin marriages are also perceived rather negatively by young Baharna women in comparison to 'Ajam and Lawatiya, which might also explain the relatively higher *mahr* found among this group. "I would never marry my paternal cousin; he is like a brother, that's incest!" explains one single Baharni women. "We are not like the Lawatiya who marry between them; that's why they have lots of diseases and eye problems." In the popular discourses, the consanguineous unions among the Lawatiya in fact appear to be a generalized pattern, with many respondents criticizing diseases such as anemia, blood problems, and blindness among them.

The consanguineous unions seem to have been reinforced since the mid-1990s with the weakening of transnational marriages. Unions between a (Shi'a) Omani and a (Shi'a) non-Omani have actually decreased since the mid-1990s with the implementation of strict laws regarding mixed marriages. As mentioned before, the marriage procedures became quite difficult since that time, requiring the Ministry of Interior's approval for such marriage, after a special investigation by the Marriage Committee. Transnational Shi'a marriages were frequent before the 1990s, especially among the Baharna, who married their fellows in the Gulf region. Interviews revealed that marriages with fellows from Iran or Pakistan were less frequent among the 'Ajam and the Lawatiya communities. However, "in the sixties, and amid the economic crisis in Oman, some Lawatiya merchants left to Irak and intermarried there with Iraqi women. They only came back to Oman with their wives and families after the war in Iraq, and mainly after the Iraqi invasion [*ghazu*] of Kuwait in 1990. These Lawatiya live today in Muscat," declares one 'Ajami respondent.

A Higher *Mahr* for Intersectarian Unions

The type of marriage, either sectarian or intersectarian, also influences the *mahr* amount. Marrying a woman from outside the Twelver Shi'a requires, in general, a higher *mahr*. A Shi'a man wishing to marry a Sunni (or Ibadi) woman can expect to pay a higher *mahr* in comparison to a sum paid within his community. Amid economic hardships and youth unemployment, it is easier for Shi'a men to marry someone from their own community who request a lower *mahr*, rather than marrying a non-Shi'a woman. A high *mahr* asked by a Sunni (or Ibadi) bride's father to a Shi'a groom can be interpreted as a price for the "loss" of his daughter's (Sunni or Ibadi) religious belonging—as wives usually convert to their husband's sectarian belonging. In intersectarian arrangements, *mahr* negotiations between the bride and the groom's families appear more tense, each family wishing to preserve its religious and cultural practices. Ahmad, a 'Ajami man from Sohar married in 2005 to a Sunni girl from Saham whom he met at the Sultan Qabous University, declares, "At the beginning, the girl's family asked for a *mahr* of 7,000 rials. Her mother asked and spoke directly to me, because my wife has no brothers, and her father passed away few months ago. But I explained that, for us, *mahr* is 4,000 rials. After long talks, I finally agreed to pay 5,000 rials." Ahmad's wife actually converted to Shi'ism; and this was the main argument for convincing Ahmad's reluctant extended family to marry a Sunni girl. In such a case, *mahr* acts as an indicator of intersectarian dynamics. Another Shi'a man explains also the high *mahr* paid by his brother from Sohar to a Sunni woman from Saham in the context of a love marriage. Present during the *mahr*'s negotiations between both families, in December 2015, he declares, "The girl's father asked for 7,000 rials, but my father told him 5,000. . . . Finally, my brother paid a *mahr* of 6,500 rials. He did not have any inconveniences because he wanted to marry his beloved woman. She also wanted 6,500 as a *mahr*; she's a doctor." Love marriage is a recent phenomenon in Oman that explains such unusually high costs paid by Shi'a men.[37] In addition to love and intersectarian marriages, giving a high *mahr* can be explained by the woman's level of education and/or employment. Women perceive their education or their professional activity as capital, prestige, and self-realization that can be reflected by a higher *mahr*.

On the other side, interfaith unions between Twelver Shi'a women and Sunni (or Ibadi) men are much less frequent in Oman.[38] "Shi'a women rarely marry Sunni. I've never heard of any Shi'a women marrying a Sunni men in Sohar or in Muscat! We don't allow it; even the *'ulama* don't tolerate it because it affects the way we raise our children," explains one Shi'a man married to a Sunni. In this regard, Ayatollah Ali al-Sistani, who represents a key reference for the overwhelming majority of the Shi'a in Oman, does not recommend the marriage of Shi'a women to Sunni men.[39] Using a gender approach, this same respondent explains the logic where women are considered the main cultural reproducers.

For him, Shi'a women are supposed to "preserve the community and always keep the traditions (*tazal muhafiza*)," adding, "[i]n Al Batinah, we actually find a lot of mix marriages between Sunni women and Shi'a men! A Sunni woman gets used to the everyday Shi'a lifestyle; she goes to ceremonies and celebrations [*munasabat*], she melts [*tazub*] with the crowd. It is easier for wives to change their sect than men. For example, my wife [Sunni] follows me today. But this is more difficult for a Shi'a woman married to a Sunni husband; because such unions end up with divorce. The Shi'a wife wants to keep her traditions like Ashura, other mourning days, the *ma'tam*, but her husband can mock her customs! He can make fun of her! Women are more sensitive, that's different for a Shi'a man. Being a male is different," he concludes. Transmitting the Shi'a cultural rituals to children is also feared by the dominant sect.

Finally, studying the *mahr* institution and its amount provides a broader analysis on the cross-sectarian and endogamous unions and on the different types of marriage. With a relatively low *mahr* in the country, the Shi'a practices appear diversified along ethnic and geographical lines. *Mahr* is thus a complex institution where ethnicity, religion, and class are intertwined. The next section also analyzes how the *mahr* ceremony allows for both the reproduction and the differentiation of the Shi'a communities in Oman.

The "Giving of the *Mahr*" (*Taslim al Mahr*) Ceremony

In addition to relatively low dowers, another significant element of the Shi'a marriage lies in the *mahr*'s celebration (called *taslim al-mahr*), which is a women-only and family party where *mahr* and gifts are exhibited and laid out in front of the guests. This party is held following the *mahr* agreement and after fixing a marriage date (or *milka*). In this women-only ceremony, extended families of both spouses and their friends gather together to show the *mahr* and presents in front of everyone. The amount is announced publicly without the "taboo of explicating" the price, and prayers are offered for its benediction. Gifts and gold are also given to the bride, and guests can admire these material objects like in an exhibition. Songs, prayers, recitations, dances, and incense manifest the symbolic and religious ritual of the union and the preservation of the community: "There was a Qur'an in a box offered by the groom's family, with a lot of other beautiful things. We put boxes on the floor decorated with flowers, with shoes, bags. We lay out the watches offered by the groom family." This material and symbolic display of generosity is seen as a distinctive social and religious marker among non-Ibadi minorities. The *taslim al mahr* ceremony thus represents a marker of social identification for minorities in Oman. Beyond the exchange of material goods between kin and close friends, the *mahr* ceremony contributes to solidifying social and religious bonds and to preserving familial hierarchies. *Mahr* negotiations are led by men who are responsible for sealing communal alliances, while women in the *mahr*'s party act as key actors in exhibiting status, wealth, and religion. A grandmother from the 'Ajam community in Sohar explains in detail the ceremony of her granddaughter, showing how material and nonmaterial goods circulate in the group to preserve a communal spirit, and where Twelver Shi'a families pray for the imam's memory:

> The bride's kin were sitting in an air-conditioning tent, at their house; and a woman was reciting some *jalawat* [songs glorifying the imams' memory].[40] Afterward, the groom's mother, sisters and kin entered with a Qur'an, money and gifts, and they also started reading *jalawat*, poems, with applauses. A woman from the girl's family took the microphone, announcing, "This is the *mahr* of the girl and the amount is 4,000 rials." Then she started counting it with other women. We usually count the *mahr* and pray for benediction; we pray for the Prophet's memory (*nusali 'ala al nabi lil zikra*). We don't count all the *mahr* but we announce the real amount. After that, the woman enumerated all the gifts offered, first, by the bride's family, then by the groom's family and friends: "This is a set from her mother, this is from her brother, this is from her sister"; "This Qur'an is a gift to the bride, with perfumes and incenses"; "This is a watch offered by the groom"; "These are rings, perfumes, incenses"; "Each set of jewelry costs 1,000 rials, and the bride received three or four sets!" During the ceremony, we didn't dance. The girl was inside, and she didn't attend the party because she had her *milka* the same day. She saw the gifts later on. For our girls, it is shameful (*'ayb*) to show up before the marriage contract.

This example shows the mix of elements that are religiously Shi'a (recitations and prayers for the imam's memory) and the displays of presents that are also found in other non-Shi'a settings, namely among the Zadjalis and some Baluchis.[41] In this party, exchanging objects between groups builds relationships and maintains collective identities. The *taslim al-mahr* ceremony hence functions as a community marker.

The *Milka*

After the *mahr* celebration, another stage in the marriage process is the *milka* (or *'aqd al qiran*), which is the religious ceremony where the marriage contract is signed in the presence of a *millik* or Shaykh. Differently from Sunni or Ibadi communities, the Shi'a settle the *milka* on particularly legitimate days. The groom (or his father) can also visit a specific person who will select the exact timing for the *milka*, as certain days are not recommended for marriage. The marriage ceremony should not coincide with the Islamic calendar months of Muharram or Safar, considered mourning days for *ahl al-bayt*.[42] Indeed, the austere ten first days of Muharram are not socially nor religiously recommended for marriage, the tenth of Muharram being the day of mourning for the killing of *ahl al-bayt* at Karbala (Ashura). The month of Safar marks the death of the Prophet and martyrdom of his elder grandson, Imam Hassan.[43] Preferred days for the *milka* could be the dates of birth of the imams. This particular Shi'a element also appears as a marker of distinction in marriage rituals among sectarian groups in Oman.

The bride's approval of the marriage is an essential condition for contracting the marriage, and the *millik* usually asks her if she accepts the marriage and the given *mahr*. The same *millik* then goes to the mosque and meets with the groom and the men to conclude the marriage. The bride is absent from the ceremony held in the mosque, where the *millik* pronounces that the *mahr*, to which both parties had agreed, had been paid. As explained by Amira, twenty-three years old, from the 'Ajam community in Sohar, "The Shaykh came to our house on the day of the *milka,* just before the men's celebration. It was in the afternoon. He came and asked me if I want the man [*tibghi al rajul*]. He came to take the *mantuq* [pronouncement] from me, and I gave him a mandate [*awaklo*]. We put a Qur'an between us. I sat next to him; we opened the Qur'an on the verses of the Fatiha; and I put my legs in rosewater and *rihan* [basil] while sitting on two pillows. The water must have a green color; it can be mixed with anything that is green. I was entirely covered, with a mirror next to me. Women from the family were present, in addition to the groom's father and my father. The Shaykh asked me: 'Do you accept this person and do you accept the *sadaq*?' He repeats it three times, but I only answer the third time, it is just a matter of modesty [*haya*]. The amount of the *mahr* is not mentioned. He came for fifteen or thirty minutes before going with the fathers to the mosque." The presence of green-colored water is found generally in Shi'a marriages in Oman.[44] Another Shi'a element concerns the triple repetition of the marriage acceptance formula in front of the marriage contractor by the bride, but also by the groom at the mosque.[45]

While not physically present at the mosque with the men assembly during the *milka*, Amira recounts the male ceremony by showing a video on her phone that her fiancé sent her: "These men here are essentially from the family's circle; . . . these are my maternal uncles, these are my paternal uncles, this is my grandmother's uncle. . . . During the *mantuq*, men are aligned and sing while moving their shoulders. In Al Batinah, all men make these moves, inspired by maritime songs. Traditionally, men hit the groom, but they did not hit my fiancé this time!," she says laughing. Hitting the groom (by males from the bride's side) is a ritual to remind the husband of the woman's male support in case of any misbehavior or ill-treatment to the woman. Pictures and direct videos sent by the groom to the bride during the ceremony appear as a new medium for sharing information between the young couple and signal how technology is bringing changes to contemporary marriage practices.

Later at night, the groom heads toward the bride's house for the exchange of rings, which is also a recent phenomenon in Omani marriages: "It is only a party for me and him," which means a private and intimate party, with the presence of only close family members. Amira narrates this event: "I was sitting, covered entirely in green, with a mirror. When he entered, women started ululating. . . . He then lifted my veil, but he didn't know how to lift it; he was so afraid! It's the first time he sees my hair; it's acceptable because I'm his wife now." Amira then describes other rituals, in particular the egg-breaking ritual, which symbolizes the woman's fertility:[46] "His mother broke an egg while reciting some verses. She has to break the egg with the big finger [al-isba' al kabir]. We usually break eggs, pour it on the feet of the wife and the husband; then we wash it with rose water and basil." She adds that after the egg breaking, "We cut the cake, then he puts the shabka composed of a necklace, a bracelet, a ring and earrings [taraki], that he offered me. He did not know how to put my necklace . . . he was so shy. At this moment, women recite verses: 'Pray on Muhammad, and Peace of Allah upon him' [sali 'ala Muhammad, salamu Allah 'alayhi]. We then exchanged rings and take photographs of the rings [dibal] while holding each other's hands. He then prays on my shawl and kisses it."

New modern elements have thus been incorporated in the milka "party," such as the cake, the exchanges of rings, and the wedding photography. These elements are also observed among non-Shi'a marriage ceremonies in a context of global modernity. At the same time, the particular Shi'a markers in such ceremony remain the prayers and the anashid in the memory of the imams, notably when the green shawl is put above the spouse's head while reciting prayers for the Prophet, for Hassan, and for Hussein.

The Wedding Ceremony: Class Distinctions among the Shi'a

After signing the marriage contract, the wedding ceremony ('irs) is the final step of the matrimonial process. The 'irs is a ceremony that publicizes the marriage in front of everyone. It is generally a wedding ceremony for women (called haflat al harim) and remains an arena for displaying wealth and "celebrating distinctions" (Pauli 2011). Marriage ceremonies have actually been transformed from a modest event into a lavish celebration; a phenomenon also observed among Sunni and Ibadi communities. A low mahr is therefore accompanied by expensive wedding elements, reflecting women and family's status, especially among the Baharina and Lawatiya. The relatively limited amount of mahr observed among the Shi'a is thus accompanied by a rapid commercialization of weddings. The net result is that the party has now become far costlier compared to the mahr. Whereas the mahr amount of the Shi'a in Oman is relatively low and contributes to maintaining the communal endogamy, the lavish wedding ceremony appears more as a sign of class distinction.

In Oman, the wedding ceremony underwent tremendous changes in the past decades in amounts, but also in material performance. New elements were introduced such as the wedding hall (*qaʿa*) and the *kosha* (podium scene or couch where the newlywed sit). "The wedding hall started ten years ago. What a waste! It takes a lot of time to organize it, and goes away in few hours. This girl wants a *kosha* and the other girl wants a velvet tent! All these things are external to our customs, like the ballrooms and things coming from the movies and from our openness to other Arab countries who themselves imported it from Europe," explains one ʿAjami man. This comes in contrast to the male ceremony. "The men's wedding party is very simple. My son paid only 1,000 rials for the party with 400 guests, and the wedding hall was free. But the problem is my daughters who have arranged a very expensive marriage! One of my daughters will get married in October. She wants a *kosha,* in addition to another party with another *kosha*! The whole ceremony, including the hall and the *kosha* will cost more than 20,000 rials. They don't care. I did not marry this way!," explains this Lawati father. He explains that brides' fathers usually contribute to paying this ceremony.[47] In fact, "[t]he girl's party [*haflat al-banaat*] is Expensive. It's either the bride's father who pays for it, or it's half-half. I was responsible for my girl's marriage; I don't want their husband to take a loan." Because of their high economic status, Lawati fathers often participate and share the lavish wedding expenses to maintain endogamy and avoid men's debts in the community. The bride's father's contribution was also observed in a rich ʿAjami family: "Some fathers here take advantage of their daughter's *mahr.* But in my case, my father would give me 5,000 additional rials. He would give me more money every time the previous amount is spent. He helped me a lot," explains this woman whose *mahr* was established at 4,000 rials. Another woman in Sohar explains that the ballroom costs 4,000 rials. "For those who don't have money, it costs 1,000 or 2,000 rials, but reaches 4,000 with the buffet, the cake, and one-night hotel. The ceremony of my daughter will be held at Majan Hotel," says a bride's mother. The bride's white dress reached also important sums: "I bought a dress for 1,600 rials. It's better than renting it for 1,000 rials. This way, I can invest and rent it out. Half of the *mahr* was used for my dress and for the hall. I invited 520 guests," explains this Shiʿa woman who participated in paying for the hall with the groom, a recent practice present among young couples wishing to organize a prestigious event. "Before, the bride would be wearing green all over; and no one would see her. It's not like today with her white dress and five hundred guests seeing her!," explains this woman from Sohar married in the 1960s, a statement that points to the new visibility of the bride. Today, the white bridal dress constitutes an essential part of the marriage expenditures. While celebrated at the bride's house, the marriage ceremony is today held in a hotel, a club, or a hall. "In the eighties, I remember that, in our neighborhood, the bride would come walking from her father's house to her husband's house with women surrounding her all over with a green shawl that they would raise and lower by singing Persian songs, such as the famous '*White Rambo, White Njoub*'.[48] The gown was green. Today, the dress costs 2,000 rials. It is 500 or 1000 rials if rented . . . that's fire [*nar*]! People think it's *modern* but it was much nicer before," explains a 'Ajami man from Sohar. The loss of women's solidarity has been also quoted by this same interviewee who explains some other changes in marriage practices. "Today, the girl sits all day in the beauty salon without eating or drinking; she comes completely 'finished' [*minthiyya*] and exhausted at her wedding, with a blow face, depressed, fainting of fatigue. Before, the bride would stay at her house and women would dress her, discuss with her." The rituals of men's ceremony ('*irs*) have also undergone some major changes in the last decades, and this is applicable to both Shi'a and non-Shi'a groups. "Today, men only go to the mosque for the *milka* then have a dinner [*walima*], that's it! Before, men and women used to celebrate the marriage for seven days, with a lot of popular arts. Now, the '*irs* is only for women and is celebrated in a ballroom!," declares a man from Sohar. Some male wedding rituals are still celebrated. The *malid* (or *mawlid al nabi*, birth of the Prophet) appears today as a distinct Shi'a element during the wedding ceremony. It is also found in joyful calendar events, birthdays of the Prophet and his daughter (Kalinock 2003). The *malid* is one way of remembering the birth of the Prophet (*zikr al mawlid*) and praising the Prophet (*madh al-nabi*). Actually, "it is a Sufi way of remembering the birth of the Prophet; and here in Sohar, you cannot find any Shi'a wedding without a *malid*," explains an 'Ajami man. The *malid* procession is performed by a leading singer, accompanied by two rows of singers opposite each other, all praising the Prophet Muhammad through poetry and recitations. Before the *henne* ritual, where the groom's face is also covered with curcuma, a *malid* is usually performed at the groom's house or at the *ma'tam*. Then the groom celebrates the transition to adulthood by a particular ritual of tearing his clothes apart (*tamziq al thiyab*), notably the white *dishdasha*, although this practice is disappearing in Muscat and in other cities. He then cuts his hair during the *razha* (or *hilaqa*), a practice that is also disappearing. A bath in a *falaj* or garden (called *nahoussa* or *tasbouha*) ends the male rituals, accompanied by a *malid* procession. Finally, another *malid* is performed at the '*irs* dinner. "This ends the male ceremony. Then the groom joins the bride at her party," explains an 'Ajami man. Though the *malid* seems to have been present in Oman in the old days, it is today directly associated to the Shi'a, particularly in Al Batinah region. In addition to the *malid* that glorifies the Prophet and *ahl al-bayt*, recitations (*anashid*) for *ahl al-bayt* constitute a key element during the men's wedding rituals.

The Mass Wedding among the Lower Class

In parallel to major changes in the wedding celebration and organization, particularly in the commercialization of wedding, a recent trend related to mass or collective weddings (*zawaj jama'i*) is observed among the Omani Shi'a belonging to the lower strata.[49] The development of mass weddings, particularly among the 'Ajam, is a new development to counter the high marriage expenses. The wedding ceremony appears hence as an arena of class exclusion and of competition between the various Shi'a groups. The organization of mass marriages by the 'Ajam *Awqaf* (religious committee) started in 2010, with a first mass wedding that gathered nineteen grooms (only men). A second mass wedding was held in 2012 with twenty-three grooms, and a third one in 2014 with thirty-three grooms held in Muscat.[50] In Sohar, for example, the charitable *Waqf* (*Waqf al khayri*) has a special fund and committee dedicated to organizing and financing the collective weddings. However, "the *Waqf al khayri* doesn't pay for the *mahr*," explains this 'Ajami man whose brother married last year as part of a collective wedding ceremony. He then gives details on the saved amount during a collective wedding: "In a normal marriage, a groom alone pays 4,000 rials for the diner [*walima*]. But when they are ten men, each groom pays 400 rials. Plus, if the *Waqf* helps with 2,000 rials, that's 200 rials per groom. My brother paid 400 rials, there were fifteen grooms; all Shi'a, mainly 'Ajam and few Baharna." Such an example values the communal solidarity and the social cohesion for reproducing family. "We encourage collective marriages, even if it is possible to organize a marriage at home. Through these collective marriages, we want our young and single fellows to marry quickly; we don't want them to wait a long time before building a family. We want the marriage to be quick," explains a 'Ajami man from Muscat. "People accept more and more the idea of mass weddings. Men's *'irs* was in the past sacred; but men concede today because of material difficulties. A woman might tolerate men's mass wedding, provided the groom books a ballroom for her wedding! Wedding ceremonies are today for women [*al-'a'ras harimiyya*]!" Rich Shi'a businessmen can also help in financing mass weddings as a way to reduce the cost of marriage and to maintain collective Shi'a identities. In a way, Shi'a are leading the way by spreading the idea of collective weddings in Oman. More than a religious or sectarian affair, collective weddings are today becoming a social phenomenon in the country to counter the high marriage expenses, especially since the failure of creating the marriage fund that was asked by some young Omanis since 2011.[51] In January 2015, the Consultative Council announced that the marriage fund is pending, promoting at the same time mass weddings. Therefore, to counter celibacy in the country, young Omanis are finding new alternatives to finance their marriage, such as mass weddings and the development of other group-associative fundings (Safar 2015).

Conclusion

This chapter discussed how religious affiliation, ethnic belonging, and class are intertwined in complex ways, and at various moments, in *mahr* payments and in wedding ceremonies. Describing the marriage expenses, rituals, and other performances informs us about the Shiʻa matrimonial practices in Oman, revealing internal dynamics vis-à-vis other sectarian groups as well as among the Shiʻa. One of the defining features of the Omani Shiʻa marriage rests on their relatively low *mahr* fixed at around OMR 4,000 in comparison to double this amount for some non-Shiʻa groups. The Shiʻa reproduce their community through a low *mahr* that favor the communal endogamy.

The giving of the *mahr* ceremony with its displays of presents seems also to function as a community marker, although this is not inherently Shiʻa but shared with some other Sunni minorities in Oman. Particular Shiʻa elements during the marriage ceremony, namely the symbolism around the objects, the green color, the *malid*, the recitation, and prayers for the imam's memory, are however markers of Shiʻa practices. Finally, the organization of mass weddings by the Shiʻa communities represents another marker of distinction, even if other non-Shiʻa communities are today also engaging in such performances.

On the other side, however, while the Shiʻa share a common ethos that differentiates them from the Sunnis and Ibadis, marriage practices and attitudes toward the *mahr* also differ among them on the basis of ethnicity and class. Marriage is hence regarded at the same time as a marker of identification for the Shiʻa group's formation in Oman (low *mahr*, organization of mass weddings) and as a marker of distinction inside the Shiʻa communities, where intermarriages between the three Twelver Shiʻa groups remain rare, especially in Muscat. A much lower *mahr* is for example observed among the Lawatiya compared to the ʻAjam. This is nevertheless contravened by lavish weddings among the Lawatiya, considered economically very powerful in the country. The distinction between the Shiʻa in Al Batinah coast, and those in Muscat, appears also key to understanding the diversity among the Shiʻa communities.

The Shiʻa in Oman may be seen as leading the way in regard to marriage expenses in two distinct ways. First, the upper-class strata is paving the way to "modern" marriages, with a strong commercialization of the wedding ceremony combined with a lesser focus on the *mahr*. Second, the lower-class strata who struggle more to finance their marriages develop alternatives, especially with respect to how marriages are organized. Finally, the development of collective marriages, in addition to relatively low *mahr*, is gaining more social momentum across the country.

NOTES

1. *Mahr* does not necessarily have to be money but must have a monetary value. It is due to the bride prior to the consummation of the marriage. In the Qur'an, the term *sadaq*, which means gift and friendship, is rather mentioned to designate the *mahr* (see Surah al-Nisa', verse 4).

2. Amounts can reach more than OMR 15,000 (USD 39,000) in some cities.

3. The relation between marriage and trust needs to be situated within a context of growing sectarianism in the Middle East. Intermarriages act as a survival strategy for minority groups. However, Oman stands out "in sharp contrast to other countries in the Middle East where prominent Muslim preachers openly incite sectarian divisions." See https://www.france24.com/en/20171124-oman-enforces-tolerance-keeping-sectarian-divide-bay.

4. In addition to the Shi'a, other Sunni groups (of non-Arab ethnicity) such as the Zadjalis and some Baluchis in Muscat also perform the *mahr* celebration.

5. The research was part of my postdoctoral studies funded by Georgetown University (Qatar-CIRS program on *The Gulf Family*).

6. The survey was designed only for women because it is the woman's family that determines the *mahr* amount, and the groom accepts this amount. The main objective of the study was to understand women's attitudes in regard to *mahr* and to its personal use. For more details, see Safar (2018). There were no direct questions about the sectarian belonging of the respondents. However, one question (number 42) was asked about the spoken language other than Arabic: either English, French, Swahili, Buluchi, Farsi, Hindi, Zadjali, or Jabali. See https://docs.google.com/forms/d/1q6oZceyuhx2 lıTSdLuiSDH4StdtkTTsPqN6ZWKeDXLc/edit.

7. Ibadism is the moderate version of Kharijism. The Ibadi doctrine recognizes only the two first caliph, Abu Bakr Al Siddiq and Omar ibn al Khattab. "The Caliphate issue was common to all the Kharijites: they rejected the principle of heredity which privileged the Prophet Muhammad's descendants and focused on the election of the Imam. This position could be entrusted to any believer, whatever his social class or his tribe, provided he was morally and religiously irreproachable" (Valeri 2009, 10).

8. Both the actual Sultan, Haytham ben Tariq al Sa'id, and the Grand mufti of Oman, Ahmad Al Khalili, are Ibadis.

9. The percentage of Shi'a in Oman remains unclear as no official statistics are published according to religious affiliation. Authors estimate the Shi'a to number from 3–4 percent (Valeri 2010) to 5 percent (Majidyar 2013). Our Shi'a informants declared they do not exceed 3 percent. Out of a total population of 4.6 million in 2018, 56 percent are Omanis (Statistical Yearbook 2019, 67, 81). https://www.ncsi.gov.om/Elibrary/LibraryContentDoc /bar_Statistical%20Year%20Book_%207-5-2020_3d83f732-9fdf-4523-a64d-8c9dac8c19cb .pdf

10. This ethnic division is adopted by the Shi'a themselves as well as by authors working on Oman (Peterson 2004; Valeri 2010).

11. This division between the Shi'a groups is however less evident in the Al Batinah region compared to Muscat. "In Sohar, the *ma'atim* are usually mixed (*khalit*). My grandfather who is a 'Ajami Sheikh founded for example a *ma'tam* that is managed by Baharna. But in Muscat, there is a separation (*infisal*). The Lawatiya have their own *ma'atim*; the Baharna have their own *ma'atim*, and the'Ajam have their own ones" explains a 'Ajami man from Sohar.

12. Valeri (2010, 254) estimates the Lawatiya to count between 15,000 and 20,000.

13. The first members arrived from Kutch approximately 300 to 400 years ago (Peterson 2004, 41).

14. For more details on the construction of the ethnic and religious identity of the Lawatiya, see Amal Sachedina (2013).

15. The community was "distinctive for introducing new modes of education that were shaped by their ties to the Raj. From the 1940s onwards, the Lawati community had established their own local schools in the Mutrah area. Unlike the *katatib* system, the emphasis of which was on memorizing the Qur'an and Prophetic hadith, these schools were based on the modern education system. Most of the students were the sons of traders and retailers" (Sachedina 2013, 167).

16. Some of the prominent figures are Maqbul bin Ali Sultan (minister of trade and industry, 1993 till his dismissal during the 2011 events) and Fuad Ja'far Al Sajwani (minister of agriculture and fisheries 2011).

17. In 2019, Dr. Suad bint Mohammed bin Ali Al Lawatia was appointed minister of art affairs. She was also the first women in the GCC to hold the position of vice chairperson of the State Council.

18. Some small groups in Muscat, composed mainly of Lawatiya, follow Ayatollah Muhammad Shirazi (1928–2001) (Valeri 2010, 257).

19. The 'Asfour or Darwich families figure among the powerful families.

20. He also served as an ambassador to the United States and France.

21. Only three schools existed in the country before 1970.

22. Enrolled at the missionary school, a Baharni woman explains how she founded a club (*nadi*) in the seventies that was later transformed into a charity association.

23. Lujayna bint Mohsin Haydar Darwish was one of the two women elected at the Majlis Al Shura (Muscat district). By royal decree, since November 2015 she has been a member of the State Council.

24. The decree 92 (November 1993) on restricting extra-nationals' marriages was implemented to preserve the Omani identity in a context of massive immigration and increasing female celibacy rates (Safar 2015, 505, 510). For more details on the marriage decree, refer to Mandana Limbert (2010).

25. Marriages with GCC nationals were softened in 2005 and do not require a special approval (*tasrih*) from the Ministry of Interior.

26. Oman's Personal Status Law, Articles 9, 16, and 21–27, http://www.omanlegal.net/vb /showthread.php?t=8872.

27. Historically, the notary used to mention the *mahr* amount in handwritten customary marriage contracts, but this was no longer the case in the early 1970s with the emergence of the modern state and new institutional bodies (Safar 2018). Today, the Ministry of Legal Affairs delivers standardized and printed marriage forms, equally to all Omanis. No amount is inscribed in the specific column devoted to the *mahr*. Rather, the *mahr* column is always filled with an identical formula, replicated in all registries, "according to the agreement [of both parties]," without specifying the amount of the *mahr*.

28. Tribes can decrease the marriage payment inside their tribe to preserve a rate of endogamy and a statutory rank, threatened by multiple occasions of outside marriages in the modern context (Bonte et al. 2001).

29. Though women very often pre-negotiate the *mahr*'s amount, men are the ones who give the final decision on the agreed upon *mahr* and seal the (endogamous) alliance between both families and hence bond the community. More than a decision between the couple, marriage (and *mahr* in particular) is a family and community affair, an influence observed among other Omani non-Shi'a communities (Safar 2015) and Arab societies (Barakat 1993; Singerman 2007; Hasso 2011).

30. Rather than the official currency (OMR), the term *Rial* will be used in the text when quoted by the respondents who commonly employ this term. The official Omani Rial (OMR) is used to distinguished it from the Saudi, the Iranian, or the Qatari Rial.

31. An expensive gift of gold offered by the groom to the bride. It is difficult to estimate the real amount of the *shabka* as some people include it in the *mahr*. When not included, the amount reaches on average OMR 581 (Safar 2018, 139).

32. The *mahr* is split into two amounts, the *muqaddam* (first part advanced), which must be paid to the bride upon the signing of the contract and before the marriage consummation; and the *mu'akkhar* (second part deferred), which is a sum promised to the bride upon divorce or widowhood.

33. In other Arab countries, the *mu'akkhar* is generally higher than the *muqaddam*. Oman is, for this reason, an unusual case in the region (Safar 2018).

34. This attitude comes in sharp contrast with those in societies like Iran, where high *mehrieh* is generally registered as a deferred part and is correlated with high divorce rates (see Farzanegan and Gholipour 2017).

35. *Mahr* is found to be lower in kin marriages even among non-Shi'a groups in Oman (Wikan 1982). This characteristic is also observed in Shi'a communities elsewhere, notably in Lebanon (El Kheshen and Saadat 2013), in Kuwait (Al Kandari et al. 2002), and in some Muslim societies (Cuisenier 1975, 367, 571).

36. Before 1970, it appears that the Lawatiya men occasionally married women who were Baluchi or Arab, but women invariably married within the community (Sachedina 2013).

37. More particularly, respondents employed the term "*zawaj 'an tariq al hob*" (marriage through love).

38. One respondent mentioned the case of her Shi'a neighbor married to an Ibadi man who converted to Shi'ism. Another case related to a Lebanese Shi'a woman married to an Ibadi man (in 2005), and where *mahr* was much higher than the commonly paid one by the Shi'a in Oman.

39. See https://www.albawaba.com/ar/print/أخبار/السيستاني-يحرم-زواج-الشيعية-من-سني (last visited September 30, 2018).

40. In her study of Shi'a communities in London, Shanneik (2017) underlined the key role of the cantor (*mullaya*), who through her readings activates the memories and generates a collective memory.

41. For the Zadjalis, the *mahr* party is more specifically known as *haflat al haq* (*haq* meaning in Arabic "right").

42. The term "people of the house" refers to members of the prophet's family descended through his daughter Fatima Al Zahra. It refers to those who believe in the rights of the family of the prophet to be his successor.

43. Happy celebrations such as marriage ceremonies never take place during the mourning period (el-Aswad 2010, 67).

44. Green is a color very clearly associated with the Shi'a population (Doherty 2017, 63).

45. These practices are also found in Iran (Koutlaki 2010, chap. 8).

46. This ritual is observed among some communities in Oman, particularly in Al Batinah governorate. For more details on the egg symbolism during the wedding celebration in other societies, see Monger (2013, 247).

47. In other Middle Eastern societies, it is generally the groom's father's responsibility to pay for the party.

48. Other (non-Shi'a) Persian groups in Sohar, such as the Baluchis, borrowed some Persian traditions particularly the White Rambo song.

49. This practice has been also observed in the Middle East among Sunni Muslims, such as in Yemen, in Palestine (Islah 2009), in the UAE, and in Saudi Arabia.

50. See https://www.youtube.com/watch?v=xwaxbSLYGHI.

51. On May 2011, the Consultative Council (Majlis Al Shura) approved the marriage fund panel proposals. The proposals were sent to the Council of Ministers at the end of 2013; but to date the creation of a marriage fund is still under discussion. The sharp decrease in oil prices since 2014 is one element that can explain the reluctance toward this fund estimated at around OMR 50 million (USD 130 million).

REFERENCES

Al Kandari, Yagoub, Crews Douglas, and Poirier Frank. 2002. "Length of Marriage and Its Effect on Spousal Concordance in Kuwait." *American Journal of Human Biology* 14 (1): 1–8.

Al Naser, Fahad. 2009. "Al-Qīma al-Ijtimā'iya li-l-Muhūr fi-l-Mujtama' al-Kuwaytī [The Social Value of Mahr in Kuwaiti Society]." *Journal of the Social Sciences* 37 (4): 15–51.

Badareen, Nayel. A. 2016. "Shī'ī Marriage Law in the Pre-Modern Period: Who Decides for Women?" *Islamic Law and Society* 23 (4): 368–391.

Barakat, Halim. 1993. *The Arab World: Society, Culture and State.* Berkeley: University of California Press.

Barth, Fredrik. 1983. *Sohar: Culture and Society in an Omani Town.* Baltimore: Johns Hopkins University Press.

Bøe, Marianne. 2015. *Family Law in Contemporary Iran: Women's Rights Activism and Shari'a.* London: I.B. Tauris.

———. 2018. "Lived Experiences of Norway's Regulation of *Mahr* (the Muslim Dower)." *Nordic Journal of Religion and Society* 31 (1): 58–74.

Bonte, Pierre, Edouard Conte, and Paul Dresch. 2001. *Emirs et présidents: Figures de la parenté et du politique dans le monde arabe.* Paris: CNRS Editions.

Bourdieu, Pierre. 1979. *La distinction. Critique sociale du jugement.* Collection Le sens commun.

Clarke, Lynda. 2001. *Shi'ite Heritage: Essays on Classical and Modern Traditions.* Binghamton, NY: Global.

Cuisenier, Jean. 1975. *Économie et parenté: leurs affinités de structure dans le domaine turc et dans le domaine arabe.* Paris: École pratique des hautes études.

Dahlgren, Susanne. 2005. "Women's *adah* versus Women's Law: The Contesting Issue of *Mahr* in Aden, Yemen." *Égypte/Monde arabe*, Troisième série 1: 125–144.

Doherty, Gareth. 2017. *Paradoxes of Green: Landscapes of a City-State.* University of California Press.

Dresch, Paul. 2005. "Debates on Marriage and Nationality in the United Arab Emirates." In *Monarchies and Nations: Globalization and Identity in the Arab States of the Gulf,* edited by Paul Dresch and James Piscatori, 136–157. New York: I.B. Tauris.

Eickelman, Christine. 1984. *Women and Community in Oman.* New York: New York University Press.

El Kheshen, Ghadir, and Saadat Mostafa. 2013. "Consanguinity among Shi'a Population in Lebanon." *Journal of Biosocial Science* 45 (5): 675–682.

El-Sayed, el-Aswad. 2010. "The Perceptibility of the Invisible Cosmology. Religious Rituals and Embodied Spirituality among the Bahraini Shi'a." *Anthropology of the Middle East* 5 (2): 59–76.

Farzanegan, Mohammad Reza, and Fereidouni Hassan Gholipour. 2017. "Divorce and Gold Coins: A Case Study of Iran." CESifo Working Paper Series No. 6873 (November): 613–641.

Graz, Liesl. 1981. *Les Omanis: nouveaux gardiens du Golfe.* Paris: Albin Michel.

Hasso, Frances. 2011. *Consuming Desires: Family Crisis and the State in the Middle East.* Stanford, CA: Stanford University Press.

Islah, Jad. 2009. "The Politics of Group Weddings in Palestine: Political and Gender." *Journal of Middle East Women's Studies* 5 (3): 36–53.

Jones, Jeremy, and Nicholas Ridout. 2012. *Oman, Culture and Diplomacy.* Edinburgh: Edinburgh University Press.

Kalinock, Sabine. 2003. "Between Party and Devotion: Mowludi of Tehran Women." *Critical Middle Eastern Studies* 12 (2): 173–187.

Khosronejad, Pedram, ed. 2014. *Women's Rituals and Ceremonies in Shiite Iran and Muslim Communities.* Berlin: Lit Verlag, Iranian Studies.

Koutlaki, Sofia A. *Among the Iranians: A guide to Iran's Culture and Customs.* Boston: Intercultural, 2010.

Limbert, Mandana. 2010. *In the Time of Oil: Piety, Memory and Social Life in an Omani Town.* Stanford, CA: Stanford University Press.

Louer, Laurence. 2008. *Transnational Shia Politics: Religious and Political Networks in the Gulf.* Comparative Politics and International Studies Series. London: Hurst.

Majidyar, Ahmad K. 2013. "Is Sectarian Balance in the United Arab Emirates, Oman, and Qatar at Risk?" *AEI* 6 (October). https://www.aei.org/research-products/report/is-sectarian-balance-in-the-united-arab-emirates-oman-and-qatar-at-risk/.

Mauss, Marcel. 2007. *Essai sur le don.* Puf.

Monger, George P. 2013. *Marriage Customs of the World: An Encyclopedia of Dating Customs.* Santa Barbara, CA: ABC-CLIO.

Moors, Annelies. 1994. "Women and Dower Property in Twentieth-Century Palestine: The Case of Jabal Nablus." *Islamic Law and Society* 1 (3): 301–331.

———. 1995. *Women and Property in Palestine.* Cambridge: Cambridge University Press.

———. 2003. "Registering a Token Dower. The Multiple Meanings of a Legal Practice." *ISIM Newslettter* 13 (December): 85–104.

Pandya, Sophia. 2010. "Women's Shii *Maatam* in Bahrain." *Journal of Middle East Women's Studies* 6 (2): 31–58.

Pauli, Julia. 2011. "Celebrating Distinctions: Common and Conspicuous Weddings in Rural Namibia." *Ethnology* 50 (Spring): 153–167.

Peterson, John. 2004. "Oman's Diverse Society: Northern Oman." *Middle East Journal* 58 (1): 31–51.

Rezai-Rashti, Goli M., and Valentine M. Moghadam. 2011. "Women and Higher Education in Iran: What Are the Implications for Employment and the 'Marriage Market.'" *International Review of Education* 57 (3/4): 419–441.

Sachedina, Amal. 2013. "Of Living Traces and Revived Legacies: Unfolding Futures in the Sultanate of Oman." PhD dissertation, University of California, Berkeley. https://digitalassets.lib.berkeley.edu/etd/ucb/text/Sachedina_berkeley_0028E_13852.pdf.

Safar, Jihan. 2015. "Mariage et Procréation à Oman et au Koweit. Une étude générationnelle dans le contexte des Etats rentiers." PhD dissertation, Sciences Po.

———. 2018. "Explaining Marriage Payment: *Mahr* among Omanis." *HAWWA* 16: 90–143.

Shanneik, Yafa. 2017. "Shia Marriage Practices: Karbala as lieux de mémoire in London." *Social Sciences* 6 (3): 1–14.

Singerman, Diane. 2007. "The Economic Imperatives of Marriage: Emerging Practices and Identities among Youth in the Middle East." Dubai School of Government, Wolfensohn Center for Development, Middle East Youth Initiative Working Paper (6).

Singerman, Diane, and Barbara Ibrahim. 2003. "The Costs of Marriage in Egypt: A Hidden Dimension in the New Arab Demography." In *The New Arab Family*, edited by Hopkins Nicholas, 80–116. Cairo: American University in Cairo Press.

Tamadonfar, Mehran. 2015. *Islamic Law and Governance in Contemporary Iran: Transcending Islam for Social, Economic and Political Order.* Lexington, MA: Lexington Books.

Valeri, Marc. 2009. *Oman. Politics and Society in the Qaboos State.* London: Hurst.

———. 2010. "High Visibility, Low Profile: The Shi-a in Oman under Sultan Qaboos." *International Journal of Middle East Studies* 42 (2): 251–268.

Wikan, Unni. 1982. *Behind the Veil in Arabia: Women in Oman.* Baltimore: Johns Hopkins University Press.

4

Mahr Iranian Style in Norway

Negotiating Gender Equality and Religious and Cultural Belonging through Transnational Shiʿa Marriage Practices

MARIANNE HAFNOR BØE

Exploring Transnational Shiʿi Marriage through the Lens of *Mahr*

This chapter examines the lived experiences involved in contracting Shiʿi Muslim marriages in a transnational context. Through interviews on how Norway's Iranian diaspora relates to *mahr* (*mehrieh* in Persian), attention is directed toward the interviewees' negotiations of cultural and religious belonging, gender equality, as well as the financial and legal significance *mahr* represents in this setting. Although the interviewees tend to denounce *mahr* for being at odds with gender equality and marrying for love, the results of this study show that it is nonetheless maintained, even if such goes against their ideas of marriage. Hence, in a transnational setting the relevance of Shiʿi Muslim marriage practices comes to the fore in new ways, as rejected and transformed, but most commonly continued as a marker of an Iranian style marriage.

Why Study the Iranian Community in Norway?

This chapter focuses on how *mahr* (the marriage gift offered from the husband to a wife in a Muslim marriage) is performed by members of Norway's Iranian diaspora. It is based on a postdoctoral study conducted from 2015 to 2019 at University of Bergen, Norway. Before turning to the empirical results of this study, it is important to first explain why Norway's community of individuals of Iranian background was chosen for this study. The Iranian diaspora is neither the largest nor the oldest immigrant group in Norway, or in Europe for that matter.[1] Still, there are several factors that make this group an interesting case study. Compared to other non-Western immigrant groups, individuals of Iranian background are frequently seen as "resourceful" and "well-integrated" in the Norwegian setting (Alghasi 2009; Sveen 2015). Persons of Iranian background also stand out with regard to religion. A large survey on the living conditions of ten immigrant groups in Norway, conducted by Statistics Norway in 2005 and 2006, reported that religion held little significance for respondents of Iranian background (Blom and Henriksen 2008). On a scale of one to ten, with ten indicating religion's highest significance, Iranian respondents averaged a four (Blom and Henriksen 2008, 67). In comparison, persons of Iraqi background averaged a seven on the chart and those of Somali background stated that religion was of utmost importance, that is, ten. Moreover, nearly half the respondents of Iranian background reported that they no longer belong to the religion of their birth. These factors triggered my inquiry into how this group, who do not necessarily consider religion important to their lives, relate to Shiʻi Muslim marriage practices and *mahr* when getting married.

A central issue for the interviewees in this study is how to relate to their Iranian background in a diaspora situation. Floya Anthias has argued that in contrast to the term "identity," the analytical concept of belonging works better to capture nuanced aspects of difference and contestations that are relevant in this regard (2018). Rather than simply asking who an individual is or who and what they identify with, belonging allows for questions about belonging to what in a more plural sense (144). Whereas identity is used more in a possessive meaning regarding what the individual possess, belonging is always in relation to something outside the self—a place in a social or geographical sense (145). Furthermore, Anthias asserts that belonging is contested and negotiated through spaces, practices, and biographies and closely interrelated by notions of power and social divisions. Such an approach is useful not only for grasping the negotiations performed by the interviewees in relation to how they perceive and practice *mahr* but also for understanding the broader contestations of belonging that are at stake in this regard. What counts as Iranian is a highly contentious issue among members of Norway's Iranian diaspora community. This is also the case for Iranian diaspora groups elsewhere and has been the focus of research in several studies in recent years (Alghasi 2009; Gholami 2015; McAuliffe 2007; Spellman 2004). In this study, however, I examine how such issues emerge regarding transnational Iranian Shiʻi marriages, and arguably the complexities of belonging are revealed in new ways through the lens of *mahr*.

The transnational context between Norway and Iran also provides an intriguing setting for investigating practices of *mahr*. Norway and Iran represent conflicting regulations and interpretations of *mahr*. In Iran, *mahr* is mandatory to marriage registration and must be part of the marriage contract. It represents the particular importance of women in Iranian marriages as it provides leverage and financial security in the case of divorce. By forfeiting their *mahr*, women may obtain access to divorce and negotiate rights that are otherwise not guaranteed for women in the Iranian legal system (Mir-Hosseini 2000, 37–39).

In contrast to Iran, the practice of *mahr* is not approved in Norway's state-sanctioned regulation of marriage rituals. The main reason for the regulation against *mahr* is that it is seen as a contradiction to "Norwegian law and general gender equality principles" (Bufdir 2017). *Mahr* is seen as contravening civil and legal criteria for marriage, as *mahr* is primarily paid from the husband to the wife (Bredal and Wærstad 2014, 37–39). Hence, the Norwegian understanding of *mahr* in the marriage ritual regulation is that it does not reflect equality between the genders, which underlies the Norwegian Marriage Act. The Norwegian regulation does not, however, entail a ban on *mahr* as such. Hence, the parties involved in a Muslim marriage are free to make their own private agreements on *mahr*, if it is not mentioned and included in the civil marriage contract (Bøe 2018, 65). Still, the Norwegian regulation relies on the interpretation that *mahr* represents a mere gender discriminatory practice that contravenes ideals of gender equality as presented in the Norwegian Marriage Act. Consequently, this interpretation discounts the leverage *mahr* may offer women in Shi'i Muslim and Iranian marriages and the financial security it can provide in the event of divorce. On this basis, Norway and Iran's conflicting regulations pose a set of legal dilemmas for individuals who are involved in transnational Iranian-Norwegian marriages. As a result, many tend to engage in a plurality of marriages and consequently coexisting legalities in the area of marriage (Bøe 2018, 67). The implications of this situation of interlegality are not further elaborated on here. However, throughout this chapter I examine the dynamics of *mahr* for members of the Iranian diaspora in Norway and the significance that concluding a Shi'i Muslim and Iranian marriage holds in the daily lives of presumably secular and nonreligious Iranians. Before turning to the empirical research that this chapter builds on, it is relevant to include a few notes on the method as well as data collection procedures.

Method and Data Collection

In this chapter I draw on interviews and conversations with members of the Iranian diaspora community in Norway.[2] I conducted qualitative in-depth interviews with twenty-seven individuals of Iranian and Shi'i Muslim background (twenty-two women and five men) resident in Bergen and Stavanger, two cities on Norway's western coast.[3] All interviewees were adults aged between twenty and sixty, either married, divorced, or in the process of getting married or divorced.[4]

The interviewees represent two main groups in terms of immigration background: those who came to Norway to seek political refuge during the 1980s and 1990s and those who had moved to Norway for family reunion, work, or education during the 2000s. Moreover, the majority lived in urban neighborhoods on the southwest coast of Norway and belonged to the middle or upper-middle stratum of Norwegian society. Typically the interviews took place in the private homes or workplaces of the interviewees or in coffee shops, small restaurants, or other public meeting places in and around the cities of Bergen and Stavanger. I usually recorded the interviews and then transcribed and analyzed the conversations thematically in order to identify patterns and breaks in the material (Kvale and Brinkman 2009). I asked interviewees to elaborate on their ideas and practices (or nonpractices) of *mahr*. A focus in the interviews was on how members of this community negotiate *mahr* in a transnational setting. In addition to narratives about their personal backgrounds and experiences related to marriage and/or divorce, the interviewees touched upon identity issues, particularly what it meant for them to be Iranian, secular, and/or religious.

Mahr and the Lived Experiences of Shi'i Marriage

The Muslim dower (*mahr* in Arabic, *mehrieh* in Persian) holds significance in a Muslim marriage. It represents the bridegroom's payment of a specific amount of money or possessions to the bride. It is mentioned in the Qur'an several times (cf. Qur'an 2:236, 2:237, 4:4, 4:24, 4:25) and is thus seen as obligatory to Shi'i and Sunni Muslim marriages alike.

Practices of *mahr* tend to rely on factors such class, religion, gender, and locality. In Iranian marriages, *mahr* is often decided through negotiations between the bride, groom, and their guardians (*awliya'*, the plural of *wali*). *Mahr* negotiations tend to involve the families' social status, the husband's class, education, and financial situation, and the wife's legal security in the event of divorce. Both parties involved in the marriage may desire a large *mahr*, as such denotes wealth and security.

Mahr tends to be divided into prompt (*muqaddam*) and deferred (*mu'akhkhar*) portions. The prompt *mahr*—usually gold or jewelry—is paid at the time of the wedding, while the deferred portion—typically money—is paid in the event of divorce. The *mahr* consists of anything agreed upon by the bride and groom— for example, gold, money, or any other object and/or token of their matrimony. Although a wife may claim her *mahr* at any time during her marriage, it is most commonly paid if the marriage ends or is dissolved. This is not, however, always the case in Iranian marriages. Several of the interviewees in this study reported that it was common for women to give up the deferred portion of their *mahr* in order to obtain divorce. Although a woman is entitled to the deferred *mahr* if the marriage ends according to Iranian law, the deferred *mahr* is often delayed or even held back by the husband in exchange for a wife's divorce (*khul'*). Hence, *mahr* serves a bargaining function for women seeking divorce in Iran, as it may enable them greater access to divorce and make them financially secure when newly single (Mir-Hosseini 2000, 73). This is happening not only in Iran. There are also cases of Shi'i serving as a bargaining tool in European contexts, particularly in divorce cases involving couples of Iranian background (Fredriksen 2011). On this basis, *mahr* has become significant for the legal position and rights of women in Iranian Shi'i Muslim marriages and tends to serve as a source of financial and legal security for women if their marriage is dissolved.

Mahr is also significant for the relation between a husband and wife in marriage. There is a parallel between a husband's financial support and a wife's sexual availability in Muslim marriage (Quraishi-Landes 2013, 194). Still, it is important to note *mahr*'s complexity. On the one hand *mahr* can be the sale of women's sexual favors and sexual availability in marriage, while on the other hand, it can provide women with fundamental rights regarding divorce. Thus, *mahr* can offer women basic legal and financial rights in Shari'a-based legal systems, which tend to be gender discriminatory, particularly regarding divorce. For this reason, *mahr* is significant for women's position and rights within such systems, as it can enable women greater access to and financial security in the event of divorce (Mir-Hosseini 2000, 73).

Despite the centrality of *mahr*, most research on the topic in Western societies focuses on its judicial aspects in relation to international private and comparative law (Büchler 2011, 67–69; Fournier 2010; Freeland 2001; Günther et al. 2015; Løvdal 2009; Mehdi 2007; Mehdi and Nielsen 2011; Sayed 2008; Yassari 2013). However, the ways in which *mahr* connects to the lived experiences of marriage and how it is contextualized and internationally linked remain unexplored. Several researchers have therefore pointed to the need for more ethnographic research on the actual practice of *mahr* in pluralistic Western contexts (Günther et al. 2015, 34; Mehdi and Nielsen 2011, 16; Shah 2010, 125). In this chapter, I therefore respond to the call for ethnographic research on how *mahr* is practiced and developed in the European setting by reporting on how *mahr* is conceived, practiced, negotiated, and situated within a transnational Shi'i Muslim marriage.

Mahr among Norway's Iranian Diaspora

This study's interviewees spoke to three main *mahr*-related practices: rejection, transformation, and continuation. Out of twenty-seven interviewees, only five considered *mahr* to be intrinsic to marriage (four women and one man), while the remaining twenty-two (eighteen women and four men) strongly believed *mahr* to be an old-fashioned practice symbolizing the sale of women into marriage. Although the latter understanding of *mahr* is widespread, only five interviewees excluded *mahr* from their marriage; hence, twenty-two interviewees did include some form of *mahr* when they married.

Mahr *Rejected*

Reza exemplifies most of the interviewees' view of *mahr*. He referred to himself as "secular," and when marrying a non-Iranian woman in Norway he never even considered engaging in a Muslim marriage. Reza came to Norway for political refuge in the late 1980s, and at the time of our meeting he was in his late forties. In his view, the need for *mahr* was obsolete in Norway, as women and men enjoy the same rights in marriage. In the Iranian system, however, *mahr* still served an important purpose. Reza explains, "I consider *mehrieh* very negatively. For me it entails buying and selling goods. . . . I believe that if men and women had equal legal rights [in Iran], then the situation would be the same as in Norway. There would be no need for *mehrieh*. . . . I am completely against it [*mehrieh*], but in that situation [in Iran], it represents security for women" (interview, October 2015). In most cases, the size and form of *mahr* are decided based on the bride's traits—age, beauty, previous marriages, sexual experience, etc.—and her family's social status. For this reason, many Iranians—like Reza—compare the payment of *mahr* to selling a woman into marriage (Bøe 2018). Although many of the interviewees shared Reza's dislike of *mahr*, the majority still considered it important to continue *mahr* as practiced in Iran. As we will see in the next sections, the majority of this study's interviewees saw *mahr* as inherent to their Iranian marriages. In the remaining part of this chapter I bring attention to the two different but interrelated practices of *mahr* that this group of interviewees employed.

Mahr *Transformed: A Romantic Symbol of Marriage*

In Iran, symbolic forms of *mahr* are commonly used to counter the sales aspect often connected to the practice. Symbolic forms of *mahr* underline a couple's idea of a love marriage and may thus signify a move away from more traditional forms of marriage. Demanding not traditional amounts of *mahr* but rather gifts and romantic symbols—such as a thousand roses or jasmine flowers (BBC 2008; Mir-Hosseini 2000, 75)—has therefore become important to represent ideas of a love marriage instead of a mere sale of a woman in marriage. Accordingly, some of this study's interviewees disapproved of *mahr* because it contravened their ideas of gender equality and a marriage based on love. Although many still practice *mahr*, they do so in alternative ways by instead employing romantic and symbolic forms.

During the interviews, a vast range of symbolic forms of *mahr* came up. Some couples used a silver mirror, or an object taken from their *sofreh* (the marriage cloth typically used in Iranian marriages) as *mahr*, whereas others preferred a single flower or ten thousand roses as token *mahr*. The symbolic *mahr* does not, however, reflect only such romantic attributes but can also include some religion. For example, some interviewees had a copy of the Qur'an or promises of *hajj* (pilgrimage to Mecca) as their *mahr*.

Neda was in her late thirties at the time of our interview and had lived in Norway since childhood. She had divorced her first husband a few years prior and was in the process of planning a new marriage. For her first marriage, Neda had a substantial amount of money as her *mahr*; this time, in contrast, she wanted *hajj*: "[This *mahr* is] so that he and I can go and visit God's house together. The one you love and God; so beautiful, right? So, this is my demand. I do not require any gold, house, car, no. . . . As long as he is a proper guy, and takes good care of me" (interview, April 2015). Asking for *hajj* travel or other symbolic religious objects as *mahr* was a recurring theme among interviewees who self-identified as Shiʻi Muslims. For Neda it was clearly a way of combining her romantic and religious aspirations of her Shiʻi marriage. This was not, however, widespread among the interviewees as most of them would focus only on the romantic aspects of their marriage when asking for symbolic forms of *mahr*. Still, Neda's case illustrates the interviewees who mostly employed a symbolic *mahr*—women marrying for the second time who had their own income and did not factor having children into their decision. Additionally, women who had no intention of ever returning to Iran and therefore saw no need to relate to the Iranian marriage system would also make use of symbolic *mahr*. Hence, these are women who were in no need of the financial or legal security that high values of *mahr* may offer for those involved in Iranian marriages.

Symbolic forms of *mahr* are by no means a diaspora phenomenon or something that occurs only in Iran. Annelies Moors has documented this trend in a study of *mahr* practices in Jabal Nablus in Palestine (2008). Although their possibilities and trajectories for making token *mahr* registrations were highly differentiated, the women in Moors's study would register token *mahr* as "a move towards modernity" (2008, 88). However, in Iran and in Palestine, token *mahr* are in most cases registered as prompt *mahr*. In addition to the token prompt *mahr*, a significant financial amount is commonly registered as a deferred portion to serve as financial and/or legal security in the case of marriage dissolvement.

In contrast, Neda and other interviewees in this study would ask only for a symbolic *mahr*, with no additional deferred portion. Living in a country where they enjoy basic divorce rights and financial and welfare security in case their marriage is dissolved, they did not see the immediate need for additional financial security. Hence, these women—marrying for the second time and/or financially independent—turn *mahr* into a sole symbol of the romantic and/or religious characteristics of their marriage. Their symbolic use of *mahr* entails a transformation compared to what is widespread in Iran: asking for a symbolic *mahr* in combination with a financial deferred *mahr* as a bargaining chip in case of divorce. Moreover, through its sole symbolic use they turn *mahr* into something romantic and thus clearly take a stance away from certain patriarchal aspects of Iranian Shiʻi marriage that offer scarce rights for women. However, the use of symbolic *mahr* among Norway's Iranian diaspora also represents a continuation of Iranian Shiʻi marriage in some regards. Both the content they add to their symbolic *mahr* and the fact that they choose to practice *mahr* refer to a continuation of Iranian Shiʻi marriage. Particularly the use of typical Iranian marriage objects as *mahr*—like candles, mirrors, or even religious objects like the Qur'an—underlines the Iranian and Shi'i character of their marriage. What is more, including *mahr* in a Norwegian-Iranian marriage underscores the religious aspect of the marriage. In these regards *mahr* seems to represent a link between their new life in the diaspora and their Iranian background.

Through the objects and/or symbols used as *mahr*, their marriage takes an Iranian form. Hence, their practice of *mahr*—even though somewhat transformed from what is common in Iran—refers to a sense of belonging to what they see as Iranian. According to Nira Yuval-Davis, "Belonging is about emotional attachment, about feeling 'at home'" (2006, 197). Being in a situation of displacement allows individuals to initiate practices that create a sense of belonging. Such practices of belonging are, however, often contested and negotiated and may take many forms (Davis et al. 2018, 7–8). Moreover, as seen in the case of this study's interviewees who can practice only symbolic *mahr*, the abilities of various groups to negotiate practices of belonging vary according to their resources, possibilities, and inclusion in society. The transformation of *mahr* into a mere symbolic practice that emphasizes the romantic potential of marriage is thus the privileged right of the few who are not dependent on the legal and financial rights that *mahr* may entail. Still, the fact that they practice *mahr* refers to a sense of belonging to what they see as Iranian. In this way, the transformed use of *mahr* may be interpreted as parallel to the *mahr* employed by most of the interviewees, namely the continued *mahr* that will be elaborated on in the next section.

Mahr *Continued: Iranian Style*

Although interviewees reported a variety of symbolic forms of *mahr*, the majority still considered it important to continue *mahr* as practiced in Iran. As mentioned, twenty-two out of twenty-seven interviewees chose to include *mahr* in some form in their marriage contract. Bahareh was an unmarried woman in her early twenties who came to Bergen to study. At the time of our interview, she had lived in Norway for two years. During our talk, Bahareh referred to herself as secular and talked about how she had been questioning the mind-set of many people in Iran, a mind-set that she had also previously taken for granted. She talked about how she disregarded many of the customs practiced in Iran, particularly customs related to marriage that she saw as opposing women's rights. Bahareh claimed to be a firm believer in gender equality, but still considered it important to marry "Iranian style." As she explained, "If I was to marry an Iranian man here, I think the situation would be the same as if I had married him in Iran. I believe I would think that *mehrieh* was like the honor of my family, something like that. Even though I am educated and am to marry here, I will still marry 'Iranian style.' Because everything is Iranian style! It will be registered in the Iranian system, so it is reasonable to do it Iranian style" (interview,

May 20, 2015). Bahareh's reference to Iranian style signifies the complexity of marriage practices in Iran. Her use of the term is also important for understanding why a noteworthy number of interviewees maintained *mahr* even though they disregarded the practice. Most interviewees openly criticized Islam, rejected Shari'a, and disavowed everything connected to the current government in Iran. Furthermore, like Bahareh, most also defined themselves as secular or even anti-Islam.

The meaning of Iranian style is, however, interpreted in different ways. Generally, the term refers to doing something in line with Iranian customs and way of life. Iranian style thus entails different aspects of daily life, along with the relevant social, religious, and legal customs related to how weddings are conducted in Iran. While Iranian marriage traditions are somewhat based on Islam, they also draw on a diversity of pre-Islamic customs from Iran and its neighboring countries. Iranian-style marriage customs may include practices such as *sofreh 'aqd*, a marriage cloth or table decorated with objects that supposedly bring luck and fertility to the newlyweds.[5] They may also refer to *khastegari*, the process where the man and his family pay a visit to the potential bride and her family, and that of holding a silk scarf (*tureh qand*) over the heads of a newlywed couple and grating sugar cubes (*kalleh qand*) through the scarf to bring sweetness and happiness to their marriage. Additionally, poetry reading and/or Qur'an recitation and dancing are central to Iranian weddings. Iranian marriage practices thus build on a plurality of cultural and religious customs, similar to how other Iranian customs are maintained by people of Iranian background, such as Nowruz (Iranian new year), *Chahar Shanbe Suri* (the fire festival prior to Nowruz), and *Mehregan* (autumn festival). These customs hail from Zoroastrianism but no longer have any apparent religious function for many Iranians. Rather, these customs are expressions of *Iraniat*, the cultural and historical heritage inherent to Iran (Holliday 2011). Although the content of *Iraniat* has changed throughout different periods of Iranian history and can be associated with a diversity of ideas, overall it refers to notions of authenticity in the construction of Iranian identity (2011, 49–50). Corresponding to how other customs are maintained as expressions of *Iraniat*, similar ideas were connected to that of maintaining *mahr*. Although it may hold no religious significance for many interviewees, *mahr* was still considered essential to an Iranian marriage.

Iranian-style *mahr* may take many forms. Like Bahareh, many of the interviewees underscored that it was significant for maintaining family traditions. At the time of our interview, Ali was a married man in his late thirties who had come to Bergen to work in the early 2000s. He explains, "We married in Iran, but if we were to marry here [in Norway] we would also have *mehrieh*. . . . It is important for the family; it is tradition in a way. And it is important if we should decide to go back to Iran. It is part of the marriage" (interview, September 2015).

Bahareh and Ali's explanations as to why they chose to continue *mahr* include sentiments connected to gender, family, and belonging in a diaspora setting. These aspects are closely interrelated and refer to a broader sense of belonging involved in the lives of people living in diaspora communities. Anthias argues that belonging is about formal and informal attributions, both discursive and practice-based attributions that are political as well as personally efficacious (2018, 144). However, such belongings do not necessarily rely on shared values but may deal with formal membership as well as less formal social institutions, such as families and social networks (145).

For Bahareh and several other interviewees, their main motivation for practicing *mahr* was the financial and legal benefits connected to it. This motivation is an expression of what Anthias refers to as formal belonging, marked through having the marriage registered in the Iranian system. What is more, it also brings to mind the significance that gender relations and women's rights hold in transnational settings. Typically, negotiations of gender relations and home are central to the diaspora situation, and issues dealing with the rights of women in marriage have proven particularly relevant for Muslims living in the diaspora (Moghissi and Ghorasi 2010). As we have seen, the issue of women's rights is highly pertinent for the practice of *mahr* in this study as well. Bahareh's point of having the marriage registered in Iran underlines the fact that *mahr* is a mandatory aspect of an Iranian marriage contract and that a marriage is not considered lawful without it. Hence, many of the interviewees who continue the practice of *mahr* include it for their marriage to be acknowledged in the Iranian system and for enjoying the legal privileges that *mahr* may entail for women.

Although a main motivation for practicing *mahr* is based on degrees of formal or informal belonging to Iran, it is nonetheless interesting to note other motivations for practicing *mahr* in a transnational setting. Arezoo underlined the importance of continuing *mahr* as an Iranian marriage practice. At the time of our interview, she was in her mid-forties. Arezoo had come to Norway in the 1990s to marry a man of Iranian origin who lived in Norway. When Arezoo and her husband got married, they had no *mahr*. Still, she considered *mahr* inherent to marriage and lamented the fact that she had none: "Ever since we were kids, we have been influenced and affected by rituals. And the way I see it, it affects the interactions and relationship between us as humans. A challenge many have in Norway, and in my country, is that many rituals are not practiced and [therefore] forgotten. And this leads to a kind of loneliness. *Mehrieh* is part of such rituals. If you have grown up with it, and everyone around you have had *mehrieh*, then you take it for granted that you should also have it" (interview, October 2015). Arezoo then sought to link the role of *mahr* to that of other Iranian marriage practices, explaining that several things were done according to Iranian custom during her wedding, although not always in the correct manner.

Her narration of her wedding underlined the significance that Iranian marriage customs hold for her, even in Norway:

> Already from the beginning, something was wrong. The fact that we only invited about twenty people I did not know, and I never really understood what was going on that evening. We invited some people over for dinner; there was dancing, I was wearing a wedding gown, and had put on makeup and fixed my hair. But that table [*sofreh*], I had done it myself. And I'm not supposed to do it myself! People around me are supposed to do everything. And I remember I had to cook, and there were a lot of issues. . . . After getting married in Iran, you are a bride for a whole month. But here, we invited his cousin and family to stay at our place, so the day after [the wedding] I got up and cooked and worked. So well. . . . (interview, October 2015)

For Bahareh, Ali, and Arezoo alike *mahr* is closely connected to family traditions and notions of the self, and they thus underscore the compound significance that marriage customs hold for diaspora communities. Maintaining the family's expectations and ways of doing things is important for many of the interviewees' sense of belonging and refers to marking a sense of belonging through informal membership to social institutions like family and social networks (Anthias 2018, 145). As for the interviewees, continuing marriage practices is about being accepted and participating in their family's expectations and habitual ways of doing things. However, Arezoo's narration of *mahr* as an inherent part of the wedding ceremony reveals that a different sense of belonging is also at work. When she talks about what it meant for her not to have *mahr* in her transnational Iranian marriage, she refers to a feeling of "loneliness" and of "something being wrong." Thus, *mahr* clearly represent a significant aspect of an Iranian style marriage in her view. Arezoo's reaction toward the lack of *mahr* can be understood as what Anthias refers to as an affective dimension of belonging (2018, 145). Hence, *mahr* is linked to feelings of cultural competency and safety as well as practices of inclusion. The affective dimension recalls the complexities of *mahr* and the relevance it represents beyond that of a mere practical and contractual marriage issue. In other studies of diaspora communities, the roles that places, objects, groups, memories, and even smells and familiar habits may have as sites of belonging have been documented (Buitelaar and Stock 2010, 166). Correspondingly, the issue of *mahr* represents a gateway into similar issues for the Iranian diaspora in this study. Although continuously negotiated and representing different things for different people, the mere practice of *mahr* clearly evokes a sense of belonging and a feeling of home for the interviewees on different levels. Hence, merely rejecting the practice does not appear as a viable option for the majority involved in this study.

Mahr as a Marker of Iranian-Style Marriage

This chapter has presented the various ways in which individuals of Iranian background in Norway practice, perceive, and negotiate *mahr*. Although some interviewees refrained from employing *mahr*, as it contravenes their views on gender equality and marrying for love, a noteworthy majority still chose to practice *mahr* as a sign of Iranian-style marriage. Interestingly, many interviewees who continued *mahr* outside of Iran did so in order to gain legal and financial rights through *mahr* in Shi'i Iranian marriages. Hence, the notion of gender equality is highly contextual and differentiated according to the positionality of the interviewees.

The significance that *mahr* holds within the Iranian diaspora community is complex. These *mahr* cases illustrate how Shi'i Muslim marriage practices can play a significant role in the lives of individuals of Iranian background, even when conducted outside Iran. Although many refrain from religion, particularly Islam, their *mahr* show that religious practices are continued and maintained in relation to marriage, although sometimes in transformed ways.

Recent studies of Iranian diaspora communities have focused on notions of secular and religious identification in particular (Gholami 2015; McAuliffe 2007; Spellman 2004). Cameron McAuliffe, in his study of second-generation Iranians in London, Sydney, and Vancouver, explains that his interviewees are best seen as Iranian "cultural Muslims" (2007). During Nowruz and Muharram alike, the interviewees' ideas of Islam are individually negotiated as a cultural identity, much like their Iranian identity. Islam, he writes, remains "a cogent part of their Iranian identity as a set of core (national) values that inform everyday cultural and secular interactions" (McAuliffe 2007, 44). Reza Gholami makes a parallel finding in his recent study on the Iranian diaspora in the United Kingdom (2015). In it, he recounts how the Shi'i Muslim religious experience is intermeshed with and constituted by the Iranian diaspora's productive, secular discourse and practices (Gholami 2015, 195). In contrast to these studies, practices of *mahr* analyzed in this study point to a less sharp distinction between secular and religious belongings and of what counts as Islamic and Iranian for the interviewees. The fact that *mahr* is still used among Iranian migrants of Shi'i Muslim background in Norway represents a continuation of Shi'i Islam in the area of marriage, sometimes even against my interviewees' own ideas of marriage. Although there is much discrepancy over *mahr*, it continues as a marker of belonging in different ways regarding what is considered a typical Iranian marriage in a transnational setting. The interviewees referred to various dimensions of belonging as important for why they continued *mahr* outside Iran. *Mahr* thus gained relevance due to the formal, informal, and affective dimensions that the interviewees read into such practices. What is more, the interviewees remind us that practices of *mahr* are not only gendered but highly dependent on the situational and positionality of those who deploy it.

Conclusion

This study's interviewees spoke to three main *mahr*-related practices: rejection, transformation, and continuation. Although the general opinion of the interviewees was that *mahr* represented an old-fashioned practice symbolizing the sale of women into marriage, a large majority nonetheless chose to continue the practice. Some used it in transformed ways to signify a move away from more traditional forms of marriage and the sales connotation that *mahr* represents. However, even more of the interviewees continued *mahr* as an expression of Iranian style marriage in a Norwegian context. For some, it entailed relating to an informal cultural practice, a way of projecting cultural competency and adherence or even profound sentiments related to marriage, whereas for others it represented a more formal tool for obtaining rights and post-divorce financial security within the Iranian Shi'i Muslim legal system. These variations underline the differences in social location and positionality that are relevant for the kind of choices and bargaining possibility that are available for different groups within Norway's Iranian diaspora.

The diverse *mahr* practices of the interviewees in this study also bring attention to the ways in which Shi'i Muslim marriage is connected to the lives of members of the Iranian diaspora. The interviewees have offered a glimpse into how transnational marriage works as an arena where notions of gender, religion, and belonging come to the fore in new ways. What is more, this study portrays the relevance that Shi'i Muslim marriage practices hold for people who might not de facto proclaim a religious identity, but the ways in which such practices are emphasized and become important through the compound dimensions of formal, informal, and affective senses of belonging. Thus, the results of this research illustrate how *mahr* is negotiated and practiced in a transnational context, as rejected and transformed, but most commonly continued as a sense of belonging, even when conducted outside of Iran.

NOTES

1.   According to Statistics Norway (SSB), 16,462 individuals of Iranian background lived in Norway at the start of 2016 (SSB 2016); they are the tenth largest immigration group in Norway (Østby 2015). While most Iranians migrated to Norway as political refugees at the end of the 1980s (1986–1990) and in the early 2000s, a substantial number also came for family reunification, work, and education.

2.   The processing of personal data of the interviewees in this project has been notified to the Data Protection Officer for Research, the Norwegian Centre for Data Research (NSD).

3. Throughout this chapter, the term "individuals of Iranian and Shi'i Muslim back-ground" includes Iran-born persons who immigrated to Norway and Norway-born persons born with at least one Iranian-born parent. "Shi'i Muslim background" refers to individuals who are born Sh'ii Muslim. The term does not, however, necessarily denote an individual's current religious affiliation.

4. Fifteen interviewees were married, four were divorced, two had remarried, and six were unmarried.

5. *Sofreh 'aqd* usually includes herbs, cakes, a mirror, candelabras, rose water, fruit, sugar cubes, a bowl of coins, a copy of the Qur'an, a prayer rug (*jay-e namaz*), and fertility symbols such as decorated eggs, almonds, and walnuts.

REFERENCES

Alghasi, Sharam. 2009. "Iranians in Norway: Media Consumption and Identity Making." PhD dissertation, University of Oslo. https://www.uio.no/forskning/tverrfak/culcom /publikasjoner/doktoravhandlinger/2009/Avhandling-Alghasi.pdf.

Anthias, Floya. 2018. "Identity and Belonging: Conceptualizations and Reframings through a Translocational Lens." In *Contested Belonging: Spaces, Practices, Biographies*, edited by K. Davis, H. Ghorashi, and P. Smets, 137–159. Bingley: Emerald.

BBC. 2008. "Iranian to Pay 124,000 Rose-Dowry." http://news.bbc.co.uk/2/hi/middle_east /7275506.stm.

Bredal, Anja and Tonje Wærstad. 2014. "Gift, men ugift: om utenomrettslige religiøse vig-sler." Institutt for samfunnsforskning, rapport 2014: 06. https://samfunnsforskning .brage.unit.no/samfunnsforskning-xmlui/bitstream/handle/11250/2599700/Rapport _2014_6_Allkopi_v3_Ferdig_2.pdf?sequence=1&isAllowed=y.

Blom, Svein, and Kristin Henriksen, eds. 2008. "Levekår blant innvandrere i Norge 2005/2006." Statistics Norway Reports, 2008/05. https://www.ssb.no/a/publikasjoner /pdf/rapp_200805/rapp_200805.pdf.

Bøe, Marianne. 2018. "Lived Experiences of Norway's Regulation of *mahr* (the Muslim Dower)." *Nordic Journal of Religion and Society* 31: 58–74. https://doi.org/10.18261/issn .1890-7008-2018-01-04.

Büchler, Andrea. 2011. *Islamic Law in Europe? Legal Pluralism and Its Limits in European Family Laws*. Burlington, VT: Ashgate.

Bufdir. 2017. "Godkjenning av vigselsritualer." November 14. https://www.bufdir.no/Ekteskap _og_skilsmisse/Godkjenning_av_vigselsritualer.

Buitelaar, Marjo, and Femke Stock. 2010. "Making Homes in Turbulent Times: Moroccan Dutch Muslims Contesting Dominant Discourses of Belonging." In *Muslim Diaspora in the West. Negotiating Gender, Home and Belonging*, edited by H. Moghissi and H. Gho-rashi, 163–180. Aldershot: Ashgate.

Davis, Kathy, et al. 2018. "Introduction." In *Contested Belonging: Spaces, Practices, Biographies*, edited by K. Davis, H. Ghorashi, and P. Smets, 1–18. Bingley: Emerald.

Fournier, Pascal. 2010. "Flirting with God in Western Secular Courts: Mahr in the West." *International Journal of Law, Policy and the Family* 24 (1): 67–94. https://doi.org/10.1093 /lawfam/ebp011.

Freeland, Richard. 2001. "The Islamic Institution of Mahr and American Law." *Gonzaga Jour-nal of International Law* 2000–2001. http://blogs.law.gonzaga.edu/gjil/2006/03/the -islamic-institution-of-mahr-and-american-law.

Fredriksen, Katja J. 2011. Mahr (Dower) as a Bargaining Tool in a European Context: A Comparison of Dutch and Norwegian Judicial Decisions". In *Embedding Mahr in the*

European Legal System, edited by Rubya Mehdi and Jørgen S. Nielsen, 147–190. Copenhagen: DJØF.

Gholami, Reza. 2015. *Secularism and Identity: Non-Islamiosity in the Iranian Diaspora*. Farnham: Ashgate.

Günther, Ursula, Martin Herzog, and Stephanie Müssig. 2015. "Researching Mahr in Germany: A Multidisciplinary Approach." *Review of Middle East Studies* 1 (49): 23–37. https://doi.org/10.1017/rms.2015.64.

Holliday, Shabnam. 2011. *Defining Iran: Politics of Resistance*. Farnham: Ashgate.

Kvale, Steinar and Svend Brinkman. 2009. *Det kvalitative forskningsintervju*. Oslo: Gyldendal akademisk.

Løvdal, Lene. 2009. "Private International Law, Muslim Laws and Gender Equality: The Adjudication of Mahr in Scandinavian, English and French Courts." Master's thesis, University of Oslo. http://urn.nb.no/URN:NBN:no-21885.

McAuliffe, Cameron. 2007. "Visible Minorities: Constructing and Deconstructing the 'Muslim Iranian' Diaspora." In *Geographies of Muslim Identities: Diaspora, Gender and Belonging*, edited by C. Aitchson, P. Hopkins, and M. P. Kwan, 29–57. Aldershot: Ashgate.

Mehdi, Rubya. 2007. "Danish Law and the Practice of Mahr among Muslim Pakistanis in Denmark." *International Journal of the Sociology of Law* 31 (2): 115–129. https://doi.org/10.1016/j.ijsl.2003.02.002.

Mehdi, Rubya, and Jørgen S. Nielsen, eds. 2011. *Embedding Mahr in the European Legal System*. Copenhagen: DJØF.

Mir-Hosseini, Ziba. 2000. *Marriage on Trial: A Study of Islamic Family Law*. London: I.B. Tauris.

Moghissi, Haideh and Halleh Ghorashi, eds. 2010. *Muslim Diaspora in the West: Negotiating Gender, Home, and Belonging*. Surrey: Ashgate.

Moors, Annelies. 2008. "Registering a Token Dower: The Multiple Meanings of a Legal Practice." In *Narratives of Truth in Islamic Law*, edited by B. Dupret, B. Drieskens, and A. Moors, 85–104. London: I.B. Tauris.

Østby, Lars. 2015. "Flyktninger i Norge." Statistics Norway. https://www.ssb.no/befolkning/artikler-og-publikasjoner/flyktninger-i-norge.

Quraishi-Landes, Asifa. 2013. "A Mediation on Mahr, Modernity, and Muslim Marriage Contract Law." In *Law, Feminism and Religion*, edited by Marie A. Failinger, Elizabeth R. Schiltz, and Susan J. Stabile, 173–195. Farnham: Ashgate.

Sayed, Mosa. 2008. "The Muslim Dower (Mahr) in Europe: With Special Reference to Sweden." In *European Challenges in Contemporary Family Law*, edited by Katharina Boele-Woelki and Tone Sverdrup, 187–208. Antwerp: Intersentia.

Shah, Prakash. 2010. "Between God and the Sultana? Legal Pluralism in the British Muslim Diaspora." In *Shari'a as Discourse: Legal Traditions and the Encounter with Europe*, edited by Jørgen S. Nielsen and Lisbet Christoffersen, 117–139. Farnham: Ashgate.

Shanneik, Yafa. 2017. "Shia Marriage Practices: Karbala as *lieux de mémoir* in London." *Social Sciences* 6 (3): 100. https://doi.org/10.3390/socsci6030100.

Spellman, Kathryn. 2004. *Religion and Nation: Iranian Local and Transnational Networks in Britain*. New York: Berghahn.

SSB. 2016. "Innvandrere og norskfødte med innvandrerforeldre, 1. januar 2016." Statistics Norway. Last modified November 5, 2019. https://www.ssb.no/befolkning/statistikker/innvbef.

Sveen, Eirik Hind. 2015. "Iranske Houman er integreringsvinner." *NRK*. https://www.nrk.no/finnmark/iranske-houman-er-en-norsk-integreringsvinner-1.12679807.

Yassari, Nadjma. 2013. "Understanding and Use of Islamic Family Law Rules in German Courts: The Example of the Mahr." In *Applying Shari'a in the West—Facts, Fears and the Future of Islamic Rules on Family Relations in the West*, edited by Maurits S. Berger, 165–187. Leiden: Leiden University Press.

Yuval-Davis, Nira. 2006. "Belonging and the Politics of Belonging." *Patterns of Prejudice* 40 (3): 197–214.

PART THREE

Temporary Marriage

A Flexible and Controversial Institution

5

Mut'a Marriage among Youth in the Non-Shi'i Environment of Indonesia

EVA F. NISA

Mut'a marriage (temporary or fixed-time marriage) has not been popular in majority-Sunni Indonesia. The practice is religiously sanctioned by Shi'ism—especially among Twelver Shi'is residing largely in Iran. The discussion of *mut'a* in Indonesia has been closely related to anti- Shi'i sentiment. The presence of Shi'ism in Indonesia dates back to the seventh century CE, during the early formative period of Islam in the archipelago (see Rakhmat 1998). During the advent of Islam in the archipelago, the separation between Sunni and Shi'i elements was not clear. Syed Farid Alatas argues that there are two important aspects in the discussion of the elements of Shi'i culture in Indonesia:[1] "One, the vast majority of Indonesians are unaware of the presence of Shi'i customs and norms in their practice of Islam. Two, the Shi'i influences in Indonesian Islam are both the result of direct contact with Shi'i communities in India and West Asia as well as the *'Alawiyyun* factor in the [I]slamization of the Malay world" (1999, 336).[2] Therefore, even today, it is not uncommon to see Shi'i elements in the practice of Islam by Indonesian Sunnis. For example, some understandings and practices of Islam by Muslims from the largest Muslim mass organization in Indonesia, Nahdlatul Ulama (NU), have been seen as close to those of Shi'ism. This includes the famous celebration of Ashura held on the tenth of Muharram (Islamic calendar) (see Feener 2015), which marks the martyrdom of one of the Shi'i *imams* (leaders), Imam Husayn (see Feener 1999; Formichi 2014a; Zulkifli 2013).[3] In addition to this, the influence of Shi'i Islam can be seen from some classical literary works (see Saenong 2015) that emphasize a special place for Shi'i *imams*, the decorated tombs, and the practice of tomb visitation (*ziyarah*) as well as the veneration of Muslim saints (Alatas 1999, 336). Makin argues that "clear differentiation between the two in public, only began during the late New Order and reform periods" (2017, 5).[4] This, in particular, can be seen after the Iranian Revolution in 1979 (Makin 2017, 6).

Studies on Shiʻi Islam in Indonesia mostly focus on the interest in Shiʻism in Indonesia after the Iranian Revolution, particularly from the early 1980s (Formichi 2014a; Marcinkowski 2008, 50; Zulkifli 2013). Following the Iranian Revolution, especially during the 1980s and 1990s, many Indonesians studied at *hawza ʻilmiyya* (colleges of Islamic learning)[5] in Qum or at Jamiʻa al-Mustafa alʻAlamiyyah (Al-Mustafa International University) in Iran (Latief 2008, 307; Marcinkowski 2008, 40).[6] Azyumardi Azra also argues that there was a growing interest in Shiʻism among Sunni Muslims due to the Iranian Revolution (2005, 8–9). Before the Iranian Revolution, only a small number of Indonesians studied there, such as one of the most famous Shiʻi leaders in Indonesia, Umar Shahab, who is currently the chairman of the Ahlul Bait Indonesia (ABI, the Indonesian Shiʻi Community) advisory council, and Hussein Shahab (Assegaf 2015, 254; Latief 2008, 307; Zulkifli 2009, 234). Throughout the years, the number of Indonesian students pursuing study in Qum increased significantly. Zulkifli recorded that in 2000, for example, more than a hundred students went to Qum (Zulkifli 2009, 238). Many scholars assert that the Shiʻi life in Indonesia can currently be seen mainly in Java, particularly in Jakarta, Bandung, Yogyakarta, and Surabaya (Farida 2014; Marcinkowski 2008, 50). In Bandung, West Java, for example, there are two well-known Shiʻi academic institutions, Yayasan al-Jawad (al-Jawad Foundation) and Yayasan Pendidikan Islam Muthahhari (Islamic Education Foundation Muthahhari), which have played significant roles in the development of Shiʻism in Indonesia (see Farida 2014, 163).

In addition, from the early 1980s, the work of Iranian Muslim scholars has been translated into the Indonesian language (Latief 2008, 301). Marcinkowski argued that since then Indonesia has been considered as "the centre of Shiʻi revivalism in the region" (Marcinkowski 2008, 50).[7] This can be seen also through the establishment of Shiʻi centers, including the Iranian Corner, which is present in some state Islamic universities in Indonesia (Latief 2008, 300). All these developments have alarmed certain conservative groups of Muslims in Indonesia, especially Dewan Dakwah Islamiyah Indonesia (DDII, Indonesian Islamic Propagation Council), which has been particularly active in its anti-Shiʻi campaign since 1980s (Latief 2008, 324).[8] Bruinessen contends, "No doubt encouraged by its Saudi and Kuwaiti sponsors, it denounced Shiʻism as a fatal deviation from Islam and published an unending series of anti-Shiʻi tracts and books" (2002, 127).

DDII's campaign was followed by the issuance of a *fatwa* (Islamic legal opinion) by the Majelis Ulama Indonesia (MUI, Indonesian Council of Ulama) on March 8, 1984, which was directed to Muslim minorities, in particular Shiʻis. The content of the *fatwa* was mainly to warn Muslims: "MUI advise all Muslims in Indonesia who are Ahl al-Sunna wa al-Jamaʻa [Sunni] to increase alertness from the infiltration of any influence of the Shiʻi doctrines" (MUI 2011, 47). Although the *fatwa* mentioned theological arguments on the differences between Sunnis and Shi'is, it mainly related to the government's anxiety about the political impact on Indonesian Muslims caused by the followers of Khomeini who overthrew the shah and his autocratic regime during the Iranian Revolution (Formichi 2014a, 219; Latief 2008, 325; Zulkifli 2009, 249).

The persecution of Shi'is intensified during the Suharto regime. From the 1980s, Shi'is were considered as "threats to the state" due to the assumption that Shi'ism was considered an "Iran-inspired revolutionary movement" (Marcinkowski 2008, 51). Therefore, many followers had to practice *taqiyyah* (prudent dissimulation). Recent work has also focused on the persecution of some Shi'i groups in Indonesia by conservative Sunni groups. Chiara Formichi argued that Shi'i communities have become the target of violent attacks, especially since April 2000 (2014b, 1). Formichi (2015) and Makin (2017) also discuss the 2013 persecution of Shi'i intellectual group Rausyan Fikr in Yogyakarta by Majelis Mujahidin Indonesia (Indonesian Mujahidin Council), Forum Umat Islam (Islamic Community Forum), and Front Jihad Islam (Indonesian Jihad Front).

The growing number of Shi'i adherents in Indonesia (Zulkifli 2009, 232) has resulted in the issue of *mut'a* becoming a hotly debated topic in public. Scholars working on Shi'ism in Indonesia, however, often mentioned *mut'a* marriage only in passing (Latief 2008, 310; Marcinkowski 2008). Drawing on fieldwork conducted in Jakarta and Yogyakarta, Indonesia, this chapter focuses on the voices of young Shi'i adherents and sympathizers who are currently the main proponents of *mut'a* marriage practices in Indonesia.[9] With this in mind, this chapter also analyzes other major parties involved in the discussion of Shi'i marriage, especially the Indonesian government, which has strived to bureaucratize Muslim marriage. Considering this phenomenon, this chapter argues that *mut'a* marriage is still being severely rejected in this Sunni majority country. This is despite widespread attempts at normalizing *mut'a* as an Islamically permissible marriage practice by arguing that it is the solution for the perceived sexual problems of today's Muslim youth, an argument that can be found in Shi'i literature. The rejection of *mut'a* is, in general, part of the broader anti-Shi'i sentiment in Indonesian society.

This chapter is based on exploratory research. Due to the sensitive nature of the topic, especially for the Shi'i community itself, the research was difficult to conduct. It was critical to ensure that both male and female informants felt comfortable in order to avoid anxiety while sharing their experiences and thoughts about this issue. To protect the privacy of my interlocutors they remain anonymous and pseudonyms are used.[10] It is important to note that the male informants were generally more open to sharing their *mut'a* narratives, in comparison to the female informants who preferred to exercise greater caution. This relates specifically to the objectives of the practice of *mut'a*, namely sexual enjoyment (*istimta'*), which some women are often more reluctant to discuss. In addition, the prejudice attached to *mut'a* in Indonesia is akin to a religiously sanctioned form of prostitution, resulting in women feeling uncomfortable in sharing their stories. Some Shi'is also do not approve of the actual practice of this marriage in the Sunni-majority Indonesian context, despite their acceptance of the concept of *mut'a* marriage in Shi'i Islamic jurisprudence. Therefore, although women's voices are also present in this research, when discussing the in-depth experiences of *mut'a* marriages, the focus will be more on the perspectives of the male Shi'i adherents interviewed.

Unwanted Shi'is and Accusations of *Mut'a*

For the Sunni majority, especially the conservatives and radicals, the 1984 MUI *fatwa* on the danger of Shi'ism and its influence indirectly led to the labeling of Shi'is as unwanted Muslims. Shi'i teachings, including *mut'a* marriage, are commonly seen as deviant. *Mut'a* marriage in Indonesia has been one of the key elements in the discrediting of Shi'ism. In October 1997, MUI, as the highest Islamic authority, issued a *fatwa* stating that *mut'a* marriage is unlawful (*haram*). One of the factors that led to issuing this *fatwa* was the growing practice of *mut'a* marriages (see, for example, Nashifa 2015 and Tauhidi 2011), particularly among youth and university students (MUI 2011, 375). Additionally, MUI mentioned that parents, *'ulama'* (Muslim scholars), educators, community figures, and Indonesian Muslims in general were concerned that the practice of *mut'a* marriage was being used as a tool for propaganda with the aim to expand Shi'ism in Indonesia, especially among youth (see MUI 2011, 376).

MUI based their argument on the position of a woman conducting *mut'a* who, according to verse 23:5–6, cannot be considered a wife. MUI *'ulama'* also quoted two Hadith that *mut'a* marriage was originally unlawful in Islam, but there was a dispensation (*rukhsa*) during the time of the Prophet Muhammad (MUI 2011, 378). The practice was allowed due to the needs and emergency context at the time and was particularly directed to Muslim warriors who were separated from their wives for long periods of time.[11] MUI believed that in later times, due to the absence of the *'illat* (cause), the dispensation had been annulled (MUI 2011, 378). In addition, MUI mentioned that *mut'a* marriage is against Indonesian Marriage Law, UU Perkawinan No. 1 of 1974 and Kompilasi Hukum Islam (Compilation of Islamic Law), which relates to marriage registration. According to female judge Atifaturrahmaniyah, who holds several strategic positions in various Islamic courts in Indonesia, Islamic courts have not handled *mut'a* marriages to date. The Compilation of Islamic Law in Indonesia, which regulates Muslim marriages, does not include *mut'a* marriage. Unregistered marriages in Indonesia, on the other hand, violate Indonesian family law Article 2 No. 2 of

1974, stating that "every marriage is required to be registered according to the regulations of the legislation in force." This phenomenon is different from Iran. Haeri (2005) mentioned, "Traditionally, a temporary marriage does not require witnesses or registration, though taking witnesses is recommended. . . . At present, however, the Islamic regime in Iran requires it to be registered." The Compilation of Islamic Law that regulates Muslim marriages in Indonesia also states in Article 5 No. 1, "To guarantee the order of marriage for Muslims, every marriage must be registered."

Furthermore, MUI also believes that *mut'a* marriage is against the main essence of marriage, namely to create a family and for procreation. Here, the *'ulama'* specifically refer to the main objective of *mut'a*, which is sexual enjoyment (*istimta'*) and differs from the objective of permanent marriage, which emphasizes procreation (*tawlid al-nasl*), as mentioned in the Shi'i literature (see Mutahhari 1981).

In contrast, Shi'i adherents and sympathizers in Indonesia hold a different position regarding the practice of *mut'a* marriage. Following the opinions of Shi'i scholars, *ahl al-tashayyu'* (Shi'i adherents) do not believe that the Islamic texts have abrogated the practice of *mut'a* marriage. They maintain the legitimacy of *mut'a* marriage based on the teachings of the Qur'an, particularly verse 4:24, and the Prophet's sayings (see Haeri 2005; Mutahhari 1981; Naqvi 2012).

Shi'i communities and organizations, such as Ikatan Jamaah Ahlul Bait Indonesia (IJABI, The Indonesian Association of the Family of the Prophet), founded in 2000 in Indonesia, and Ahlul Bait Indonesia (ABI, the Indonesian Shi'i Community), founded in 2010, uphold that *mut'a* marriage is lawful in Islam. An article on *mut'a* marriages on the official website of ABI (www.ahlulbait indonesia.or.id) contends that the difference regarding *mut'a* marriage between Sunni and Shi'ism is "[for Shi'ism] the permissibility and lawfulness of it [*mut'a* marriage] is valid until the Day of Judgment."[12]

Ustadz A. M. Safwan, the current director of Rausyan Fikr, a Shi'i intellectual group founded in 1995, contends that Shi'i leaders in Indonesia believe that *mut'a* marriage is part of the sacred teachings of Islam.[13] However, he argues, "many of them [including Shi'i intellectual and leading Shi'i scholar Jalaluddin Rakhmat, the former leader of IJABI] maybe do not agree with the current *mut'a* marriage practices [especially in Indonesia] which tend to focus on channeling one's lust." The ruling regarding *mut'a* marriage is also available at one of the most popular Shi'i websites in Indonesia, http://id.al-shia.org, which is the Indonesian version of the Twelver Shi'i website http://al-shia.org and has become an important reference for Indonesian Shi'is. The explanation of *mut'a* marriage on this website mentions, "Shi'a Imamiyah [also known as the Ithna 'Ashariyah, Twelvers or the followers of the twelve *imam*s of Shi'a] argue that the lawfulness of *mut'a* marriage is still valid and there is no saying of the Prophet Muhamad that abrogates it. This opinion is in contrast with the four *madhhabs* [schools of Islamic legal thought] (*madhahib* of Sunni) which forbid it because [they believe that] the provision was removed."[14]

Shi'i adherents and sympathizers in Indonesia follow the position of leaders within IJABI and ABI regarding *mut'a* marriage and other references, including online *fatwa* that can be found on the authoritative Shi'i websites. Shahid, a forty-four-year-old Shi'i adherent, says, "For a Shi'i like me, *mut'a* is lawful. There is no problem for Shi'i adherents to have *mut'a* marriage. The issue of *mut'a* in Shi'ism is not whether the verses in the Qur'an or Hadith have abrogated the practice, but whether it is part of noble behavior or not [*patut atau tidak patut*]. Therefore, its emphasis is more on *akhlaq* [morality in Islam]."

Recently, there is a growing phenomenon of the practice of *mut'a* marriage among youth, especially university students (Nashifa 2015; Tauhidi 2011). The following section discusses the practice of *mut'a* marriage by Indonesian youth.

Youth: *Mut'a* as a Solution?

Youth have been the backbone of the development of Shi'ism in Indonesia. Throughout its history, the Shi'i movement in Indonesia has been strong among students (Bruinessen 2002, 131). Marcinkowski also argues, "Shi'ite Indonesians are often well-educated and many of them are university graduates" (2008, 54). Therefore, it is not surprising that the issue relating to *mut'a* marriage among Shi'i youth is pervasive. In Iran in 1990, then-president Hashemi Rafsanjani suggested that *mut'a* marriage could be an alternative approach for male-female relationships, particularly for young Muslims living in modern societies (Haeri 1992, 202). In addition, through his pro-*mut'a* advocacy, Rafsanjani demonstrated his attention to the suppression of women's sexuality. Rafsanjani invited Iran-Iraq War widows to conduct *mut'a* marriages to legally fulfil their sexual instinct given by God (Haeri 2014, 220). Although the impact of Rafsanjani's statement could also be felt outside of Iran, as argued by Haeri (1992, 203), Rafsanjani's statement, in particular on *mut'a* for youth as a legal sexual outlet, was less popular than that of Murtaza Mutahhari in Indonesia. Ustadz A. M. Safwan says, "The same kind of understanding [on how *mut'a* can be seen as a legal sexual outlet for young people], which has been popular in Indonesia, did not originate from Rafsanjani, but from Murtaza Mutahhari who wrote about the practice earlier and his writings have been translated in Indonesian."

Mut'a teaching has become widespread due to the penetration of Shi'i *da'wa* (proselytizing) at Indonesian campuses. Zakaria, a twenty-four-year-old postgraduate student, says, "I came from a NU cultural background. When I was small, I only knew that Shi'ism is the enemy of Sunni. I became more interested in Shi'ism when I did my undergraduate degree at the State Islamic University. Through my intellectual circles, reading some books by NU figures, such as Said Aqil Siradj and

Gus Dur, I realized that the difference between both is insignificant. Since reading their work, my mindset about Shi'ism has changed."

Many of the young Shi'is I met echoed Zakaria's experience. They were particularly interested in Shi'ism because of Shi'i Muslims' contributions toward the development of Islamic intellectuality. Zakaria says, "I found that Islamic intellectuals have grown in Shi'ism, especially in the domain of philosophy. There are so many Shi'i intellectual Muslims who produced great books during their times. In addition, a great city like Cairo was also built by Shi'is. The role of Shi'i is amazing in building Islamic civilization. This has made me admire Shi'ism even more."

The student circles of Shi'ism usually focus not on studying Shi'i theology but on the intellectual traditions, especially Islamic philosophy and mysticism. For example, student discussions at Rausyan Fikr, which are usually attended by students from universities around Yogyakarta, especially State Islamic University (UIN Sunan Kalijaga) and Gadjah Mada University (UGM), focus on discussing the work of Shi'i intellectuals, such as Mulla Sadra, Murtaza Mutahhari, and 'Ali Shari'ati (Formichi 2015, 287; Makin 2017, 8–9).

Rausyan Fikr named one of its main programs Madrasah Muthahhari Institute, which is dedicated to the study of Islamic philosophy and mysticism in the format of a boarding school for university students. There is a gender divide in Shi'i student circles. Usually male students outnumber females.

Mut'a not *Zina'*

The most common reason used by those who conduct *mut'a* marriages is to prevent *zina'* (adultery and fornication), which is considered a sin in Islam. Supporters of the practice mention that Islam forbids dating; therefore, rather than having illicit male-female relations they prefer to have *mut'a* marriage. In some Indonesian cities, especially Yogyakarta—which is known as the city of students, it is not uncommon to find male and female students in their twenties having several experiences of *mut'a* marriages (see Tauhidi 2011). *Mut'a*, for its proponents, is regarded as an important practice aimed at guarding male and female Muslim dignity, based on Islamic teachings. The proponents often emphasize that *mut'a* has a *shar'i* base and is therefore a legitimate Islamic practice. For many, *mut'a* is considered safer than the common practice of dating, which does not have a *shar'i* base. Firdaus, for example, says, "The tradition of dating is clearly *haram* (unlawful) and must be shunned. . . . Rather than following the tradition of dating which is usually based on lust and deceit, it is safer to frame dating within a contractual agreement (*mut'a*)" (2007, 8).

The practice of *mut'a* marriage among youth has been modified to adjust to their needs. For example, some couples whom I met during the fieldwork admitted that they chose to postpone sexual intercourse with their husband or wife until they finished their university studies. Many scholars have noted that "a provision unique to *mut'a* marriage is the possibility of an agreement for nonsexual intimacy: the temporary spouses may agree to enjoy each other's company as they see fit, except for having sexual intercourse" (Haeri 2014, 54). Maliha, a twenty-three-year-old university student, says, "I conducted *mut'a* marriage for a good cause, Mbak [Sister] Eva. I do not want to be sinful. This marriage is to protect me. I can hold my husband's hand now without feeling sinful because he is my husband. While if I only date him, holding hands and staring at each other is sinful. However, we decided to postpone sexual intercourse until we finish our studies. We have almost finished our studies. So, this is perfect."

While some young Shi'is, like Maliha, see *mut'a* marriage as a "passport" to celebrate their lawful relationship, for example, so they can hold hands, the majority attempt to hide their status of *mut'a* marriage due to prejudice and the negative image of *mut'a* marriage in Sunni-majority Indonesia. Therefore, some Shi'i figures and older generations often emphasize the importance of avoiding demonstrating their status in public spaces. One of these figures, Ustadz 'Ali, says, "These young couples with *mut'a* marriage should not show their closeness in public spaces. This can create *fitnah* [in this context bad impressions] and might also jeopardize them because of the negative image of Shi'ism."

Maliha's position on the importance of *mut'a* marriage in preventing her from committing *zina'* is echoed by some Shi'i adherents of the older generation, who give permission to their children and relatives to conduct *mut'a* marriage. Shahid, for example, shared his thoughts when I asked him whether he would agree if his relatives conduct *mut'a* marriage:

> First, I would test the man who will marry my relative in the *mut'a* way—whether he knows the teachings regarding *mut'a*. If there are some hindrances to conduct *da'im* [permanent] marriage, then *mut'a* marriage can be a solution, especially for university students who are at the stage of maturity [*sedang matang-matangnya*]. At the same time, it is very difficult for them to have *da'im* marriage, because of the huge cost of having this kind of marriage. *Mut'a* marriage helps them. These students can create a commitment that both parties, for example, will refrain from having sexual intercourse.

Some young Shi'is consider *mut'a* marriage as a solution to adjusting to the contemporary wedding-related preparations before a wedding reception. The trend of posing for pre-wedding photos, which are often attached to wedding invitations and showcased during the wedding celebrations, is one factor. For some practicing Shi'is as well as Sunnis, pre-wedding photos are considered unlawful due to the often-intimate poses between an unmarried couple. This is usually negotiated by first conducting *mut'a* marriage for the sake of the *da'im* marriage celebration. Namira, a twenty-five-year-old newlywed, for example, says, "My husband and I decided to have a *mut'a* marriage before our wedding celebration because there were so many things that we needed to prepare prior. One of them was pre-wedding photos. We wanted to have that, but our parents did not approve because we could not be together in the pictures as we had not yet married. *Mut'a* marriage saved us. We had a *mut'a* marriage before all of the processions, so when we did all of the poses for pre-wedding photos, we did not do sinful things." Once the preparations for the procession of her *da'im* marriage finished, Namira ended her *mut'a* marriage and transformed it into a *da'im* marriage. The transformation of *mut'a* to *da'im* has become quite common among young Shi'is. Those who feel that they can fund a large celebration for their "proper" wedding also often transformed their *mut'a* marriage to *da'im* marriage.

The relatively manageable requirements for *mut'a* marriage have driven young Shi'is to conduct this kind of marriage. Some components, such as a bride's dowry (*'ajr* or *mahr* in permanent marriage) is relatively manageable for these students. The *'ajr* is usually based on an agreement between both parties, and the amount is generally higher for longer contracts. However, for university students the *'ajr* is adjusted to their circumstances as students. Shahid shares his knowledge on the practice of *mut'a* marriage among university students within his circles: "Usually among university students that I know, the *mahr* is quite simple. It can even be a book or the Holy Qur'an which will be useful for both parties [husband and wife]."

Like *da'im* marriage, *mut'a* marriage does not require witnesses (Haeri 1986, 125), although at present, as Haeri (2005) emphasizes, taking witnesses is recommended. Additionally, as mentioned above, this type of marriage does not require marriage registration (see also Haeri 2014, 55). This kind of condition suits young student couples well. Syauqi, a twenty-four-year-old university student, says, "[m]ut'a marriage is not complicated [*ribet*]. We do not need to register it and we do not need witnesses for this. It suits my condition as a university student."

The most often mentioned obstacle is the requirement of permission from the *wali* (guardian) of a virgin woman. Although there are some varying opinions regarding the permission from *wali* among Shi'i *'ulama'* (see Haeri 2014, 54), many Shi'i adherents in Indonesia follow the *'ulama'*, who argue that a virgin woman requires permission from her guardian before she may conduct a *mut'a* marriage. Others also mentioned that the permission of a guardian is usually not emphasized, especially for university students who usually live far away from their parents. Adina, a twenty-five-year-old university student, says, "my parents do not know about my *mut'a* marriage. I could not imagine if they know about this."

In response to the problem of a guardian, some university students decided to marry divorced women (see below) because Shi'i *'ulama'* do not stipulate that permission is required from the guardian of divorced or widowed women due to the belief of their greater autonomy (Haeri 2014, 54).

The practice of the solemnization of *mut'a* marriages among the Indonesian youth in this study is also relatively simple. While the solemnization of permanent marriage in Indonesia is usually done by state-appointed *penghulu* (marriage registrar) or *'ulama'*, *mut'a* marriage does not have such a requirement. Haeri also notes that Rafsanjani once proposed that "the young men and women who might feel shy about going to a *mulla* [Shi'i *'ulama'*] to register their temporary marriage need not do so. They could agree among themselves (i.e., have a private contract) 'to be together for a month or two'" (Haeri 1992, 203).

Muslim youth who have conducted *mut'a* marriage usually ask fellow students who are knowledgeable of Islam to marry them. They do not ask Shi'i *'ulama'* or leaders to marry them. Ustadz A. M. Safwan says, "What I know is that there are around five to seven students of Rausyan Fikr who have *mut'a* marriages . . . in practice they arranged the solemnization by themselves. I knew that they married only after the solemnization. I have never solemnized any *mut'a* marriage so far. In addition, for male students *mut'a* marriage is also considered less burdensome because there is no obligation to provide *nafkah* [daily maintenance]."

Is It a "*Halal*" Prostitution?

Mut'a marriage has been criticized by many as legalized prostitution. Critics include Sunni Muslims as well as some of the Shi'i community, especially by "more Westernised and educated urban Iranian middle-class women, and some men too" (Haeri 1992, 213). The opponents of *mut'a* marriage in Indonesia also see this type of marriage as *halal* prostitution. The term *halal* is often used because of the understanding that the practice is lawful according to Shi'i Islamic jurisprudence. Critics argue that those who conduct *mut'a* marriage try to camouflage their illicit behavior. There have been cases where *mut'a* has been used by non-Shi'i adherents or sympathizers. Pak Arman, a forty-three-year-old male Shi'i who works as a civil servant, for example, says, "I have heard about these *mut'a* cases many times from my colleagues. I think those who practice it just want to cover up their bad behavior. This kind of *mut'a* marriage has been used also as an alibi for those who have extramarital relationships. If they are caught, they will say that they married in the *mut'a* way."

This kind of criticism by Shi'is against the *mut'a* marriage institution, which is often misused not only by Sunni but also by many Shi'i adherents, is often heard in Indonesia. Haeri analyzes the ambiguities of the institution of temporary marriage and asserts the presence of "a wide range of manipulations, negotiations, and interpretations of the institution" (1986, 125). Marcinkowski also argues that in Malaysia, a neighbor of Indonesia, "the misuse of *mut'ah*, 'temporary marriage,' for instance—mostly by individuals who were not even Shi'is themselves—led to severe accusations against local Shi'is as a whole" (2018). The same phenomenon can also be seen in Indonesia.

In 2012, there was a case of two university students (twenty-seven-year-old male and twenty-three-year-old female) in the Bengkulu province of Indonesia who were caught in a rented house by the leader of the community and locals due to their extramarital relationship. Both of them admitted to the relationship; however, the man claimed that he married his partner in the *mut'a* way. To convince the leaders of his community and the locals who sought their explanation, the man showed a book titled *Perkawinan Mut'ah dalam Tinjauan Hadits dan Perspektif Masa Kini* (Mut'ah Marriage within Hadith and the Contemporary Perspective). He declared, "What we did is legally valid. Our *mut'a* marriage is in this book. Before this, I once married my first wife in the *mut'a* way too" (quoted in Dwinka 2012).

Aspects mentioned by opponents that make *mut'a* marriage comparable to *halal* prostitution include the process of solemnization, which is often performed secretly, the absence of witnesses and absence of the prospective bride's guardian (Nashifa 2015; Tauhidi 2011). The following sections focus on Amran's and Idham's experiences of *mut'a* marriages. Their experiences demonstrate the way young Shi'i adherents negotiate the rulings regarding *mut'a* marriage, including what *mut'a* marriage means for young Shi'is living in urban modern Indonesia. Amran's and Idham's trajectories toward having *mut'a* marriages are different as they come from different family backgrounds. Their experiences demonstrate the customs of Shi'i adherents who practice *mut'a* marriage to prevent unlawful relationships between the opposite sex before marriage. However, Idham's story is slightly more pragmatic.

Amran is a twenty-seven-year-old postgraduate student who has practiced *mut'a* marriage for one year. His *mut'a* marriage agreement is for one and a half years. When I asked Amran whether he will renew his marriage contract, he said, "*No in-sha'-Allah* [if God wills]. After this contract finishes, we will have *nikah da'im*. We want to start a real family. We want to have children." Amran's statement is resonant with that of Ustadz A. M. Safwan, who says, "Most of those who have *mut'a* marriages [that I know] will eventually have *da'im* marriages with their *mut'a* partner."

Amran is from the Indonesian province of South Sulawesi, and his father is of Hadrami descent. He has a Shi'i family, therefore, he did not face problems when he decided to have a *mut'a* marriage. In fact, his parents supported his decision. His *mut'a* wife also comes from a Shi'i family and from the same province. The couple both study at a state university in Jakarta. Although they both have strong Shi'i backgrounds, Amran admitted that before conducting the *mut'a* marriage he had to learn the related teachings from both religious leaders within his community and books. He said that his parents and his *mut'a* wife's parents allowed them to conduct a *mut'a* marriage under the condition that they first gain a deep level of knowledge regarding the practice. Amran recounted his experience of having *mut'a* marriage: "I feel more comfortable after having this *mut'a* marriage. Just imagine, first you pray, but then you commit *zina'*, even if it is only small [by staring at women] or even big. We have this *mut'a* marriage because both of us want to follow God's rule. Because both of us are still students, we decided not to have children first. We postpone the 'real' *istimta'* [while smiling] or [sorry] sexual intercourse. We do not live together neither."

Amran's *mut'a* marriage journey is relatively unproblematic because both his parents and his in-laws are Shi'i adherents who believe in his intentions. After his marriage contract was finished, I contacted him again and he informed me that he had married his wife permanently. He also shared his sister's *mut'a* marriage experience: "I have a sister and I have allowed her to conduct *mut'a* marriage several times. But I have one condition for her and her *mut'a* husband [or husbands]—that they both have to understand the *mut'a* teachings in Shi'ism before having one."

Responding to those who are against *mut'a* marriage and see it as *halal* prostitution, Amran contends, "It is not prostitution, of course. *Mut'a* marriage is a marriage facility for those who want to get to know their prospective permanent life partners. I believe *mut'a* is the solution for our contemporary time. Rather than dating or committing *zina'*, which is unlawful in Islam." The reason for *mut'a* marriage for Amran was clear—he perceived *mut'a* as lawful marriage to prevent an unlawful relationship with the opposite sex. Many young Shi'i adherents want to follow the same trajectory as Amran. However, they usually face opposition from their parents, who prefer immediate permanent marriage for their children.

Idham is a postgraduate student at an Islamic university in Yogyakarta. He is originally from Madura, a region in East Java province. He has a strong NU background and became interested in Shi'ism in 2014 after being involved in the study of diverse groups in Islam, reading books on Shi'ism, and finally being active in Shi'i study circles. Idham has had two experiences of *mut'a* marriage, each for one semester or six months. At the time of the interview, both of his *mut'a* marriage contracts had ended. He recounted his first *mut'a* marriage: "Once I worked in a publishing company. There was a woman working in this company. I met her every day. We then decided to have a *mut'a* marriage because we stared at each other's face every day and, of course, this is sinful." Both of Idham's previous *mut'a* wives were divorced women. Idham argued that it was easier with divorced women because then he did not have to ask the permission of their guardians. He gave each of them one million rupiah (around fifty-five pounds) as a dowry. He said, "They understood that I was a student." Both of them were also Sunni. Idham explains his decision to marry Sunni women: "It was very difficult to find Shi'i women. I tried, but they did not want, or they did not 'need.' In fact, it is not easy to find women who want to have a *mut'a* marriage, except I think if she is a prostitute. But, of course, I do not want to marry a prostitute. . . . My previous wives were divorced women, they basically needed me. I mean they needed 'a shoulder.' So, with them I think I had this *nikah kebaikan* [marriage for a good cause]."

The difficulties to find a woman who wants to conduct *mut'a* marriage, as Idham mentioned, are also shared by many Shi'i adherents, especially finding virgin women. Many guardians of virgin women, from both Sunni and Shi'i backgrounds, are often reluctant to allow their virgin daughters to marry in the *mut'a* way. One of the community leaders of the Shi'a in Indonesia, who believes that *mut'a* is lawful, for example, says, "I am one of the people who does not agree to marry my daughter in the *mut'a* way. I would prefer a *da'im* marriage for them." *Mut'a* marriage with a widowed or divorced woman is easier because they believe that she does not require the guardian's approval.

In contrast to Amran, Idham had to face significant personal challenges because his parents are not Shi'i adherents. Asking divorced women to conduct *mut'a* marriage with him was one of his strategies to overcome difficulties in having this type of marriage because it meant that he would not have to involve many others in the solemnization process of his marriage. In fact, Idham contended that young Shi'is often have the same kind of trajectory.

Idham also shared his struggles during his *mut'a* marriages. He had to practice *taqiyyah* (concealing his Shi'i faith and *mut'a* marriage due to a hostile environment) because according to him most Indonesians are not ready to accept this kind of practice. He did not live with his wives. During the time of the interview Idham said, "I do not want to have *mut'a* marriage again. I have a new orientation to have children. The Indonesian public have not accepted the practice of *mut'a* marriage, so it is difficult."

Mut'a and Its Damage

The image of Shi'ism has been severely attacked by the opponents through the *mut'a* practice (see also Halimatusa'diyah 2013, 141). For example, the Salafi website Muslimah.or.id explains the danger of *mut'a* marriage in its article titled "Marry Me!!! . . . I Will Contract You." The article closes by pointing at the deviant teaching of Shi'ism: "*Wahai para pecinta kebenaran hakiki janganlah tertipu dengan Syi'ah karena hakekatnya Syi'ah bukanlah bagian dari Islam*" (You the lovers of the true truth, you should not be deceived by Shi'ism because the truth is that Shi'ism is not part of Islam; Nashifa 2015). Fahim, a thirty-four-year-old Shi'i adherent, says, "*Mut'a* is often stigmatized negatively among the Indonesian community. It is still considered as *'ayb* [disgrace] among Muslims in general in Indonesia. Therefore, when we see one practice is considered *'ayb* by the majority it would be safer to try to avoid it."

Many Shi'i adherents and sympathizers in this study also believe that the issue of *mut'a* has jeopardized the development of Shi'ism in Indonesia. Ustadz A. M. Safwan says, "although there are good effects of *mut'a* marriage, the *mudarat* [damage] of this issue is more prevalent, especially relating to bad opinions regarding the sacred purpose of *mut'a* marriage. *Mut'a* marriage is often used [by anti-Shi'i groups] as their strategy to shut off Shi'i intellectual spaces." Therefore, it is noteworthy that in Indonesia, there are some Shi'is who are against the practice of *mut'a* marriage, especially in a context, where there is no necessity or emergency conditions that drive them to justify *mut'a* marriage. This can be seen from the presence of some married Shi'is who conduct *mut'a* marriage with divorced or widowed women without the knowledge of their first wives.

Conclusion

A major concern of Muslims in Indonesia is male and female relationships, especially free lifestyles including dating culture among young Muslims living in modern society. At the same time, having a permanent marriage ceremony in Indonesia is demanding, particularly due to its high cost. This condition has led young Shi'i adherents and sympathizers to believe that *mut'a* marriage can save them from committing the sin of *zina'*. However, practicing *mut'a* poses challenges as well. Those who have experienced *mut'a* marriage often complain that the Sunni Indonesian cultural atmosphere is not ready to accept this practice. This has worsened since the practice of *mut'a* marriage is often misused not only by Sunni Muslims but also by Shi'i adherents and sympathizers themselves who use *mut'a* marriage for their own benefit. Negative cases of *mut'a* marriage covered by the media have added to the negative image of *mut'a* and have tarnished the image of Shi'ism more generally.

Consequently, young Shi'is who have *mut'a* marriages find themselves having to practice *taqiyyah*, which is not easily done. This condition has led to the widespread assumption among *mut'a*-married young couples that their *mut'a* marriage is a bridge to a permanent marriage, as in the case of Namira, Amran, and Idham. Usually when students are ready to build a family, including registering their marriage and having children, they will consider *da'im* marriage.

In contrast, the opponents of *mut'a* marriage in Indonesia, who can be regarded as the majority of Indonesia's Sunni population, see this type of marriage as violating the sanctity of marriage. In general, however, the rejection of Indonesian Sunni Muslims toward *mut'a* marriage is related to the anti-Shi'i sentiment that has become more prevalent in recent times—which is also evidenced in the persecution of Shi'i adherents and sympathizers in many places in Indonesia. By closely analyzing the practice of *mut'a* marriages among Shi'i adherents in Indonesia, it is evident that they accept the concept, but not all support the practice of *mut'a* marriage in Sunni-majority Indonesia. It can be said that Indonesian Sunni Muslims and some young Indonesian Shi'i adherents and sympathizers are not ready to accept *mut'a*. Additionally, the rise of anti-Shi'i sentiment in Sunni-majority Indonesia has propagated a negative image of *mut'a*. Shi'i elites and organizations in Indonesia are often reluctant to deal with and encourage youth to practice *mut'a* marriage as a result of the damage that *mut'a* marriage can bring to the existence and development of Shi'ism in Indonesia, in particular due to the way anti- Shi'i groups use this issue as part of their strategy to attack Shi'ism.

NOTES

I am grateful to Annelies Moors and Yafa Shanneik for their invaluable feedback. I am also indebted to Nur Choerul Rizal, my research assistant, for his generous assistance. Research for this project is partially funded by European Research Council Advanced Grant for "Problematizing 'Muslim Marriages': Ambiguities and Contestations" (grant number 2013-AdG-324180) and Global Religion Research Initiative "Gender and Divorce among Muslims in Contemporary Indonesia."

1. He emphasized the importance of distinguishing between Shi'i culture and mores and the Shi'i school of jurisprudence (*madhhab*). Alatas contends, "While the vast majority of Indonesian Muslims belong to the *Sāfi'ī madhhab* aspects of *Sī'ah* Islam can be found in their culture and mores, these having been implanted in the region centuries ago" (1999, 335).

2. The *'Alawiyyun* factor in this context refers to the role of *'alawiyyah* Sufi orders, followed by the *Sayyids* (descendants of the Prophet Muhammad) of Hadramawt (Yemen) or Hadrami *Sayyids*, in the Islamization of the Malay-Indonesian Archipelago, East Africa, and Southern India (see Ho 2006). Alatas argues, "The *Sayyids* of Hadramawt share a common history with the Shī'ī school and to some extent it is this commonality that caused Shī'ī elements and tendencies among the descendants of Hadrami *Sādat* émigrés in the Malay-Indonesian Archipelago to surface, particularly after the Iranian revolution of 1978" (1999, 323).

3. For a good account of Ashura, see also Ayoub (1978), Nasr (2006), and Chelkowski and Dabashi (1999).

4. Here he refers to the late 1990s, especially from 1998 until the present.

5. This includes Malaysians (see Marcinkowski 2018).

6. Al-Mustafa International University also has a branch in Indonesia (see also Daneshgar 2014, 197) and has been active in offering scholarships to Indonesian students who want to undertake studies toward a bachelor's, master's, or PhD degree. See http://www.uinjkt.ac.id/id/iran-tawarkan-beasiswa.

7. Region here refers to Southeast Asia.

8. DDII was founded in 1967 by Mohammad Natsir (d. 1993), the fifth prime minister of Indonesia, and his colleagues (Bruinessen 2002; von der Mehden 2018). As a missionary organization, DDII was influenced by the puritan Wahhabi-Salafi interpretation of Islam (van Bruinessen 2002; von der Mehden 2018). Saudi Arabia was the backbone of the development of DDII in Indonesia. The kingdom provided funds including scholarships to DDII students to continue their studies in Saudi Arabia. Since 1973, DDII

has been the representative of Rabitat al-Alam al-Islami (Muslim World League) in Indonesia (Hasan 2002, 152).

9. There have been many studies, including those conducted by Indonesian scholars, on the practice of temporary marriages in Puncak, Cisarua, and Bogor (West Java) by Arab male tourists with local Indonesian women (see, for example, Haryono 2011; Suhud and Sya'bani 2014; Arivia and Gina 2015). The term used for this practice varies, including *kawin kontrak* (contract marriage or temporary marriage), *nikah wisata* (visiting marriage), and *mut'a* (marriage). The men come from different countries. Many of them are Sunni Muslims coming from Sunni-majority countries, especially Saudi Arabia. The presence of these Saudi men coming to Indonesia, especially during the summer holiday period, to conduct visiting marriages has led the Saudi Arabian government to issue warnings to Saudi men regarding the consequences of temporary marriages. The majority of those who conduct this kind of marriage are Sunni Muslims. Therefore, it is a mistake to use the term *nikah mut'a*. MUI uses the term *nikah wisata* in their *fatwa* issued in 2010. The *fatwa* states that visiting marriage is *haram* (unlawful) "because it is part of *nikah mu'aqqat* [temporary marriage] which is [can be regarded as] one form of *nikah mut'ah*" (MUI 2011, 562–566). In the same year, the Saudi Grand Mufti also declared that a marriage with the intention of divorce, such as *misfar* marriage (a marriage conducted in the context of travel and ending when a man returns to his country), is *haram*. He believed that it can be regarded as thinly disguised *mut'a*, which is condemned by Sunnis (see Cuno et al. 2018). Besides *misfar*, another type of temporary marriage is *misyar* (ambulant marriage) (see Ibrahim and Hassan 2009; Marcotte 2010). This kind of practice of marriage, conducted by Sunni Muslims, is beyond the scope of this chapter. See https://english.alarabiya.net/en/perspective/features/2015/04/18/Saudi-Arabia-grappling-with-the-surge-in-temporary-marriage.html; http://www.arabnews.com/node/323345.

10. This is except for important figures within the diverse Shi'i organizations in Indonesia who are willing to have their names mentioned.

11. The Sunni *madhhab* (schools of Islamic law) believe that the Prophet Muhammad prohibited *mut'a* after the Battle of Khaybar in 629 CE and the second caliph 'Umar b. Khattab (634–644) reaffirmed the prohibition.

12. See https://www.ahlulbaitindonesia.or.id/berita/index.php/s13-berita/perbedaan-dan-persamaan-nikah-permanen-daim-dengan-nikah-mutah/.

13. For a good account of Rausyan Fikr, see Formichi (2015).

14. See http://id.al-shia.org/.

REFERENCES

Alatas, Syed Farid. 1999. "The Tarīqat al-'Alawiyyah and the Emergence of the Shī'ī School in Indonesia and Malaysia." *Oriente Moderno* 18 (79): 323–339.
Arivia, Gadis, and Abby Gina. 2015. "Culture, Sex and Religion: A Review of Temporary Marriages in Cisarua and Jakarta." *Indonesian Feminist Journal* 3 (1): 23–30.
Assegaf, Umar Faruk. 2015. "Aspects of Shī'īsm in Contemporary Indonesia." In *Shi'ism in South East Asia: Alid Piety and Sectarian Constructions*, edited by Chiara Formichi and Michael Feener, 251–268. Oxford: Oxford University Press.
Ayoub, Mahmoud. 1978. *Redemptive Suffering in Islam: A Study of the Devotional Aspects of Ashura in Twelver Shī'īsm*. The Hague: Mouton.

Azra, Azyumardi. 2005. "Islamic Thought: Theory, Concept, and Doctrines in the Context of Southeast Asian Islam." In *Islam in Southeast Asia: Political, Social and Strategic Challenges for the 21st Century*, edited by K. S. Nathan and Muhammad Hashim Kamali, 3–22. Singapore: ISEAS.

Bruinessen, Martin van. 2002. "Genealogies of Islamic Radicalism in Post-Suharto Indonesia." *Southeast Asia Research* 10 (2): 117–154.

Chelkowski, Peter J., and Hamid Dabashi. 1999. *Staging a Revolution: The Art of Persuasion in the Islamic Republic of Iran*. New York: New York University Press.

Cuno, Kenneth M., Zafer Öter, and Abed Awad. 2018. "Marriage." In *The Oxford Encyclopedia of Islam and Women*. http://www.oxfordislamicstudies.com/article/opr/t355/e0288?_hi =0&_pos=1#match.

Daneshgar, Majid. 2014. "The Study of Persian Shī'īsm in the Malay-Indonesian World: A Review of Literature from the Nineteenth Century Onwards." *Journal of Shī'a Islamic Studies* 7 (2): 191–229.

Dwinka, Angga. 2012. "Digerebek, Mahasiswa Ngaku Nikah Mut'ah" [Raided, University Students Admitted That They Have Already Married in *Mut'a*]. *Bengkulu Ekspress*. http://bengkuluekspress.com/digerebek-mahasiswa-ngaku-nikah-mutah.

Farida, Anik. 2014. "Respon Organisasi Massa Islam terhadap Syiah di Bandung Jawa Barat" [Islamic Organization's Responses to Shii Muslims in Bandung, West Java]. *Journal Penamas* 27 (2): 159–176.

Feener, R. Michael. 1999. "Tabut: Muharram Observances in the History of Bengkulu." *Studia Islamika* 6 (2): 87–130.

———. 2015. "Alid Piety and State-sponsored Spectacle." In *Shi'ism in South East Asia: 'Alid Piety and Sectarian Constructions*, edited by Chiara Formichi and Michael Feener, 187–202. Oxford: Oxford University Press.

Firdaus, Robitul. 2007. *Kalau ada Mut'ah Kenapa harus Pakai Kondom* [If There Is *Mut'a*, Why Should You Use a Condom?]. Yogyakarta: Pondok Pesantren Universitas Islam Indonesia.

Formichi, Chiara. 2014a. "Shaping Shī'a Identities in Contemporary Indonesia between Local Tradition and Foreign Orthodoxy." *Die Welt Des Islams* 54 (2): 212–236.

———. 2014b. "Violence, Sectarianism, and the Politics of Religion: Articulations of Anti-Shī'a Discourses in Indonesia." *Indonesia* 98: 1–27.

———. 2015. "One Big Family? Dynamics of Interaction among the 'Lovers of the Ahl al-Bayt' in Modern Java." In *Shi'ism in South East Asia: Alid Piety and Sectarian Constructions*, edited by Chiara Formichi and Michael Feener, 269–291. Oxford: Oxford University Press.

Haeri, Shahla. 1986. "Power of Ambiguity: Cultural Improvisations on the Theme of Temporary Marriage." *Iranian Studies* 19 (2): 123–154.

———. 1992. "Temporary Marriage and the State in Iran: An Islamic Discourse on Female Sexuality." *Social Research* 59 (1): 201–223.

———. "Mot'a." In *Encyclopaedia of Iranica*. http://www.iranicaonline.org/articles/mota.

———. 2014. *Law of Desire: Temporary Marriage in Shī'ī Iran*. Rev. ed. Syracuse, NY: Syracuse University Press.

Halimatusa'diyah, Iim. 2013. "Being Shī'īte Women in Indonesia's Sunni-Populated Community." *South East Asia Research* 21 (1): 131–150.

Haryono, Bagus. 2011. "Kawin Kontrak di Indonesia: Fungsional Bagi Siapa?" [Contractual Marriage in Indonesia: Functional for Whom?]. *Journal Sosiologi* 26 (1): 1–14.

Hasan, Noorhaidi. 2002. "Faith and Politics: The Rise of the Laskar Jihad in the Era of Transition in Indonesia." *Indonesia* 73: 145–169.

Ho, Engseng. 2006. *The Graves of Tarim: Genealogy and Mobility across the Indian Ocean.* Berkeley: University of California Press.

Ibrahim, Rozita, and Zaharah Hassan. 2009. "Understanding Singlehood from the Experiences of Never-Married Malay Muslim Women in Malaysia: Some Preliminary Findings." *European Journal of Social Sciences* 8 (3): 395–405.

Latief, Hilman. 2008. "The Identity of Shī'a Sympathizers in Contemporary Indonesia." *Journal of Indonesian Islam* 2 (2): 300–335.

Makin, Al. 2017. "Homogenising Indonesian Islam: Persecution of the Shia Group in Yogyakarta." *Studia Islamika* 24 (1): 1–32.

Marcinkowski, Christoph. 2008. "Aspects of Shi'ism in Contemporary Southeast Asia." *Muslim World* 98 (1): 36–71.

———. 2018. "Southeast Asia, Shia in." In *Oxford Islamic Studies Online.* http://www.oxfordislamicstudies.com/article/opr/t343/e0018?_hi=3&_pos=3.

Marcotte, Roxanne D. 2010. "Gender and Sexuality Online on Australian Muslim Forums." *Contemporary Islam* 4 (1): 117–138.

MUI. 2011. *Himpunan Fatwa MUI sejak 1975* [Collection of MUI Fatwa since 1975]. Jakarta: Penerbit Erlangga.

Mutahhari, Murtadha. 1981. *The Rights of Women in Islam.* Teheran: World Organization for Islamic Services.

Naqvi, Ali Raza. 2012. *Shia Marriage Law.* Islamabad: Islamic Research Institute.

Nashifa, Isruwanti Ummu. 2015 "Kawini Aku!! . . . Kau Kukontrak" [Marry Me!! . . . I Contract You]. *Muslimah.or.id.* https://muslimah.or.id/7948-kawini-aku-kau-kukontrak.html.

Nasr, Vali. 2006. *The Shia Revival: How Conflicts within Islam Will Shape the Future.* New York: Norton.

Rakhmat, Miftah F., ed. 1998. *Catatan Kang Jalal: Visi Media, Politik dan Pendidikan* [Kang Jalal's Notes: Media, Political and Educational Vision]. Bandung: PT. Remaja Rosdakarya.

Saenong, Faried F. 2015. "Alid Piety in Bugis Texts on Proper Sexual Arts." In *Shi'ism in South East Asia: Alid Piety and Sectarian Constructions,* edited by Chiara Formichi and Michael Feener, 99–113. Oxford: Oxford University Press.

Suhud, Usep, and Noorfie Syahri Sya'bani. 2014. "Halal Sex Tourism in Indonesia: Understanding the Motivation of Young Female Host to Marry with Middle Eastern Male Tourists." *Journal of Economics and Sustainable Development* 5 (25): 91–94.

Tauhidi, Muhammad Pizaro Novelan. 2011. "Kawinilah Aku Kau Kukontrak: Potret Nikah Mut'ah Sepasang Syiah" [Marry Me I Contract You: A Portrait of a Shii Couple's *Mut'a* Marriage]. *Eramuslim.* https://www.eramuslim.com/berita/tahukah-anda/kawinilah-aku-kau-kukontrak-potret-nikah- mut-ah-sepasang-syiah-1.htm#.WVS8XooxWt9.

von der Mehden, Fred R. 2018. "Dewan Dakwah Islamiyah." In *The Oxford Encyclopedia of Islam and Politics.* http://www.oxfordislamicstudies.com/article/opr/t342/e0149?_hi=1&_pos=1.

Zulkifli. 2009. "The Education of Indonesian Shī'ī Leaders." *Journal of Islamic Studies* 47 (2): 231–267.

———. 2013. *The Struggle of the Shī'īs in Indonesia.* Canberra: ANU E Press.

6

Between Love and Sex, Modernity and Archaism

Iranian Students' Discourse in the Netherlands about *Sigheh*

SOPHIE-YVIE GIRARD

Temporary marriages are a heated topic of discussion, both inside and outside of Iran and among different social and religious circles. A temporary marriage—or *sigheh* in Farsi[1]—is a written or oral marital contract between a man (either married or unmarried) and an unmarried woman (never married, divorcée, or widow) for a limited period of time, varying customarily between one hour and ninety-nine years. It includes a specific payment (dower) the woman is to receive from the man (Haeri 1992, 211). In Iran, these marriages are authorized legally by the Iranian government and religiously by Shiʻi Islam (Haeri 1986, 124; 1992, 210).

In everyday life, *sigheh* is one among many forms of relationships a man and a woman enter into in Iran, and as will be explained in this chapter, it exists next to permanent marriages, boyfriend/girlfriend relationships, and so-called "white marriages." A special form of temporary marriages is the *sighe-ye mahramiat*, the nonsexual *sigheh*. In this chapter, I investigate the way in which the (sexual) *sigheh* relates to these other forms of relationships in the discourse of Iranian students living in the Netherlands. Research is based on interviews, informal conversations, and activities undertaken with twenty-three Iranian students— twelve female and eleven male students—living and studying in the Netherlands, who with a few exceptions moved there relatively recently. Three of them were openly religious, and most of the students originated from a middle-class family. How do they qualify the different types of relationships? What are the determining factors? How do their conceptions about love, sex, and sin shape their discourse? What role does their gender, their religiosity, and their social class play in the evaluation of *sigheh* and the other types of relationships?

In the following pages, I first briefly outline the legal and social background underlying *sigheh* in Iran, focusing on its relevant religious, political, and gender-related underpinnings. I then analyze the students' discourse when they compare temporary marriages to, respectively, permanent marriages, the nonsexual *sigheh*, the boyfriend/girlfriend relationship, and white marriage. In doing so, I also analyze the elements that shape the students' discourse about *sigheh* and compare their views with the Iranian legal, religious, and social norms and rules.

A Short Note on *Sigheh*

Sigheh is a topic of great debate among and within different circles, not only outside but also within Iran, where it is both contested and supported by feminists, secular and religious scholars, and public opinion (Shrage 2013, 109). *Sigheh* is a particular type of marriage (Haeri 1986, 124), about which Shi'i and Sunni views differ considerably. Shi'i Islam accepts and may even promote temporary marriages, based on their approval by the Prophet and in the Qur'an 4:24 (Haeri 1986, 124). Sunni Islam, in contrast, considers these marriages as "sex for hire" and underlines their prohibition by the second caliph Omar (Shrage 2013, 108).

Politically, a shift occurred in Iran with the change in government after the Islamic Revolution in 1979, which saw a transition from the Pahlavi monarchy to the Islamic Republic of Iran (Haeri 1992, 212–213). While the former Pahlavi regime opposed temporary marriages, identifying them as "an archaic aspect of religion," the post-1979 regime encouraged this practice as a progressive, modern Islamic institution (Haeri 1986, 124; 1992, 212).

In terms of gender, another shift occurred with the 1990 speech by one of the former Iranian presidents, Hashemi Rafsanjani. By claiming that women can enter a relationship when they feel the need to, he extended a positive view of sexuality in Shi'i Islam to also acknowledge female sexuality (Haeri 1989, 72; 1992, 201). More generally, temporary marriages were considered as a solution to the problem of youth who had become sexually mature but who encountered problems entering a permanent marriage because of, for instance, the length of their studies and the costs involved in a permanent marriage (Moors 2013, 146). While not radically departing from the Shi'i tradition, Shi'i religious leaders needed to engage with the rapid pace modernization, the "borrowing from the West," and "the rise in public consciousness of women's issues" and rethink this tradition (Haeri 1992, 204, 210).

On a societal level, according to most of my student interlocutors, the problematic factor with *sigheh* is its association with sexuality, an issue that Shahla Haeri already pointed at in her work. In the Islamic ideology, uncontrolled sexual drives are seen as a threat to the social order, and the "[*mahram/namahram*] paradigm, or rules for segregation and association of the sexes" constitutes an important principle of the Iranian social organization (Haeri 1986, 124, 126). Two elements related to the issue of virginity are important here. First, there is a tension between "religion and popular culture," as the latter expects women to be virgins when they first enter a permanent marriage, even though engaging in a temporary marriage is legally and religiously accepted in Iran (Haeri 1986, 124; 1992, 210, 213). Second, there is an underlying discourse of chastity and purity in Iranian society, which according to the students I interviewed makes a woman entering a *sigheh* marriage "cheap" or "lower class." In this context, a "pure" woman is one who abstains from sexual desire and activity. Female sexuality is more accepted among religious scholars than within social norms.

Sigheh and ezdevadj-e da'em

Most of my respondents frequently compared temporary to permanent marriages—also known as *ezdevadj-e da'em*. In doing so, they often referred to the discourse about women's rights on the one hand, and the discourse about love on the other. With regard to the place of women's rights in these two marriages, the students held divergent views. Two of them argued that in both marriages women's rights are not much taken into account. According to them, in Iran women's rights are always more limited than those of a man, irrespective of whether they are engaged in a temporary or a permanent marriage.

Two other students believed that women have fewer rights in temporary than in permanent marriages, as after the time limit of the marriage has passed the man does not have any further responsibilities toward his former *sigheh* wife. This makes it an easy option for a man to enjoy a sexual relationship without making any commitments whatsoever toward the woman. One of these students also stressed the importance of taking the Iranian context into account. In the case of a divorce, a woman always has very limited rights with respect to child custody. However, as this student stated, in a permanent marriage she can at least use her dower as a bargaining chip for child custody.

This statement indicates that the students are influenced by the negative social representation of *sigheh*. They are not very well informed about its actual legal regulations, since using the dower as a medium of exchange can also be done in the context of the dissolution of a temporary marriage.[2] The point is, rather, that the dower is much higher than the payment in the case of temporary marriages. The function of the dower in permanent marriages is to provide some form of protection for the wife in order to compensate for her legally inferior position. As the amount often goes beyond the husband's immediate means, women can use it as a bargaining chip, for instance, to negotiate the terms of their child's custody (Mir-Hosseini 1992, 35). In the case of temporary marriage, the payment usually does not involve such large sums of money and hence its bargaining power is more limited.

The students also considered *sigheh* an unequal institution because a man is allowed to take several temporary wives at the same time. Moreover, even if he is permanently married, he can also still legally take a *sigheh* wife and

cannot be accused of adultery. This is in contrast to a married man who wants
to take a second permanent wife. In this case he needs the approval of his first
permanent wife, as one of the students pointed out. The only thing a woman
can do in case she wants to avoid her husband taking a *sigheh* wife is to stipulate it in the marriage contract, a tactic that is occasionally used by women,
according to one of the students. Whereas my interlocutors highlighted more
the unequal rights of men and women in the context of temporary marriages,
gender inequalities nonetheless are also part and parcel of permanent marriages. Also in a permanent marriage, men can marry up to a total of four permanent wives if they have the approval of their first permanent wife, whereas
women can have only one husband at a time (Haeri 1989, 60).

In other words, it seems that the legal inequalities inherent to permanent
marriages are not as much highlighted by my interlocutors as those inherent to
sigheh. This could be explained by the earlier mentioned negative social representation of temporary marriages, that is, as an institution that permits a sexual relationship in exchange for money. However, another element that can
explain the students' view is the association between permanent marriages and
love. Since permanent marriages are considered to be based on mutual love and
faithfulness, men are not expected to marry more than one permanent wife,
even though doing so is legally permitted (Haeri 1989, 60).

The question of adultery ties in with this. There is, in fact, a difference in
defining adultery as my interlocutors do and how the Iranian legal system does
this when it comes to temporary marriages. One female student explained that
if a married man engages in a sexual relationship with another woman and if
this relationship does also not take place within the frame of a temporary marriage, it is officially considered adultery. If a man does *sigheh*, however, this relation becomes legal and Islamic and is not adultery. However, in the eyes of many
of the students they always consider it wrong and even adulterous to start another
relationship besides the permanent spouse, independently of the type of marriage involved. It is the right to polygamy permitted in Islam and by the Iranian
government that represents an important issue for many of my interlocutors,
both male and female, for whom faithfulness to one person is very important.
My interlocutors took a strong ethical stance when they talked about *sigheh*
involving a married man, a standpoint that is more important than the legal
point of view.

Two female students, in contrast, argued that women have more rights in
temporary than in permanent marriages, mainly because the custody of a child
born out of a *sigheh* marriage would be granted to the woman and because the
woman could also end the temporary marriage whenever. This is, however, a
much more positive image of *sigheh* than the actual legal rules allow for. Legally,
if a woman gets pregnant within a temporary marriage "the child is of the bed"
and thus the father, provided he acknowledges the temporary marriage, gains

custody (Haeri 1989, 55). Furthermore, the temporary marriage contract is revocable only by the husband (Haeri 1989, 57), which is not entirely the case in a permanent marriage. In fact, in permanent marriages a woman can sometimes get a divorce if she establishes one of the legally recognized grounds (Mir-Hosseini 1996, 149). This again points to the lack of legal knowledge about *sigheh* marriages.[3] Some of my interlocutors told me that they had heard about temporary marriages from their teachers in school, from their professors at university, or from popular movies screened in Iran. Most of them did not seem to be interested in gathering more information about the practice. One reason could be that they did not foresee themselves to engage in such a marriage. Hence, it was not relevant for them to know about its exact regulation.

Next to a focus on women's rights, there was another discourse present in the talks of the students already briefly alluded to—the place of love in permanent and temporary marriages. Despite the fact that both marriages are Islamic Shi'i marriages (Haeri 1989, 30), permanent marriages enjoyed a greater level of acceptance among the students—both religious and secular—and this was clearly related to the place that love takes within this marriage. *Sigheh* was often associated with pure sexual desire, while *ezdevadj-e da'em* was more frequently associated with love. The time frame of these marriages—theoretically forever in permanent but limited in temporary marriages—could be one reason to explain this. For some students this dissimilarity in temporality made a difference in the very objective of the two marriages, *sigheh* being mostly about having a sexual relationship, while in permanent marriages concern about the other's future and willingness to share it are central. Thus, in their eyes love has no place in *sigheh*, whereas it is the main element in a permanent marriage.

Once more, the influence of the socially dominant discourse in Iran that associates *sigheh* with pure sexual desire was reflected in the students' talk. The strong sexual component of *sigheh* in fact made it difficult for some of my interlocutors to consider it a type of marriage. They considered marriage as a holy union that not only includes sexual intercourse but strongly relates to the love toward the other person. On a legal level, they also noted the fact that a *sigheh* marriage does not need to be registered and does not appear officially in the passport. It thus remains unknown if a person is already engaged in another relationship at the same time. In a permanent marriage, on the contrary, the name of the spouse appears in the partner's passport.

It seems that the attempts of the religious clerics and the Iranian government to put the (sexual) extramarital relation between a man and a woman into the religiously more accepted frame of marriage in order to show the "moral 'superiority' of this form of sexual relation over its 'chaotic' and 'decadent' Western counterparts" (Haeri 1992, 220) did not have much effect, at least not among my interlocutors. For them, the goals of permanent and temporary marriages are very different, if not opposed, which makes it difficult for my interlocutors to call the second one a marriage.

Sigheh and Sighe-ye Mahramiat

The so-called *sighe-ye mahramiat* or nonsexual *sigheh* is, in contrast, a special form of *sigheh* that may well have a strong link to permanent marriage. According to Haeri, many Iranians differentiate between the sexual and nonsexual *sigheh*, the latter being a sort of "permissible familiarity" that aims to create a fictive affinal kinship to enable women to interact more freely with previously unrelated men (1986, 128, 138). While in her view the sexual *sigheh* follows a legal structure and can be seen as a law "imposed from the above," the nonsexual *sigheh* is "imagined" and "continuously improvised upon by the people themselves" (Haeri 1986, 128). In Iran, a set of informal rules and practices evolved around the nonsexual *sigheh*, making it a convenient cultural solution to the prescribed segregation codes of the sexes (Haeri 1986, 138).

During my research, I met one female student who had engaged herself in a *sighe-ye mahramiat* with the man who later became her husband. Originating from a religious and traditional family, she explained that the reason to enter into such a marriage was to get to know her future husband before actually marrying him. According to her, this is a rather common practice in religious families in Iran. This fits well with Haeri's findings that "[*sighe-ye mahramiat*] has been widely performed among the more traditional Iranians of all classes and backgrounds" (1986, 138). As another male student said it can be compared to a permissible form of dating before entering a permanent marriage. Families may well encourage their children to first enter a *sighe-ye mahramiat* to see if they are compatible with their future spouses.

The female student who had done a *sighe-ye mahramiat* explained that the man and woman engaging in such a temporary marriage decide how far their relationship will go. By keeping their relationship limited, the consequences in case of a marriage breakup are less substantial than in a permanent one. The dissolution of such a temporary marriage will harm the reputation of the spouses to a lesser extent since people would say that "they were very little *mahram* [they did not have any sexual contact]."

Due to the nonsexual nature of *sighe-ye mahramiat*, its purpose differs from that of the sexual *sigheh*, according to some of the students I interviewed, who stressed the nonsexual nature of this type of temporary marriage. The final objective of *sighe-ye mahramiat* is permanent marriage and spending one's life with the other person. Thus, it is seen as very different from the sexual *sigheh* because it is considered an agreement for nonsexual companionship during which spouses can enjoy being together in many different ways other than actual sexual intercourse (Haeri 1986, 137).

This clear separation made in Iranian society and among my interlocutors between *sighe-ye mahramiat* and any kind of sexual activity is both interesting and paradoxical since from a legal and religious point of view *sighe'e mahramiat* does not necessarily exclude sexuality (Haeri 1986, 138). Nevertheless, from a social point of view sexual intercourse in such a temporary marriage is strongly condemned. The differences between the Iranian legal system and the religious laws, on the one hand, and the norms of the Iranian society, on the other, are thus again evident.

Since *sighe-ye mahramiat* is nonsexual, it enjoys a better reputation than the sexual *sigheh* among most Iranians and among my interlocutors themselves. A female student claimed that because its aim is "to not commit sin" and that contrary to the sexual *sigheh* there is also "an agreement that you do not take advantage of the woman," it is "maybe . . . the only version [of temporary marriages] that you could accept." Apparently, as sexual intercourse is not seen as part of the *sighe-ye mahramiat*, it does not directly evoke the discourse of abuse and misuse, as is the case for the sexual *sigheh*.

Even though *sighe-ye mahramiat* is more accepted than its sexual counterpart, it is often kept secret. This secrecy is sometimes enhanced by the oral nature of such a marriage since the families discuss the terms of the temporary marriage, including its length, dower, and conditions, only between themselves and conclude it only in presence of their closest family members, without registering the union. According to a male student, the *sighe-ye mahramiat* will become official only once the persons concerned permanently marry. Thus, even though sexuality is not part of *sighe-ye mahramiat*, it remains hard to openly engage in it since it can be associated with something shameful. In fact, depending on the family this temporary marriage is mostly done only for a very brief period, such as two or three weeks. Also, some families do not allow the man and the woman to see each other in public spaces and insist on private meetings, as they fear other people "gossiping," as one male respondent explained.

Being a type of temporary marriage, *sighe-ye mahramiat* follows the same rules as the sexual *sigheh*: legally and religiously there is no restriction regarding sexual intercourse. The only factor preventing sexual relations within *sighe-ye mahramiat* is the unspoken social rule that dictates that they should not occur. Still, the a sexual relationship can never be fully excluded.

Sigheh and *Dust Dokhtar/Dust Pesari*

Some of my interlocutors considered *sigheh* as a sort of Islamic relationship. According to one of my female interlocutors who is herself religious, the purpose of entering into such a marriage is to "have a relationship, but [without doing] *gunah* [sin]." How does the concept of sin affect temporary marriages? In

Iranian society, as a religious male student told me, one of the greatest sins is to have a sexual relationship outside of the marital frame. For more religious people, *sigheh* is then considered a way to escape from sin. This student's opinion differs from the more widespread societal discourse that sees sexuality outside of a permanent marriage—and thus also *sigheh*—as highly undesirable.

One issue concerning *sigheh* thus lies in its social unacceptance, which makes it difficult, if not impossible, in particular for younger people, to enter into such a marriage. One female religious student stated that it could actually be very beneficial also for women, but only in a favorable social context. Women who are economically independent, "who want to live in a modern way, but who still want that [their actions remain] *shar'i* [following the Islamic rules]" could benefit from *sigheh*, she added. Her opinion seems to be influenced by the discourse of the Islamic regime, which upholds temporary marriages "as a progressive institution, . . . especially suited to the needs of modern society" and as "one of the most advanced and farsighted aspects of Islamic thought, indicating Islamic understanding of the nature of human sexuality" (Shrage 2013, 109).

For some of my less religious interlocutors, however, the necessity of putting a relation into the frame of a temporary marriage was not clear. "Temporary marriage is in reality . . . the Islamic version of being a girlfriend and a boyfriend," a male student stated. "Why is it even necessary for the people who want to be in a relationship to do a temporary marriage?" In a similar vein, another male student argued that if you want to be with someone, there is no need to put it in the frame of a temporary marriage.

My interlocutors not only discussed *sigheh* as a form of Islamic relationship but also compared it with the boyfriend/girlfriend relationship—*dust dokhtar/dust pesar*—as formed in Europe. A male student stated that the European boyfriend/ girlfriend relationship and *sigheh* both resemble a temporary contract since they are limited in time frame. A female student considered them more in terms of a commitment between two persons to stay together for a while, which may also include having a sexual relation and living together. Their commitment lasts until the moment they decide to split up. The difference, in her opinion, is that *sigheh* is officialized and registered (although it can be done unofficially and kept in secret), whereas the boyfriend/girlfriend relationship between a man and a woman is done secretly in Iran, as people are not allowed to officially enter an extramarital relationship (Holm and Bowker 1998, 116). Still, it is interesting to note that some of my interlocutors compared *sigheh* with the "Western style promiscuity and 'free love'" that is despised by more religious Iranians and in particular by clerics, who promoted *sigheh* as "a divinely sanctioned and 'rewarded' activity," much more desirable than the "decadent" Western relationship (Haeri 1992, 213). For some of my interlocutors, these two types of relations did not seem to be very different.

The boyfriend/girlfriend relationship was, in fact, a recurrent topic during my talks with the students. As many of them told me, engaging in such a relation in Iran has become more common. However, having a boy- or girlfriend does not necessarily include sexual relations; all sorts of relationships can be considered in the boyfriend/girlfriend frame in Iran. A male student explained that in Iran two young religious persons may go out together and not even hold hands but call themselves boyfriend and girlfriend. At the same time two less religious persons may engage in a sexual relationship with their boy- or girlfriend. Thus, according to the degree of religiosity of the couple (and one's personal values and limits), they may engage in or abstain from sexual practices in the boyfriend/girlfriend relationship.

Many of my interlocutors were actually in a relationship, while some of those who were married had been in a relationship with their future husband before marriage. One female student, for example, had spent seven years with her boyfriend before marrying him. Some of them did, however, keep this hidden from their families.

My findings indicate that when entering in a relationship *sigheh* is often not considered to be an option. According to many of my interlocutors, it is "something absurd," with most young people not even considering it when thinking about a way to have premarital sex. They may not consider *sigheh* as a bad thing, but for today's youth "it is ridiculous," one male informant said. *Sigheh* then is becoming a topic of derision among the younger generation. Quite a few students also claimed that doing *sigheh* is simply meaningless to them. One male student argued that for a nonreligious young person *sigheh* has "no meaning at all." Another one said that if he likes a woman he will tell her and does not see the necessity to engage in a temporary marriage. In the opinion of these students, *sigheh* is "for those who believe" and who do "not want to get out of [the Islamic frame]." All my interlocutors agreed that since temporary marriages are strongly linked to Islam, only more religious people would engage in them. One student, himself religious, explained that religious persons would seek the advice of Ayatollahs and follow their words in order not to commit any forbidden act. Moreover, my findings also show how *sigheh* is slowly being replaced by other forms of relationships, such as the boyfriend/girlfriend relationship. Reflecting on this, a male student pointed out that in his opinion *sigheh* is in fact forgotten "because an alternative came by the name of *dust dokhtar / dust pesar*," which satisfies those who do not see a need to do a *sigheh* anymore.

According to most of my interlocutors, even though both are not considered desirable and are often kept secret, *dust dokhtar / dust pesar* is currently more acceptable than *sigheh* in Iranian society as having a boy- or girlfriend does not necessarily mean being engaged in a sexual relationship. What comes to people's mind when they hear that someone has such a relationship is that "they spent their leisure time together, eat an ice cream and at the most they kiss," one student stated. If someone is known to be in a temporary marriage, in contrast, the thought of sexuality will always be present: "It is as if *sigheh* had been based on sexual intercourse," another male student concluded.

Again then, the fact that *sigheh* is so strongly associated with sexuality makes it less acceptable than the "Western style promiscuity and 'free love'" that is despised by the religious leaders and scholars (Haeri 1992, 213). Another factor that favors boyfriend/girlfriend relationships is, according to one student, its link to modernity. He explained that in Iran everything modern is embraced and everything traditional rejected, which makes *sigheh* less attractive. This strong attachment of Iranian society toward modernity is historically lined to the attempts of the Pahlavi regimes (1925–1979) to modernize and Westernize Iran by integrating "Western customs and manners" (Haeri 1992, 207–208, 214). One part of this process was the intent to marginalize temporary marriages by identifying them "as an archaic aspect of religion" (Haeri 1992, 212). This lack and further loss of respectability for *sigheh* under the Pahlavi regime (Haeri 1992, 213) still has an effect today.

Sigheh and Ezdevadj-e sefid

"White marriages" or *ezdevadj-e sefid* are a quite recent and not very well-known phenomenon that emerged recently in Iran. None of the students I interviewed mentioned Iranians practicing white marriages in the Netherlands. They are a phenomenon of Iran. As one of the students told me, white marriages are becoming more prevalent in Iranian society, especially among the higher classes in the northern part of Tehran, and younger people are increasingly partaking in them. Another student explained that white marriages are quite similar to permanent marriages, with the couple accepting to live together, even forever. However, the difference is that they do not want to conclude an official marriage. In other words, a white marriage refers to the cohabitation of two persons who do not have official marital documents. Another student further explained that in Iran, when someone is permanently married the name of his or her spouse appears on the passport's first page, followed by the name of the children on the next page. A white marriage, however, does not appear in the passport. In the view of this student such a marriage is closer to a Western form of partnership than to an actual marriage, which is sometimes preferred by the younger generation who do not have sufficient resources for a permanent marriage and do not accept temporary marriages.

The Iranian government is not in favor of this type of marriage and is seeking a way to end the practice, so the student said. White marriages are also a matter of discussion in the Iranian society. He stated that "[the] religious part of the society can maybe accept *sigheh*, but it cannot accept this [*ezdevadj-e sefid*]" since living together under one roof without being officially married does not correspond to Islamic values.

Some of the students also made a distinction between *sigheh* and *ezdevadj-e sefid*, but in a different way. A male student claimed that in his opinion, since the appearance and the rise in popularity of white marriages, *sigheh* has become an even more old-fashioned custom. Temporary marriages were used forty to fifty years ago so people could live together under one roof, he continued, but since white marriages appeared these are now gradually replacing *sigheh*.

One female student, in contrast, pointed to the similarities between temporary and white marriages. She stated that in both cases two persons live together; with *sigheh*, it involves very religious persons who feel the need to obtain a temporary marriage before living together. On a legal level, according to her, both types of marriages do not benefit from specific rights. But this is not entirely true. White marriages are indeed not recognized by the Iranian government, with cohabitation prohibited in Iran.[4] Temporary marriages, on the other hand, are officially acknowledged; hence, specific rights between the partners exist, such as the dower the man has to give to the woman and the legal recognition of children born out of this marriage (Haeri 1989, 53, 60). In the case of children born in a white marriage, they would not be considered legitimate as they would be born outside the frame of an officially recognized marriage.

Most of my interlocutors did not see much resemblance between temporary and white marriages or rather considered them as two contrasting ways of being together. *Sigheh* is very much associated with sexual desire and tradition, an old-fashioned way to live together under one roof, as a male student put it. White marriages, in contrast, are associated with the discourse of modernity and love. Younger people consider them as a modern relationship and refer to love as a main reason to conclude this type of marriage. Doing so enables them to live together and to get to know each other while avoiding the economic and personal commitments and pressures of permanent marriage.

Conclusion

My aim has been to investigate and analyze the ways in which the (sexual) *sigheh* relates to other forms of relationships—permanent marriages, nonsexual *sigheh*, boyfriend/girlfriend relationships, and white marriages—in the discourse of Iranian students living in the Netherlands. I have demonstrated how love, sex, sin, modernity, and gender equality shape their views and how their social and religious background has to be taken into account.

My findings indicate that when it comes to *sigheh* and these other forms of relationships, the students' views differed in some ways from the official Iranian legal, religious, and social norms and rules. Temporary marriages may be legally and religiously permitted in Iran (Haeri 1986, 124; 1992, 210), but my interlocutors made a distinction between the different contexts in which *sigheh* takes place. The students considered *sigheh* still useful for younger religious persons who do not want to commit sin, wishing to have a (sexual) relationship within the framework of Islam. It is interesting to see that both female and male students saw *sigheh* as more acceptable in the case of an unmarried man than in the case of a permanently married man, even if the latter is legally allowed (Haeri 1986, 124). Foregrounding their personal ideals of mutual fidelity rather than the law, the students took a more ethical than a legal stance about *sigheh*. Men's right to polygamy becomes questioned not only by women but also by men, which tallies with the ideal of the monogamous nuclear family based on love and partnership. These findings go along with research on changes in Iranian family structures that noted a decrease in polygamous relationships, especially among higher educated men (Azadarmaki and Bahar 2006, 598). This change can be interpreted as a shift toward a more gender egalitarian view.

Religiosity did have a certain influence on the students' evaluation of temporary marriages when they compared these to permanent marriages and girlfriend/boyfriend relationships.[5] Whereas the students who were not openly religious argued that in both permanent and temporary marriages women's rights are hardly taken into account, but even less so in temporary marriages, openly religious students considered women's rights acknowledged in temporary marriages. When comparing *sigheh* to girlfriend/boyfriend relationships, the openly religious students considered *sigheh* as a sort of Islamic relationship that would enable religious persons to enter a (sexual) relationship without committing sin since this relationship would take place within a legally and religiously permitted marital framework. Less religious students, however, did not consider it necessary to put a boyfriend/girlfriend relation within a marital framework.

Most of my interlocutors originated from the Iranian middle class. It is likely that this had some influence on their evaluation of *sigheh* and the other forms of relationships. Although not all of them disapproved of *sigheh*, many considered temporary marriages an old-fashioned and outdated custom that are replaced by other types of relationships. The fact that some of the students did not reject white marriages may also fit with their middle-class background. Indeed, as we have seen, white marriages are most prevalent within the upper class of northern Tehran, and thus it could be easier for them to identify with this type of relationship.

Their points of view seem to also resonate with those of the urban middle-class population living under the Pahlavi regime, which Haeri describes as influenced by the "desexualised language" promoted by the Pahlavi regime (1992, 208–209). It is particularly interesting that my interlocutors also considered its link to sexuality to be the problematic part of a temporary marriage. Moreover, the students had a more positive attitude toward *sigheh* when it took a less sexualized form of *sighe-ye mahramiat*. In a same vein, the Iranian girlfriend/boyfriend relationship, which is also not necessarily sexual but instead frequently associated with love, was regarded as a more acceptable form of relationship. Although they grew up after the Iranian Revolution of 1979 and under the Islamic Republic, my interlocutors still seemed to be influenced by the "desexualized language" of the Pahlavi regime (Haeri 1992, 208–209). At the same time, there has also been a change in attitude toward *sigheh* within the same social class. Whereas Haeri's urban middle-class Iranians living under the Pahlavi regime opposed *sigheh* (1992, 208–209), most of my interlocutors were more ambivalent in that they accepted it as long as it was concluded for love, showing similarity with a permanent marriage and a more equal relationship. That is, *sigheh* is accepted when it moves from a discourse of sexuality to a discourse of love.

My findings also indicate that temporary marriage is not so much a major topic of discussion among the younger generation. Instead, it is increasingly considered as an old-fashioned institution that has lost its meaning. Other forms of relationships not only are preferred but also seem to have slowly replaced *sigheh*. For example, permanent marriages were favored by the students due to their association with love rather than with sexual desire, as is the case for temporary marriages. The same applies to the boyfriend/girlfriend relationship. Although white marriages as a form of cohabitation outside of an official framework go against the social norms of Iranian society, they are considered as resembling the boyfriend/girlfriend relationship since they also represent the idea of a romantic relation. Both boyfriend/girlfriend relationships and white marriages represent a challenge to Iranian society and state authorities. The growing importance of the boyfriend/girlfriend relationship and to a lesser extent white marriage among the younger generation of Iranians indicates that the control of youths' sexuality in general, and female sexuality in particular, by Iranian society and the government is diminishing (Sadeghi 2008, 250). As this is happening simultaneously with greater criticism of permanently married men who engage in temporary marriage, this may point to more egalitarian gender relations.

NOTES

1. Following Shahla Haeri, I opt for the Persian terminology *sigheh* when referring to temporary marriages and use it as a verb and as a noun, according to the Iranian practice (Haeri 1986, 128).

2. See Shahla Haeri (1989), who interviewed some women having used the dower of their temporary marriage as a bargaining chip.

3. This was also the case for the openly religious students. Among the students who argued that women's rights are not much acknowledged in either permanent or temporary marriages, only one was openly religious. The two students, who argued for the greater acknowledgment of women's rights in temporary marriages, are both committed Muslims.

4. See *Los Angeles Times* (2015).

5. As mentioned before, the number of openly religious students who were my interlocutors was, however, very small, which makes these research findings explorative.

REFERENCES

Azadarmaki, Taghi, and Mehri Bahar. 2006. "Families in Iran: Changes, Challenges and Future." *Journal of Comparative Family Studies* 37 (4): 589–608.

Haeri, Shahla. 1986. "Power of Ambiguity: Cultural Improvisations on the Theme of Temporary Marriage." *Iranian Studies* 19 (2): 123–154.

———. 1989. *Law of Desire: Temporary Marriage in Shiʻi Iran.* Syracuse, NY: Syracuse University Press.

———. 1992. "Temporary Marriage and the State in Iran: An Islamic Discourse on Female Sexuality." *Social Research* 59 (1): 201–223.

Holm, Jean, and John Bowker. 1998. *Making Moral Decisions.* New York: Continuum.

Los Angeles Times. 2015. "'White Marriage' a Growing Trend for Young Couples in Iran." https://www.latimes.com/world/middleeast/la-fg-iran-white-marriage-20150529-story .html.

Mir-Hosseini, Ziba. 1992. "Paternity, Patriarchy and Matrifocality in the Shariʻa and in Social Practice: The Cases of Morocco and Iran." *Cambridge Anthropology* 16 (2): 22–40.

———. 1996. "Women and Politics in Post-Khomeini Iran: Divorce, Veiling and Emerging Feminist Voices." In *Women and Politics in the Third World*, edited by Haleh Afshar, 149–169. London: Routledge.

Moors, Annelies. 2013. "Unregistered Islamic Marriages: Anxieties about Sexuality and Islam in the Netherlands." In *Applying Shariʼa in the West: Facts, Fear and the Future of Islamic Rules on Family Relations in the West*, edited by Maurits S. Berger, 141–164. Leiden: Leiden University Press.

Sadeghi, Fatemeh. 2008. "Negotiating with Modernity: Young Women and Sexuality in Iran." *Comparative Studies of South Asia, Africa and the Middle East* 28 (2): 250–259.

Shrage, Laurie. 2013. "Reforming Marriage: A Comparative Approach." *Journal of Applied Philosophy* 30 (2): 107–112.

7

"Laboratory *Sigheh*"

The (Dis)Entanglements of Temporary Marriage and Third-Party Donation in Iran

TARA ASGARILALEH

ANNELIES MOORS

Temporary marriages, or in Farsi *sigheh*, are marriages that have the date of dissolution included in the marriage contract. Whereas such temporary marriages are prohibited according to the Sunni schools of law, for the Twelver Shiʿa, the dominant school of law in Iran, concluding a temporary marriage is permissible. Historically, such marriages were considered as a means to regulate (male) sexuality. This is in contrast to marriages that are concluded for an indeterminate period of time, "permanent marriages," which have the formation of families and procreation as major function.

In this chapter we focus on a very different, perhaps unexpected way in which temporary marriages have been and still are discussed and used—in the framework of assisted reproductive technologies (ARTs). Iran is one of the few Muslim countries where third-party gametes donation, embryo donation, and surrogacy are widely practiced. In some cases, a specific form of temporary marriage, which we refer to with the term "laboratory *sigheh*," is used in order to legitimate such ARTs practices. "Laboratory *sigheh*" refers to a temporary marriage that is concluded for the period during which the fertilization of an egg and sperm takes place in a laboratory setting without any physical contact between the two parties involved.

Our focus is on how concluding a temporary marriage may be used in the case of female and male infertility, in particular, with respect to third-party gametes donation in Iran. In order to gain insight into the relationship between temporary marriage and third-party donation, we need to bring two sets of literature together, that is writings on temporary marriage and the burgeoning field of research on ARTs. Doing so will help us to trace both how laboratory *sigheh* has emerged as a phenomenon and the consequences of its use within the framework of third-party gametes donation. We add to this the insights we have gained from conversations with experts working at fertility clinics that focused on the emergence and partial demise of the use of temporary marriages in relation to infertility treatment.

In the following we start with a brief discussion about the multiple meanings of temporary marriages in Iran for the various parties involved, prior to its employment as laboratory *sigheh*. Here we discuss the attempts to revitalize temporary marriage after the 1979 Islamic Revolution, the various interpretations and positions held by the men and women entering in such a relationship. We then address how ARTs have developed in Iran, taking not only the differences between Sunni and Shiʻa traditions into account but especially the variety of perspectives presented by senior Shiʻa clerics, which also focus on the question of whether it is necessary to conclude a temporary marriage or not. We analyze the effects of third-party donation for the production of filiation and the legal right and duties of donors and recipients, as well as the consequences of concluding a temporary marriage for the selection of donors. We end with a discussion of the concerns and reflections of biomedical experts about filiation, biological relatedness, and social parenthood and the solutions they suggest.

This last part of our contribution is based on exploratory fieldwork conducted in Tehran by Asgarilaleh between April and June 2019.[1] During fieldwork she observed clinical settings and interviewed medical professionals at two major clinics in Tehran that offer treatments to couples seeking medical treatments for infertility, one public and one semiprivate/semipublic. She conducted in-depth interviews with seven ARTs experts including a bioethicist, a lawyer, a social science scholar, as well as medical doctors and held informal conversations with the biomedical experts in the aforementioned clinics and in several other clinics (mostly private ones) where access was granted through our interlocutors. Next to this, informal talks were held with people who either faced (in)fertility problems themselves or had family and friends with infertility issues.

The Multiple Meanings of Temporary Marriage

While prohibited within Sunni Islam, temporary marriage is a flexible and for some controversial Twelver Shiʻi institution that may be arranged and interpreted in a variety of ways.[2] It is a contractual arrangement between a man and an unmarried (single, divorced, or widowed) woman who agree, often privately, to marry each other for a specific period of time. The husband is to pay a sum of money (*ʻajr* or *mahr*) but has no maintenance obligations toward his temporary wife, and the parties do not inherit from each other.[3] Children of the union are fully legitimate and have the same legal rights to filiation, maintenance, and inheritance as children in a permanent marriage.[4] At the end of the contract, no divorce procedures are needed, but the woman has to observe a waiting period, *ʻiddah* (of two months or two menstrual periods), to ascertain paternity in the case of pregnancy. Temporary marriages may be extended for an unlimited number of times. Whereas in Iran all marriages need to be officially registered, this often does not happen in the case of temporary marriages.[5] Nonregistration does not, however, make such marriages invalid but may make it difficult to prove the existence of such a marriage and hence the filiation of children (Haeri 1989, 55; Yassari 2019, 74).

Historically, temporary marriages have been particularly popular at pilgrimage sites and with traveling merchants who contracted temporary marriages when they stayed in another city for a few weeks or months (Haeri 1989, 78, 81). During the reign of the Pahlavi dynasty, the institution of temporary marriages became increasingly marginalized, its occurrence largely limited to some shrines and poor urban areas (Afary 2009, 279). Temporary marriages did not tally with the Pahlavi regime's aim at modernization along Western lines, which included attempts to propagate modern, monogamous families (Balslev 2019, 164; Kashani-Sabet 2011, 69). Many middle-class urban women perceived temporary marriage as a relic of the past, as a threat to the stability of the family, as a cover for forms of prostitution, and, more generally, as an institution that is detrimental to the position of women (Haeri 1992, 205, 216–219).

After the Islamic Revolution, in contrast, the regime made attempts to revive temporary marriages. During and after the Iran-Iraq War they were considered an opportunity for young war widows to remarry (Afary 2009, 284). More generally, the regime also set out to actively propagate temporary marriages, reframing them as a progressive institution suitable for modern society. In the early 1980s Ayatollah Mutahhari had already presented it as an Islamic option for young people, such as students, not yet ready for a permanent marriage (Haeri 1989, 96). Ten years later Iranian president Hashemi Rafsanjani made a similar argument, but with a twist. He did not simply, in line with Shi'a teachings, consider sexuality as a positive force but also explicitly acknowledged female sexuality, arguing that there was nothing wrong with women themselves taking the initiative to propose temporary marriage. Temporary marriage was presented as a quintessentially modern Islamic institution (Haeri 1992, 222).

The points of view of men who engage in temporary marriage generally concur with the dominant Shi'a view of temporary marriages as a legitimate form of sexual pleasure for men, as good for society's health, and as providing religious reward. Women involved in temporary marriages presented a variety of perspectives. Whereas some agree with the dominant Shi'i perspective, others challenge the popular notion that women engage in it for financial reasons and men for sexual pleasure, with some underlining their active role in arranging for a temporary marriage (Haeri 1989, 204–208). Moreover, young people may also use temporary marriages instrumentally to circumvent state regulation to avoid interference by the morality police if they are in each other's company (Afary 2009, 286).

Yet engaging in a temporary marriage may well be risky for women. Culturally, there is considerable disapproval of temporary marriages and of the women
(but far less so of the men) who engage in these. In circles where women are
expected to be virgins when they enter into their first permanent marriage,
engaging into a temporary marriage may jeopardize their chances of a respectable permanent marriage. Also, women who enter into a temporary marriage
hoping to achieve a meaningful and affectionate relation and companionship
may well be disappointed (Haeri 1989, 201, 202).

Structurally such marriages often concern relationships that are unequal
not only in terms of gender but also in terms of class, with the women usually
from the lower classes (Moruzzi and Sadeghi 2006, 25). Still, for lower class
divorced women a temporary marriage may be their only option to escape the
marginality of their status, while for better-off divorced or widowed women a
temporary marriage may be socially acceptable (Afary 2009, 64). Also, a recent
exploratory study (Aghajanian et al. 2018, 6) observed that some of these temporary marriages turn out to be committed longer-term relationships. Next to
the traditional pattern of older married men seeking young women as temporary wives, temporary marriages are also concluded by middle-aged widowed or
divorced men and women who seek companionship and a sexual partner but
do not want to go through a permanent marriage and by young never married
adults who enter into a temporary marriage to legitimate an intimate, romantic
relationship while postponing a permanent marriage as they are intent to first
pursue their education and start a professional career.

Whereas the main aim of temporary marriages is making sexual pleasure
religiously licit, there is also a form that is explicitly nonsexual (Afary 2009,
60; Haeri 1989, 80). In this case a temporary marriage is concluded to circumvent the rules of gender segregation. According to Islamic tenets, the ways in
which men and women are to behave toward each other (such as whether women
need to cover and whether a man and a woman can be socially close in each
other's company) depend on whether they, having reached puberty, are able to
marry each other (*namahram*) or not (*mahram*; pl. *maharim*). Gender segregation
is required only in the case of the former (Clarke 2007a, 382; Tremayne 2009, 147).
The category of *mahram* includes kin in the direct line (such as parents and
children) and close lateral kin, that is, siblings, siblings of the parents, and children
of siblings (brothers and sisters, uncles and aunts, nephews and nieces) and,
second, close relations of affinity (spouses of their parents and children, parents and children of their spouses). This does not change after the marriage has
ended; that is, even a brief temporary marriage can have lifelong consequences.
Also, a man cannot marry two sisters simultaneously.[6]

For men and women who are *maharim* to each other, close social contact is
permissible as they are within the incest taboo and unable to marry each other.
Hence, a nonsexual *sigheh* may, for instance, be concluded when *maharim* men

and women need to travel together when they go on a pilgrimage or tourist vis-its, or in the case of employment that entails close social contact, such as in households with domestic workers, or when engaged in other forms of close cooperation (Haeri 1989, 91–95). It may also be used in a somewhat more ambig-uous way, by couples during their engagement, in particular in more religious and conservative circles. In that case such nonsexual *sigheh*, allowing for some intimacy but not for a full sexual relationship, would enable these couples to spend time together, without concerns that their relationship would, in their own eyes and in those of their social circle, be considered illegitimate (Haeri 1989, 97–98). Yet there is also a very different way in which temporary marriage has come to be used, that is, with respect to third-party donation for involun-tarily childless couples.

The Development of ARTs in Iran

In Iran having children is important, at the individual and collective levels, and infertility carries a major stigma. To be culturally accepted and religiously licit, these children need to be born within a valid marriage, whether permanent or temporary. It is through such marriage that paternity, maternity, and more gen-eral filiation (*nasab*) are produced.[7] After the Islamic Revolution of 1979 the rul-ers at first propagated a strong pronatalist stance. A decade later, however, the state started to support population regulation, which was accompanied by efforts to make fertility treatment more widely available (Tremayne 2009, 144). When it became evident that this policy had resulted in a very strong decline in birth rates, state institutions halted support for population regulation.[8]

There are major differences between Sunni and Shi'a jurisprudence with respect to whether forms of ARTs such as third-party donation are acceptable as fertility treatment. In Sunni Islam, only IVF with the egg and semen of the mar-ried couple is permitted. The first *fatwa* on IVF by Al-Azhar shaykh Islah al-Haqq in 1980 stated that conception needs to take place within marriage and there should be no confusion of family lineage or mixing of genealogy (Inhorn 2006b, 432–433). Sunni jurisprudence considers the use of third-party gametes in a lab-oratory as similar to unlawful sexual intercourse (*zina*) and the resulting child as illegitimate.[9] Whereas some individual Sunni scholars may be more lenient, there is a uniform ban on ARTs in the Sunni-majority countries in the Middle East (Inhorn et al. 2012, 229–230).[10] In Lebanon, ARTs has remained unregula-ted because of the great diversity of religious traditions, which makes legislation very difficult, while in Iran some forms of ARTs have been state regulated and supported (Clarke 2012, 273–276).

Structurally, the Shi'a tradition allows for a broad range of opinions.[11] Shi'a Islam distinguishes between lay believers and those with religious knowledge who are capable of independent interpretation of the scriptures (*ijtihad*) and are to provide guidance to lay populace. A limited number of these clerics (*mujtahids*) are recognized by their peers and followers known as *marja' al-taqlid* (pl. *maraji'*, source of emulation). Each Shi'a believer needs to adhere to the opinions of such a living high-ranking religious authority. These *maraji'* may differ in opinion, and individuals have the option to change their allegiance (Clarke 2012, 269; Tremayne 2009, 153).

Whereas until the later 1990s the Shi'a held opinions similar to the Sunnis, this changed when in 1999 Ayatollah Khamenei (the successor of Ayatollah Khomeini) issued a *fatwa* that was a major rupture with existing thought about third-party donation (Clarke 2012, 270; Clarke 2009, 117; Tremayne 2009, 148). He allowed for all third-party donations in the case of infertility as a means to overcome marital discord, under the condition that there was no forbidden act (*fe'el-e haram*) such as touch and gaze (*ghiyab-i lams va negah*). In his view, only physical sexual intercourse outside of marriage constituted *zina* (an illegitimate sexual relation). This was not the case if conception took place by bringing together egg and semen in a laboratory setting; the resulting child would be legitimate (Garmaroudi 2012, 165; Mahmoud 2012, 81). No marriage, whether temporary or otherwise, was required.

Khamenei's *fatwa* opened the door for infertility clinics to offer a wide range of fertility treatments, including the use of third-party gametes, and made it religiously licit for infertile couples to engage in such treatments. However, whereas some Shi'a senior clerics agreed with the *fatwa* of Ayatollah Khamenei, others did not. In particular, his views on the permissibility of sperm donation were controversial (Abbasi-Shavazi et al. 2008, 5–6; Tremayne 2009, 149).[12] It is true that third-party donation would allow for a variety of solutions to infertility, but it also engendered problems with respect to lineage and filiation. According to the Shi'a tradition, it is the biological-genetic substance, the egg and the semen, that produce filiation (*nasab*); the donors of the sperm and egg are considered the legal parents of the child (Clarke 2007a, 394). Rights and duties such as rights of inheritance and maintenance duties pertain to the donors of the gametes, not to the recipients. In a similar vein, the child becomes *mahram* (falling within the incest taboo) to the donors, but not to the recipients of the gametes, the social parents (Tremayne 2009, 148–149).[13] This explains why Shi'a senior clerics were particularly critical of sperm donation. Whereas the child is related both to the father and to the mother, it is the father's lineage that takes precedence both culturally and in terms of Shi'a legal constructs. They were generally more lenient in the case of embryo transfer, that is, when fertilization had taken place outside of the womb and it involved the egg and semen of an already married couple (Abbasi-Shavazi et al. 2008, 8; Garmaroudi 2012, 165; Mahmoud 2012, 82).

In 2003 traces of these positions were visible when state authorities became involved. That year the Iranian parliament overruled Ayatollah Khamenei's *fatwa*, which had permitted extramarital conception and unrestricted third-party donation. The new law, approved by the Council of Guardians, outlines who are allowed to donate and receive embryos.[14] Embryo donation to overcome male and female infertility is permissible if it involves the sperm and egg from another married couple (Abbasi-Shavazi et al. 2008, 7; Tremayne 2009, 156). Egg donation is allowed as long as the husband marries the egg donor temporarily, but sperm donation is prohibited (Inhorn 2006b, 437). What happened in practice?

Sigheh and Donor Selection

Also prior to the development of ARTs people resorted to various means to overcome infertility. As polygamy is permitted in Islam, in the case of female infertility the husband can enter into a temporary marriage with an unmarried woman. In the context of a patrilineal descent system, the children of such a marriage are considered as belonging to their father's lineage (Haeri 1989, 87–88).[15] Using temporary marriage in the case of female infertility was widely accepted as in that case the child's lineage is largely maintained (Mahmoud 2012, 79).

In the case of the husband's infertility, a temporary marriage may also be concluded, but as polyandry is not allowed in Islam, the process is more complicated and the results are less unequivocal (Clarke 2012, 271–272; Mahmoud 2012, 81). In that case a woman would need to be divorced from her infertile husband, marry someone else after the end of her waiting period ('*iddah*), once pregnant would need to be divorced from her new husband, and then, after the delivery of the child, she could remarry her first husband.[16] The waiting period after divorce is intended to determine who is the father of the child. In this case the resulting situation is more complicated as the child will live in the household of the social father, while it is legally related only to the sperm donor.

With the development of ARTs it became possible in the case of female infertility to bring together the sperm of the husband with the egg of a fertile female donor, and in the case of male infertility the egg of the wife with the sperm of a fertile male donor in a laboratory setting. As mentioned above, according to Khamenei's *fatwa* under such circumstances (where there was no touch or gaze) it was no longer necessary to conclude any kind of marriage. Yet other high-ranking religious scholars did not consider this acceptable. According to some of them a nonsexual temporary marriage would need to be concluded for the duration of the procedure (from egg retrieval to fertilization in the laboratory and insertion of the fertilized egg in the womb of the infertile wife) (Abbasi-Shavazi et al. 2008, 5; Inhorn 2006b, 436; Tremayne 2009, 148).

Opting for or against a nonsexual laboratory *sigheh* ties in with the process of donor selection. In the early days of ARTs people often resorted to kin donation. Tremayne (2009, 152) points to a preference for the sister of an infertile wife as egg donor and the brother of an infertile husband as sperm donor.[17] In a later publication she also mentions donations by opposite-sex siblings, that is, a husband with an infertile wife may use the egg of his sister, while a wife with an infertile husband may use the sperm of her brother, although most people would disapprove of this for cultural reasons (Tremayne 2018, 101). Also, intergenerational donation occurred, that is an infertile husband using his father's sperm (Tremayne 2018, 102).[18] In all these cases it would be impossible to conclude a temporary marriage as their partner would fall within the boundaries of the incest taboo, which would make the marriage invalid.

However, over time it has become less common for infertile couples to use kin donors. On the one hand, couples often want to keep their infertility secret (especially in the case of male infertility), which would push them to resort to a stranger donor (Tremayne 2009, 153; 2012, 149). On the other hand, many clinics no longer allow their patients to select their own donors (Tremayne 2018, 101). Medical doctors are concerned that self-selection may engender problematic family relations, while consanguineous practices of donation may propagate genetic diseases (Mahmoud 2012, 84). In some cases those who engage a stranger donor, usually for a fee, may want to enter into a temporary marriage. However, this also has drawbacks. It would make it difficult to maintain confidentiality, as there needs to be a direct agreement between the man and the woman (Tremayne 2009, 151).

According to Tremayne (2012), when the donor is a stranger whether the child is accepted or not by the social parent depends on whether it is the husband or the wife who is infertile. In the case of egg donation there is generally no hostile reaction,[19] but in the case of sperm donation the child is far more often rejected by the social father (Tremayne 2012, 147). As there is a greater stigma attached to male than to female infertility, keeping the donor confidential or even anonymous carries greater weight in the case of the use of stranger sperm. Infertile couples would want to keep donation secret in order to present the child as "their own child" (Tremayne 2009, 151, 158–159). Another reason to insist on the anonymity of the donor may well be that it is relatively easy to acknowledge filiation and to establish a legal relation of the child with the social parent if the biological father of the child, in this case the donor of the sperm, is unknown (Yassari 2019, 76–77).

Expert Views

The experts we talked with held a variety of points of view about whether and how temporary marriage may facilitate ARTs and in particular third-party gametes donation.[20] In some ways third-party donation still turned out to be a gray zone. Whereas one of the medical experts stated matter-of-factly that third-party donation is legal in Iran, others were well aware that the 2003 law was more restrictive. Yet they would also simultaneously acknowledge that nonetheless a wide variety of third-party gametes donation, including sperm donation, takes place in private clinics.

Such a sense of ambiguity also emerged in the perspectives of patients. According to Abbasi-Shavazi et al. (2008, 19) some women would at first consider gametes donation *haram* (religiously prohibited) but would change their mind when they realized that it was acceptable to the clinics. Some clinics would ask their patients to consult their own religious experts, but not all couples did so, and some simply assumed that if the clinic is doing it, it is allowed (Tremayne 2018, 99). Others would simply change their religious allegiance to a cleric who would find the particular treatment they were considering permissible or were not concerned about religious permissibility at all.

The experts generally expressed a negative view about the use of temporary marriage in the case of third-party donations. Those working in private clinics pointed out that opting for a temporary marriage was far removed from the worldview of their better-off middle-class clientele. They themselves, as modern professionals, held similar views, considering temporary marriage as an undesirable, outdated institution. Still, one of them, a bioethicist, held a partially different position. He considered temporary marriages as a suitable means for people with a religious background to enter into a licit relationship before marriage. Others, however, argued that nowadays young people simply enter into a relationship without being concerned whether such a relationship would be considered legitimate in religious terms (see also Afary 2009, 360). Moreover, also this bioethicist was not in favor of using temporary marriage in the case of third-party donation. As some others, he considered doing so as resorting to "legalistic tricks" (*hiyal*), as an insincere practice as there is no intention to marry, using phrases such as "it is all fake" and "it is only a *suuri* [formal] act." To those who would want to conclude a temporary marriage for religious reasons, they would point out that there was no obligation to do so, as Ayatollah Khamenei had clearly stated in his 1999 *fatwa*. If there is no touch or gaze, there is no need to enter into any kind of marriage.

But there was also a very different argument that the experts would refer to, an argument that would entail a more ethical (rather than a purely legalistic) position, and that went beyond their personal sensibilities about temporary marriage. The problem with temporary marriage is that it does not really allow for confidentiality. As one of the medical experts pointed out, his clinic had earlier used *sigheh* in the case of egg or sperm donation but had stopped doing so as those involved may enter into some kind of relationship with the donor anyway. Such confidentiality is important because, especially for men, infertility is a strong tabooed subject. A major argument for confidentiality is the issue of filiation (*nasab*), which is central to Islamic jurisprudence and also greatly valued culturally. As argued above, filiation, which is based on genetic substance, is important both in material terms, such as for inheritance and maintenance, and for immaterial aspects, such as distinguishing between those who are *mahram* and *namahram* (in- or outside of the incest taboo).

It is because of such complications that scholars such as Tappan (2012) have questioned the desirability of third-party donation. In his view it is necessary to pay more attention to the broader question of biomedical ethics beyond simply discussing *fatawa*. He is in agreement with bioethicists such as Abdulaziz Sachedina, a Muslim public intellectual based in the United States, who opposes traditional legalistic interpretations of Islam. Rather than focusing on *fatawa* in a legalistic manner, he proposes an ethical approach and argues for the need to develop an Islamic bioethic (that is, ethical justifications for medical practices grounded in Islamic beliefs). This includes engaging in the balancing act of weighing an act's possible harm and benefit, taking the contextual setting of time and place into consideration (Tappan 2012, 120).

Sachedina is highly critical of third-party gametes or donor embryo donation. Jurists and clinicians who allow for these acts "are weighing the treatment of the suffering of the patients above and beyond the other stakeholders, namely, the possible children and the society at large" (Tappan 2012, 124). According to Sachedina children have the right to an "unblemished lineage" in Islam. Because of the stigma against children "without proper lineage," these children will face lifelong discrimination and financial instability, while they are also deprived of important genetic information about their biological parents and run the risk of accidental incest (Tappan 2012, 123).

The experts at the clinics, however, also used ethical arguments for the importance of maintaining confidentiality (or even anonymity) of donors; that is, they considered confidentiality desirable in order to avoid problems both for the social parents and for the child. As one of them, a social scientist, explained, in the Iranian context it may not be so helpful for the child to have the right to know when he or she turns eighteen. Because of the system of filiation, it is possible to fully integrate the child into the new family only if the donor is unknown. At the same time, clinics try to find solutions for the risk that such a child may inadvertently marry someone within the prohibited categories (*maharim*). In some clinics, the sperm of a particular donor can be used only for a limited number of cases to avoid accidental incest. Clinics may also use some kind of confidential micro-donor registration system, while some argued for the need for a national donor registry system that would safeguard confidentiality.[21]

It is not so much that experts overlook the rights of children but that they are faced with a dilemma: certain measures that may protect the rights of children in some ways (the knowledge of their biological parents) may also produce problems in a context in which there is a taboo on third-party donation and where it is difficult to transfer rights and duties permanently to the social parents. The experts presented different lines of argumentation to work toward a solution. One pointed out that some religious scholars supported the idea to consider the donation of egg or sperm as a form of organ donation. This would then make it easier to produce filiation with the social parents. Interestingly, this would fit with how some women talked about donating their eggs. They considered it a good deed to help someone else, did not consider their eggs as particularly valuable, and did not seem to consider themselves as the mother of the child (Tremayne 2009, 155).

The experts often pointed, rather similar to Sachedina, to the need to develop a form of social or dynamic jurisprudence, a particular strand of Shi'a thought that admits for jurisprudential interpretation that recognizes the influence of time and place and the need to find Islamic solutions to contemporary problems (Mir-Hosseini 1998). As one of the experts pointed out, applying such an approach may in cases that are controversial in the eyes of the rulers be difficult, but in his view gametes donation and social parenthood would not fall into that category.[22]

Related to this, the religious law expert suggested in a somewhat ambiguous way the possibility to consider gametes donation as falling under the umbrella of adoption. Yet he simultaneously reflected that the religious authorities may not want to recognize gametes donation as such because of concerns that the negative image attached to adoption may also stick to gametes donation. Interestingly, Iranian law already allows for a form of formalized caretaking that resembles adoption. The 2013 Act on the Protection of Children without a Guardian or with an Unfit Guardian builds on and replaces the 1975 law that for the first time regulated the permanent integration of such children (abandoned, orphaned, or with unfit parents) into a new family, using a non-Islamic term for this form of caretaking, *sarparast* (Yassari 2019, 87). These "social parents" need to fulfil particular conditions, such as being married for over five years, with one of them over thirty years of age.[23] As the child does not automatically inherit from them, they also need to guarantee the child's material security after their death by transferring a sum of money to the child or by making an irrevocable testamentary disposition (up to one-third of the inheritance, the maximum amount Islamic law allows for) (Yassari 2019, 92). The child will also get the social father's last name.

There remains, however, the issue of filiation, as rules of filiation remain governed through biological and not through social parenthood. This issue of *maharim* engendered a debate in the Iranian parliament about whether the social parent (*sarparast*) could marry the adopted child. The Council of Guardians considered the proposal by a parliamentary committee to completely prohibit this (as being against Iranian morality), an infringement of Islamic *fiqh*. It was, however, willing to consider a compromise, making nonmarriage a condition for being appointed as *sarparast* (Yassari 2019, 94). As this proposal still allowed for exceptions (if in the best interests of the child). Islamic scholars then proposed to establish marriage obstacles through Islamic means (Yassari 2019, 95).

One such Islamic way was to establish milk kinship between the child and the new parents (see also Clarke 2007b). Milk kinship is established when a woman who is not the biological mother nurses a child. This produces a particular form of "limited" kinship; that is, the rules of marriage prohibition (allowing for more intimate social relations in the household) are applied. However, it does not produce other rights, such as inheritance. In the case of milk kinship, the nursed boy is not allowed to marry the nursing woman and the nursed girl is prohibited from marrying the husband of the nursing woman. These marriage impediments are further extended to consanguine kin in a similar way as with kinship filiation. In this way social parents can become *mahram* to the child, when the child is nursed by their female relatives.[24]

Another Islamic means to produce a marriage impediment is the conclusion of a nonsexual temporary marriage (Yassari 2019, 96), which, just like in the case of a permanent marriage, turns previously unrelated persons into *maharim* yet is also deemed controversial among religious and legal scholars.[25] The child may be temporarily married, if a girl, to the father of the *sarparast* and, if a boy, to the widowed mother of the *sarparast*; in both cases the *sarparast* would be barred from marrying the child himself, even after the end of the temporary marriage (see also Rahbari, forthcoming). That is, the termination of the temporary marriage does not end the *mahramiyat* that it created between the child and the social parents. Whereas the experts we talked with did not refer to such Islamic means to regulate family relations, and while it is not clear whether and to what extent people make use of these means in practice, an issue also raised by Shariati-Nasab (2014), it points to an Islamic way in which filiation (*nasab*) may be employed flexibly. However, this does require the confidentiality or even anonymity of the donors, as otherwise there is a risk that the donors may want to claim their rights to the child.[26]

Conclusion

The religious establishment in Iran allows both for temporary marriage as well as for a range of infertility treatments, including third-party gametes donation. In this chapter we have traced how temporary marriage and third-party donation have become entangled and disentangled in the course of time. Temporary marriages were and still are a flexible institution. The use of such marriage in the case of third-party donation (what we labeled laboratory *sigheh*) can be considered both as a rupture with and as a continuation of earlier ways in which temporary marriages have been employed. It is a rupture with the dominant use of temporary marriage, aimed mainly at sexual pleasure rather than procreation. Yet at the same time laboratory *sigheh* can also be considered as yet another form of nonsexual temporary marriage.

Entering into a laboratory *sigheh* enables and obstructs particular kinds of third-party gametes donation. As some senior clerics do not agree with Khamenei's 1999 *fatwa* but insist on the conclusion of a temporary marriage for the duration of the fertilization procedure, for those who follow the opinions of these clerics laboratory *sigheh* may be a solution. Yet at the same time concluding such a temporary marriage would form an impediment for donor practices that were in common in the earlier days of third-party donation—that is, the use of egg and sperm of close kin. Concluding a laboratory *sigheh* in the case of stranger donors evokes another problem. In particular, in the case of sperm donation there may be a tension between concluding a laboratory *sigheh* and attempts of recipients of the donor sperm to maintain confidentiality.

The broader issue to address is how the religious field is implicated in ARTs and what forms of religious reasoning are employed. Some experts argue against a legalistic perspective that foregrounds *fatawa* and allows for the instrumental use of temporary marriage of whatever kind. Instead they work with a concept of religion that is more ethically oriented and argue for the development of an Islamic bioethics. Other experts propose the possibility of some kind of synthesis, making tactical use of long-standing Islamic formats, such as milk kinship and temporary marriage, within an ethical perspective that sets out to broaden the scope for and acceptability of social parenthood. Still the major empirical question then remains whether and to what extent such religious reasoning is valued by the couples themselves.

NOTES

1. The University of Tehran assisted Asgarilaleh in building contacts with experts in the field of assisted reproductive technologies and facilitated her access to this field. She asked and obtained verbal consent from all respondents, while the University of Tehran provided her with formal written permission for her research activities. This part of the research is the work of Asgarilaleh. We use the term "we" in the text only to increase readability.

2. Sunni authorities agree that temporary marriage was permitted at the time of the Prophet Muhammad but that the second Caliph Omar prohibited it in the seventh century. The Shi'a hold the opinion that since the Prophet did not ban temporary marriages, it is not permissible to forbid it (Yassari 2019, 73).

3. The Qur'anic term for the payment to the bride in the case of temporary marriage is *'ajr*, and for permanent marriage *mahr* or, in Farsi, *mehriyeh*. However, many Shi'a scholars and laypeople use the term *mahr* in both cases (Haeri 1989, 220n6).

4. In practice it may, however, be difficult to prove such marriages, as in contrast to permanent marriages, men who deny such a marriage are not required to take the oath of damnation (Yassari 2019, 60).

5. The Marriage Act of 1931 permitted temporary marriages but required them to be registered (Afary 2009, 150).

6. Note also that for a man his stepdaughter will become *mahram* only when the marriage with her mother has been consummated.

7. *Nasab* refers to both agnatic and uterine relations of filiation. However, in many contexts the agnatic element is stressed, such as when tracing genealogy (Clarke 2007b, 289).

8. The population growth rate declined from 3.9 percent during the 1976–1986 decade to around 1.5 percent during the 1996–2006 decade (Abbasi et al. 2008, 3). Moruzzi and Sadeghi (2006, 23) also point to the importance of women's greater access to education and employment.

9. The majority of Sunni medics and patients also consider third-party donation as resembling adultery, fear the risk of incest and the mixing of lineage, and consider it unfair to the donor children as they will be stigmatized (Inhorn 2006b, 440–441).

10. These state authorities are often supported by state-appointed *muftis* or collective *fatwa* bodies. As Clarke (2012, 273–274) argues, the contrast of Shi'a and Sunni theological positions should not be overstated; what matters is how religious and state authorities are related.

11. Most Shi'a clerics do not regard ARTs involving a third party as analogous to adultery as it does not involve sexual intercourse (Garmaroudi 2012, 158).

12. Prominent Shi'a clerics in Iraq often advised caution against third-party donation practices, viewing them as largely unacceptable, while some allowed them only if a temporary marriage had been concluded (Abbasi-Shavazi et al. 2008, 5–7).

13. The exception is that the child takes the name of the infertile father.

14. The Council of Guardians ensures that legislation passed by parliament fits with Islam and with the constitution.

15. Even if up till a certain age mothers may be the caretakers of the child, the father is the child's legal guardian.

16. Childlessness can legally and religiously be cited as justification for divorce under Article 9 of the Iranian Family Protection Law (Hasanpoor-Azghdy et al. 2015, 410). Couples who fail to have children may become targets of gossip about infertility, most often focusing on the wife.

17. Whereas egg donors in temporary marriage should be widows or divorcees, this rule was often not followed (Tremayne 2009, 148, 152).

18. There is, however, a major difference whether a woman uses the sperm of her husband's brother or that of her own brother, as in the latter case the child would be legally related to a different patrilineage, except if the wife and her infertile husband are from the same patrilineage, such as if they are paternal parallel cousins.

19. Also because it is possible for the birthing mother to claim milk kinship to the child if she nurses it (see Clarke 2007b).

20. They included three medical experts in the field of infertility treatment, one professor of medicine and fertility consultant, one bioethicist, one social scientist, and one medical expert/specialist in family law. They were all affiliated with private-public or private fertility clinics.

21. There are parallels here with debate elsewhere, such as in Europe (e.g., Hart 2018).

22. See also Clarke (2012) for the need to discuss the relation between religious scholarly opinions and state policy making.

23. Also for single women over thirty, but they can only adopt girls (Yassari 2019, 90).

24. Yassari (2019, 95) refers, for instance, to Ayatollah Makarem Shirazi who supported this.

25. See, for instance, Shariati-Nasab (2014).

26. Whereas they would need to do so through a court order and the courts are to take the best interest of the child into account, the outcome is not predictable (Yassari 2019).

REFERENCES

Abbasi-Shavazi, Mohammad Jalal, et al. 2008. "The 'Iranian ART Revolution' Infertility, Assisted Reproductive Technology, and Third-Party Donation in the Islamic Republic of Iran." *Journal of Middle East Women's Studies* 4 (2): 1–28.

Abu-Lughod, Lila. 1986. *Veiled Sentiments: Honor and Poetry in a Bedouin Society.* Berkeley: University of California Press.

Afary, Janet. 2009. *Sexual Politics in Modern Iran.* Cambridge: Cambridge University Press.

Aghajanian, Akbar, Sajede Vaezzade, Javad Afshar Kohan, and Vaida Thompson. 2018. "Recent Trend of Marriage in Iran." *Open Family Studies Journal* 10: 1–8.

Balslev, Sivan. 2019. *Iranian Masculinities: Gender and Sexuality in Late Qajar and Early Pahlavi Iran.* Cambridge: Cambridge University Press.

Clarke, Morgan. 2007a. "Closeness in the Age of Mechanical Reproduction: Debating Kinship and Biomedicine in Lebanon and the Middle East." *Anthropological Quarterly* 80 (2): 379–402.

———. 2007b. "The Modernity of Milk Kinship." *Social Anthropology* 15 (3): 1–18.

———. 2009. *Islam and New Kinship: Reproductive Technology and the Shariah in Lebanon.* Berghahn Books.

———. 2012. "Islamic Bioethics and Religious Politics in Lebanon: On Hizbullah and ARTs." In *Islam and Assisted Reproductive Technologies: Sunni and Shia Perspectives*, edited by Marcia Inhorn and Soraya Termayne, 261–284. New York: Berghahn.

Garmaroudi Naef, Shirin. 2012. "Gestational Surrogacy in Iran: Uterine Kinship in Shia Thought and Practice." In *Islam and Assisted Reproductive Technologies: Sunni and Shia Perspectives*, edited by Marcia Inhorn and Soraya Termayne, 157–194. New York: Berghahn.

Haeri, Shahla. 1989. *Law of Desire.* Syracuse, NY: Syracuse University Press.

———. 1992. "Temporary Marriage and the State in Iran: An Islamic Discourse on Female Sexuality." *Social Research* 59 (1): 201–223.

Hart, Linda. 2018. "Anthropology of Kinship Meets Human Rights Rationality: Limits of Marriage and Family Life in the European Court of Human Rights." *European Societies* 20 (5): 816–834.

Hasanpoor-Azghdy, S. B., M. Simbar, and A. Vedadhir. 2015. "The Social Consequences of Infertility among Iranian Women: A Qualitative Study." *International Journal of Fertility and Sterility* 8 (4): 409–442.

Inhorn, Marcia. 2006a. "He Won't Be My Son." *Medical Anthropology Quarterly* 20 (1): 94–120.

———. 2006b. "Making Muslim Babies: IVF and Gamete Donation in Sunni versus Shi'a Islam." *Culture, Medicine and Psychiatry* 30 (4): 427–450.

Inhorn, Marcia, and Daphna Birenbaum-Carmeli. 2008. "Assisted Reproductive Technologies and Culture Change." *Annual Review of Anthropology* 37: 177–196.

Inhorn, Marcia, Paquale Patrizio, and Gamal Serour. 2012. "Third-Party Reproductive Assistance around the Mediterranean." In *Islam and Assisted Reproductive Technologies:*

Sunni and Shia Perspectives, edited by Marcia Inhorn and Soraya Tremayne, 223–260. New York: Berghahn Books.

Inhorn, Marcia, and Soraya Tremayne. 2012. *Islam and Assisted Reproductive Technologies: Sunni and Shia Perspectives.* New York: Berghahn Books.

Kashani-Sabet, Firoozeh. 2011. *Conceiving Citizens: Women and the Politics of Motherhood in Iran.* Oxford: Oxford University

Mahmoud, Farouk. 2012. "Controversies in Islamic Evaluation of Assisted Reproductive Technologies." In *Islam and Assisted Reproductive Technologies: Sunni and Shia Perspectives*, edited by Marcia Inhorn and Soraya Termayne, 70–92. New York: Berghahn.

Mir-Hosseini, Ziba. 1998. "Rethinking Gender: Discussions with Ulama in Iran." *Critique: Journal for Critical Studies of the Middle East* 7 (13): 45–59.

Moruzzi, N. C., and F. Sadeghi. 2006. "Out of the Frying Pan, into the Fire: Young Iranian Women Today." *Middle East Report* 241: 22–28.

Rahbari, Ladan. Forthcoming. "Complicating or Facilitating Adoption Using Temporary Marriage in Contemporary Shi'a in Iran." *Hawwa. Journal of Women in the Middle East and the Islamic World.*

Shariati-Nasab, Sadegh. 2014. "Mahramiat dar farzand-khandegi." *Journal of Tahghighat-I Hoghoghi* 17: 235–254.

Tappan, Robert. 2012. "More Than Fatwas: Ethical Decision Making in Iranian Fertility Clinics." In *Islam and Assisted Reproductive Technologies: Sunni and Shia Perspectives*, edited by Marcia Inhorn and Soraya Termayne, 103–130. New York: Berghahn.

Tremayne, Soraya. 2009. "Law, Ethics and Donor Technologies in Shia Iran." In *Assisting Reproduction, Testing Genes: Global Encounters with Biotechnologies*, edited by D. Birenbaum-Carmeli and Marcia Inhorn, 144–164. New York: Berghahn Books.

———. 2012. "The Down Side of Gamete Donation: Challenging Happy Family Rhetoric in Iran." In *Islam and Assisted Reproductive Technologies: Sunni and Shia Perspectives*, edited by Marcia Inhorn and Soraya Termayne, 130–157. New York: Berghahn.

———. 2018. "Assisted Reproductive Technologies and Making and Unmaking of Kin in Iran: Transformations or Variation of a Theme?" In *International Handbook on Gender and Demographic Processes*, edited by Nancy Riley and Jan Brunson, 95–106. Dordrecht: Springer.

Yassari, Nadjma. 2019. "Iran." In *Filiation and the Protection of Parentless Children: Towards a Social Definition of the Family in Muslim Jurisdictions*, edited by Nadjma Yassari, Lena-Maria Möller, and Marie-Claude Najm, 67–102. Dordrecht: Springer.

ACKNOWLEDGMENTS

The contributions to this volume were, with one exception (Asgarilaleh and Moors), presented at the two-day international conference Global Dynamics of Debating and Concluding Shi'a Marriages, held in August 2017 at the University of Amsterdam. The conference was jointly organized by the editors of this book. At the University of Amsterdam this research is part of the ERC-funded research project on "Problematizing 'Muslim Marriages': Ambiguities and Contestations," grant no. 2013-AdG-324180. This publication has also received funding from the ERC under the European Union's Horizon 2020 research and innovation program (grant agreement no. 724557, "Creating an Alternative *Umma*: Clerical Authority and Religio-political Mobilisation in Transnational Shii Islam"). For their contributions we thank the other presenters and discussants at the conference: Annemeik Schlatmann, Rawand Osman, Roshan Iqbal, Iman Lechkar, Kathryn Spellman, Joseph Alagha, Moulouk Berry, Omar Fassatoui, and Tiba Bonyad. We are also grateful to Jasper Chang at Rutgers University Press and to Péter Berta, book series editor, as well as the three peer reviewers. Their support and efforts have ensured an outstanding scholarly publication.

CONTRIBUTORS

TARA ASGARILALEH is a PhD candidate in the sociology department of the University of Cambridge. Her PhD project is a part of the Reproductive Sociology Research Group (ReproSoc) program at Cambridge and is funded by the Wellcome Trust. She was a part of the Muslim Marriages project (funded by the European Research Council) in the Anthropology Department of the University of Amsterdam (2018–2019). She obtained a bachelor of science in sociology from the University of Tehran, Iran in 2014 and graduated from the Research Master Social Sciences (RMSS), funded by Amsterdam Merit Scholarship, at the University of Amsterdam in 2017. For the RMSS, she wrote her thesis on organ transplantation and unrelated kidney donors in Iran, based on ethnographic fieldwork in Tehran. With her PhD project (supervisor: Prof. Sarah Franklin), she examines how involuntarily childless couples, men in particular, can access and do actually use assisted reproductive technologies (ARTs) in the sociocultural, legal, religious, and medical context of contemporary Iran. Through her ethnographic study she hopes to bring new insights into (in)fertility and men's perceptions of fertility and reproductive precarity in the use of ARTs in Iran and how this relates to dominant notions of masculinity.

MARIANNE HAFNOR BØE is associate professor in the study of religions in the Department of Cultural Studies and Languages at University of Stavanger in Norway. She completed a PhD at the Centre for Women's and Gender Research at the University of Bergen in 2012 and continued as a postdoctoral researcher in archaeology, history, cultural studies, and religion at UiB. Her postdoctoral research project was titled "Religious Laws and Everyday Life," funded by the Research Council of Norway. She has done ethnographic research in both Norway and Iran and has published widely on practices of Muslim family law in Iran and Norway, on Shi'i Islam and Shi'i Muslim communities in Norway, and on the combination of Islam and feminism. Among her publications are *Family Law in Contemporary Iran: Women's Rights Activism and Shari'a* (2015) and the article "A Minority in the Making: The Shia Muslim Community in Norway," coauthored with Ingvild Flaskerud in *Journal of Muslims in Europe* (2017). She also published *Annotated Legal Documents on Islam: Norway* (2018) and *Feminisme og Islam* in Norwegian (2019).

SOPHIE-YVIE GIRARD is an anthropologist living and working in Europe.

MARY ELAINE HEGLAND is professor emerita of cultural anthropology at Santa Clara University in California, where she taught courses about women, gender, and sexuality; family and kinship; aging and the elderly; and anthropology of the Middle East. Traveling to Iran in 1966 as a Peace Corps volunteer to teach English in Mahabad, she was drawn to Persian culture and Iranian people and continued her focus on Iran by studying anthropology. She flew to Iran in June 1978 for her PhD dissertation fieldwork, therefore experiencing the Iranian Revolution firsthand, and stayed until mid-December 1979. After a forced gap of some twenty-four years until 2003, she has returned to Iran seven times since, the last in 2018. Her main geographical focus for field research is Iran, although she has also conducted research in Turkey, Afghanistan, and Tajikistan as well as among Iranian Americans in the United States. Her publications have dealt with women, gender, politics, revolution, ritual, local political culture, Shi'i Muslim women's gatherings, aging and the elderly, and change. Her book *Days of Revolution: Political Unrest in an Iranian Village* was published in 2014 and won two book awards. Her current research focuses on marriage, sexuality, and change.

ANNELIES MOORS is professor of contemporary Muslim societies in the Department of Anthropology, University of Amsterdam. She studied Arabic at the University of Damascus and anthropology at the University of Amsterdam. She has done extensive fieldwork in the Middle East (especially Palestine) and the Netherlands and has published widely on gendered visibility and multiple belongings (Islamic fashion and anti-fashion, face veiling), material kinship and material religion (wearing gold, marriage contracts), gendered mobilities (migrant domestic labor), and controversies on Islam and Muslims in Europe and beyond (dress and marriage, cultural politics and everyday life). From 2001 to 2008 she was the Amsterdam ISIM chair, where she directed the program on Muslim cultural politics. More recently she was the PI of an NWO grant on "Muslim Activism" and of an ERC advanced grant on "Problematizing 'Muslim Marriages': Ambiguities and Contestations." See further https://sites.google.com/site/anneliesmoors/.

EVA F. NISA is a senior lecturer of anthropology in the College of Asia and the Pacific at the Australian National University. She is also adjunct research fellow in religious studies at the School of Social and Cultural Studies and honorary research associate of the Faculty of Graduate Research, Victoria University of Wellington. She is a scholar of Islamic studies, anthropology, religion, and gender, researching how global currents of Islam reshape the lives of Muslims in Southeast Asia. Her research interests include Islam and Muslim societies, Islamic cultural economy, gender relations, gender and religion, Muslim marriages and divorces, female Muslim judges, the global politics of moderate Islam, religion and media (social media), Islamic thought, digital Islamic economy and Islamic philanthropy, Qur'anic exegesis, Muslim fashion, and Muslim refugees and migration. She has more than eleven years' experience in conducting research on the anthropology of Islam and Muslim societies in Southeast Asia, particularly Indonesia and Malaysia. She has published her work in a number of peer-reviewed journals. She is serving on the editorial board for *The Asia Pacific Journal of Anthropology (TAPJA)* and is working with Prof. Lyn Parker on the *Encyclopedia of Women and Islamic Cultures* for Southeast Asia and East Asia.

JIHAN SAFAR obtained her PhD at SciencesPo (Paris) in 2015. She continued her postdoctoral research on marriage and fertility issues in the Gulf countries (Oman, Kuwait, Qatar, Saudi Arabia). She is a researcher at the GLMM (Gulf Labour Markets and Migration) working on fertility behaviors and perceptions among Qataris.

YAFA SHANNEIK is lecturer in Islamic studies at the University of Birmingham. She researches the dynamics and trajectories of gender in Islam within the context of contemporary diasporic and transnational Muslim women's spaces. She is working on a project that explores women's narratives of transnational marriage practices performed by Iraqi and Syrian women who have settled in Europe and other countries in the Middle East since the 1980s. It focuses on the historical developments and contemporary understandings of family and gender relations. It particularly examines approaches of marriage practices among displaced Iraqi and Syrian Muslim women and foregrounds questions of identity, home, and belonging of women constituted through local, national, and transnational scales of migration experiences. She has published several articles on gender and Islam and migrant identities in Europe and their marriage practices, including "Shia Marriage Practices: Karbala as lieux de mémoire in London" in *Social Sciences* (2017) and "Reformulating Matrimony: Islamic Marriage and Divorce in the Contemporary UK and Europe" in *Journal of Muslim Minority Affairs* (2020).

ANNA-MARIA WALTER has worked in the socially very heterogenous area of Gilgit, northern Pakistan, for her doctoral research. She has written on empathic attunement as a fieldwork method, different aspects of gendered emotions, mobile phones as a tool of intimacy, as well as changing ideas of love and marriage in South Asia. Her monograph *Intimate Connections* is scheduled to be published in 2021. She served as part-time lecturer at the Institute of Social and Cultural Anthropology, LMU Munich, for several years and is now a research fellow at the University of Oulu, Finland. Her postdoctoral projects expand on methodological questions of digital technologies as remote connections to the field, conceptions of the self through social media use, and arenas of feminist partaking in pleasure and spirituality in high altitude spaces.

INDEX